C000171124

The Political Economy of the Environment

The Political Economy of the Environment

The Case of Japan

SHIGETO TSURU

THE ATHLONE PRESS
LONDON

First published in 1999 by
THE ATHLONE PRESS
1 Park Drive, London NW11 7SG

© Shigeto Tsuru 1999

British Library Cataloguing in Publication Data
*A catalogue record for this book is available
from the British Library*

ISBN 0 485 11528 X

Typeset by Refinecatch Limited, Bungay, Suffolk
Printed and bound in Great Britain by
Cambridge University Press

Contents

Preface   vii

1   Methodological Introduction   1
    'Value in Use' and 'Value in Exchange'   1
    Shifting the Boundary between the 'Internal' and
        'External'   3
    Concession to the Prevailing Position of the
        Real-Physical Aspect   8
    The Concept of 'Social Costs' Reviewed   11
    The Concept of 'Kōgai' Defined   24

2   Historical Analysis – The Prewar Period   27
    The Initial Stage of Japan's Industrialization   27
    Representative Incidents of Kōgai – The Case of the
        Copper Mining Industry   32
        The Ashio Copper Mine   33
        The Besshi Copper Mine   36
        The Case of the Hitachi Mine   40
    Summary   45

3   Historical Analysis – The Postwar Period I   48
    'Creative Defeat'   48
    Earlier Lessons Forgotten   54
    The Other Side of Affluence   58

4   Historical Analysis – The Postwar Period II: Major *Kōgai*
    Incidents   70
    Pollutions Compounded in the City of Yokkaichi   70
    The Tragedy of Minamata   79
    The Second Minamata Disease in Niigata   96

The *Itai-Itai* Disease of Cadmium Poisoning   101
Noise Pollution of the Osaka International Airport   107

5   From Stockholm (1972) to Rio (1992)   116
    A Turning Point for the Japanese Economy   116
    Stockholm, Before and After   119
    The Keyword Changes from 'Kōgai' to 'Kankyō'   124
        The OECD Review   124
        The Environmental Agency Established   127
    Conservation of Nature   129

6   Progress and Setback in Standards, Compensation and
    Assessment   140
    Standards for Pollution Control   140
    Compensations   145
    Environmental Impact Assessment (EIA)   150

7   Pharmacological and Other Pollutions   158
    The Arsenic Milk Poisoning   158
    The Kanemi Rice-oil Disease   163
    The 'SMON Scandal'   170
    The Toroku Mine *Kōgai*   178
    The Hexavalent Chromium *Kōgai*   185

8   Implications of Globalized Environment Problems:
    Sustainable Development   193
    'The Earth Summit' of 1992   193
    The Basic Environmental Law of Japan (1993)   202
    The Basic Environment Plan   206
    Environmental Impact Assessment   208
    Export of *Kōgai* and its Reversal   210
    Kōgai of US Military Bases in Japan   216
    Warming of the Earth   219

9   A New Life-Style Sought   224

Notes   239

Bibliography   257

Index   265

Preface

My interest in environmental problems originated in the 1930s while I was in the United States and was struck by the stark contrast between what was happening then in the Tennessee Valley and what had continued to harass the residents along the Watarasé River in Japan – both having a major copper mining centre in the upstream regions. Later, I had an occasion to read David Lilienthal's *TVA, Democracy on the March* (Harper & Brothers, 1943); and impressed as I was by the multi-purpose strategy of river-basin development with its implication of 'democracy on the march,' soon after the war I began organizing the 'TVA Study Group' among resource specialists, economists and political scientists in order to discuss the possibility of concretely applying some of the TVA principles to a number of regions in Japan. Out of this activity was born the Environmental Disruption Research Group (*Kōgai kenkyu iinkai*) in 1963, which was headed by myself and which from 1971 sponsored the quarterly publication (called *Kōgai Kenkyu*).

Ever since these early postwar years I have continued to be involved in environmental problems; and in the course of my empirical, often on the spot, researches I became convinced that the 'internal' logic of a particular institutional mechanism (such as the free enterprise market system) has to be remedied for the purpose of dealing with environmental disamenities. It is for this reason that I have chosen the title *The Political Economy of the Environment*, spelling out in some detail my methodological considerations in Chapter One. And, it may be suggested to those readers who wonder how these methodological considerations lead to a set of policy proposals for an environmentally sound new life style that they go directly to the last chapter and capture the intent of my practical recommendations.

I should probably bring to the reader's attention the date when I finished writing the closing chapter of the book, which was April 1998.

Shigeto Tsuru
Tokyo, Japan

January 1999

CHAPTER ONE

Methodological introduction

'VALUE IN USE' AND 'VALUE IN EXCHANGE'

In the consideration of environmental problems today it is relevant to recall the distinction Adam Smith made between 'value in use' and 'value in exchange.' He wrote:

> The things which have the greatest value in use have frequently little or no value in exchange; and on the contrary, those which have the greatest value in exchange have frequently little or no value in use. Nothing is more useful than water; but it will purchase scarce any thing; scarce any thing can be had in exchange for it. A diamond, on the contrary, has scarce any value in use; but a very great quantity of other goods may frequently be had in exchange for it.[1]

If phrased in somewhat more specific terms, the distinction Smith proposed could be stated as one between 'whatever possessing intrinsic value of its own as an object of human satisfaction' and 'whatever that is actually or potentially subject to pricing in the market.' The former statement is much broader in scope than the latter, including within it not only conventional goods and services for consumption but also such things as natural beauty and rare species of wild animals and plants. The latter statement, on the other hand, though narrower in scope, has had the historical tendency of expanding its coverage, extending itself occasionally to cover those items the property of which can hardly be said to be salutary for human beneficial use, such as opium and baneful drugs.

In the discussion of economic problems in general I have found the distinction Smith made between 'value in use' and 'value in exchange' useful and often employed the contrasting terms of 'the real (or physical) aspect' versus 'the value (or institutional) aspect.' The *real* aspect is physical, transcending specific forms of socio-economic institutions, whereas the *value* aspect is social in the sense that it reflects an historically specific mode of production, such as a predominantly exchange economy. Not only is it important to distinguish between these two aspects, but it is also of no less relevance, especially in dealing with environmental problems, to recognize the need to integrate the two while noting possible conflicts between them.

Advances in productive powers – the real aspect – may be likened, for example, to a rise in the *temperature* of H_2O, while the specific institutional arrangement of productive relations – the value aspect – may be likened to the *forms* of H_2O, such as ice, water and steam. A particular *form* of socio-economic institutions is likely to have a certain degree of historical stability often extending over a number of centuries, while having a certain internal logic characteristic of its own. In turn, such logic tends to have controlling effects over the physical or real aspect, as in the example of an exchange economy stimulating the spread of the division of labour, thus the specialization of particular skills.

On the other hand, the real aspect also has its own logic basically subject to natural laws which, as Francis Bacon said, 'could be mastered only through the faithful compliance with them.' And history records the process of a gradual but steady development of man's knowledge and his mastery of nature, thus that of his own universal productivity. It is of special significance that this process, which can be likened to the increase in temperature of H_2O, was either accelerated by a particular socio-economic institutional form or retarded (or actually held back) by another particular institutional form. Furthermore, the process spoken of, which is the real aspect, is not necessarily passive to the value (or institutional) aspect; but just as a rise in the temperature of H_2O causes the transformation of the form from solid to liquid, the rise in human productivity can have a dynamic effect on the transformation of socio-economic institutions.

The distinction made by Smith between 'value in use' and 'value in exchange' can be further developed as I have done above. More recently, however, especially in connection with the discussion of environmental problems, a relevant distinction has been proposed between 'appropriable' resources and 'inappropriable' ones.[2]

> A commodity is called appropriable when firms or consumers can capture its full economic value. . . . In a well-functioning competitive market, we would expect that appropriable natural resources would be efficiently priced and allocated. . . . An inappropriable resource is one whose use is free to the individual but costly to society. In other words, inappropriable resources are ones involving externalities.[3]

We may relate this distinction to the earlier one of Adam Smith's. Since appropriable resources can be priced and their full economic value captured by potential buyers, they may be classified in the category of 'value in exchange.' Inappropriable resources, like air quality and mountain views, on the other hand, cannot be individually appropriated, and generally be classified as 'value in use'; and since they could often be subject to negative externalities for the society, they are of special relevance to environmental economics. We shall come back to this problem later. But first, we have to clarify what is meant by 'negative externalities' mentioned above.

There are three major categories of economic activity unit: i.e. the household, the business firm and the nation state. Each one of them cannot escape from the operative logic of the society in which it functions. In a capitalist society, for example, the household (or the individual) sells its labour power as a commodity, receives the market-determined wage in return and seeks to maximize its satisfaction as a consumer; the business firm, typically taking the form of private capital, attempts to maximize its profit; and the nation state pursues what is usually called the 'national interest.' Each economic category 'internalizes,' as it were, those elements in the physical environment which are relevant to its activity and discharges what is not needed into the outside realm.

This discharging into the outside realm has the possibility of causing nuisance either to individual persons or to the community at large. The latter type is called 'public nuisance' and was dealt with by English law as early as in the sixteenth century. But the legal concern at that time was specifically with the injurious intrusion into *property rights concerning land* through the emission of obnoxious materials in general. Although such earlier legal concern was limited in the sense that it laid its main emphasis on 'anything injurious or obnoxious in relation to the property rights in land,' it did open a new way of separating the economist's vista into 'internal' and 'external.'

SHIFTING THE BOUNDARY BETWEEN THE 'INTERNAL' AND
THE 'EXTERNAL'

In actual fact, the boundary which separates the 'external' from the 'internal' has shifted significantly in the historical process for each of the activity category we have spoken of. In the case of the household, for example, self-sufficiency was the rule for each individual family in the aboriginal stage of human society. A family subsisted on whatever it could individually 'internalize' from the outside world. Then, by and by, the practice of barter began, enabling each household to obtain some of its necessities through direct exchange. The scope of domestic production gradually but steadily shrank until we came to a stage where a high degree of commercialization was attained not only in the realm of household goods but also in the wide field of services of all kinds. In a modern advanced society, being a housewife is no longer a full-time 'occupation.' Even what used to be considered by most people in Japan as a good tradition, namely, the caring of aged parents by the younger generation, is now disappearing in the trend which has created a need for 'external' provisions in the form of care services for the aged. Still further, what was at one time essentially a family-internal problem has come nowadays to be 'externalized' into an affair mediated by legal experts, as in the case of a strife between man and wife. There also has arisen what is called 'an interference of income' – a pet subject of Joseph Schumpeter, but exemplified by an experience of Keynes, who, upon coming to Washington, DC, for negotiations over the postwar economic settlement, was asked by the US counterpart official: 'where is your lawyer?' When it was explained that he had none, 'who then does your thinking for you?' was the rejoinder.[4]

In the case of business firms, on the other hand, shifting of the boundary between the 'internal' and the 'external' has been more in the direction of from the latter to the former. Most notably this is the case as regards the utilization of scientific achievements for business purposes.

What constituted the Industrial Revolution of the eighteenth and the early nineteenth centuries were technological innovations which could be described with practically no reference to the contemporary progress in the scientific world. The relationship between science and industry in those days was typically casual and unstructured. In other words, under capitalism, scientific knowledge has always been one of the *external* elements from the standpoint of a business firm.

Science, by nature, could not be an object of private ownership. It could thrive only when it was freely shared; nor did scientists know any national boundaries, let alone boundaries of private firms: they were servants only of scientific truth. This view of science and scientists could harmonize itself well with the basic philosophy of capitalism as long as the relationship between science and industry remained typically casual and unstructured and any fruits of science could be 'packaged,' as it were, into 'patentable' technology under the control of private ownership.

But in the more recent decades, especially since the decade preceding the Second World War, science itself has become the central, strategic factor in the whole complex process of technological progress, best typified by the invention of nylon by the research staff of the Du Pont Company in the mid-1930s, replacing Japan's raw silk from the position of a unique export item. It was once held that knowledge had no marginal product. But now knowledge in a broad sense of the term is a cost factor just as patents or royalties once were and still are. Science thus has come to be embraced within the hold of private capital under capitalism as an *internal* matter, with a consequence that scientists as individuals have come to be employed by profit-seeking capitalist enterprises and to be subject to the logic of private capital. This is a contradiction of no small proportions. Whereas the very effectiveness of science lies in its being shared freely, private capital, in trying to internalize science, has to restrict the very freedom of scientists which is the *sine qua non* of their successful endeavour.[5]

In this era where productive forces have advanced to such a stage that 'private capital,' willy-nilly, is forced to embrace 'science' within its fold, there have been certain important consequences, such, for example, as that science has become a cost item of a private firm. But probably most important of all, from the standpoint of capitalism, is the changing function of profit as a barometer of contribution to the progress of productive forces. The profit-and-loss systems which provided an effective mechanism of incentives for private firms under capitalism is now impaired by the very behaviour pattern of gigantic corporations (which themselves characterize the modern industrial system) which are formed on the assumption of having both the market and science embraced within its fold. For one thing, the erstwhile mechanism of rewarding an innovator with excess profits which will disappear as the innovation is spread over the entire economy is now being replaced by a mechanism which enables a firm, through administrative prices, to retain the earning advantage *to the extent that it succeeds in preventing* the spreading of innovations over the entire economy. The principle of 'as one sows, so one reaps' still remains; but the difference now is that what used to be *external* to individual firms is now *internalized* and is counted as a part of one's own sowing.

Another type of business activity, however, for which shifting of the boundary between the internal and the external has become mandatory in the recent years concerns industrial waste disposal. It was customary in the years past that business firms could discharge their industrial wastes externally with impunity, causing what is nowadays called 'negative externality.' Pigou's reference to smoke from factory chimneys possibly inflicting a heavy uncharged loss on the community was the classical example. In a more recent period of the 'scientific-revolution,' where modern large-scale industries have come to employ sophisticated techniques and highly complex materials, the pollution caused is no longer negligible in terms of damage to human health in particular. Thus, there has grown general consensus in modern developed countries to introduce in practice the so-called 'polluters pay principle,' which implies the shifting of the boundary between the internal and the external in such a way that 'negative externality' will be internalized by offending enterprises.

As we go further to consider the case of the third category of economic activity unit, that is, the nation state, we find the shifting of the boundary between the internal and the external has been especially dramatic in the post-second World War period particularly in connection with environmental problems. A call for the convening of the United Nations Conference on the Human Environment in 1972 by Ambassador Aström of Sweden at the UN Assembly meeting in 1968 marked a memorable turning point in this regard. Specific problems raised by Ambassador Aström were global in nature, such, for example, as the hot-house effect of the atmosphere and the eutrophy phenomenon in lakes and sea-coast areas. The concept of globalism, however, has been quite common among economists in the past in the sense of transnational or international relations or interactions, implying, though, still the integrity of nation states. The new approach requires transcending the boundary of nation states and is best couched in the expression of 'spaceship earth.' In fact, the idea of conceptualizing our world as a 'closed economy' in the sense that the earth has become a single spaceship without unlimited reserves of anything either for extraction or for pollution was advanced already by Kenneth Boulding and Barbara Ward in the 1960s.[6] Boulding wrote:

In a space ship, clearly there are no mines and no sewers. Everything has to be recycled; and man has to find a place in the middle of this cycle. The 'space ship earth' simply repeats this on a larger scale. . . . In the space ship economy, consumption is no longer a virtue but a vice. . . . Human welfare will clearly be seen to depend, not on the throughput of the society – that is, not on the amount it can produce and consume – but on the richness and variety of its capital stock, including, of course, the human stock.[7]

One is tempted to recall a brief description of the earth by George Dillon, an American poet of the 1930s, to wit: 'a flying, flowering stone.' The poetic intuition of grasping this earth as one 'flying stone' is remarkable enough, although the adjective 'flowering' is hardly appropriate nowadays. The spaceship simile is indeed germane. Inside a spaceship, recycling is thoroughgoing, with everything needed to be *internally* dealt with. It may be said that in the case of our earth this internality is more complete inasmuch as residents of the spaceship earth cannot bring their foodstuff from outside like pilots of an actual spaceship. In addition, there are further difficulties for the spaceship earth in that firstly the number of its residents is increasing at least up to several decades ahead and secondly there is no master pilot who can issue commands on all occasions.

These constraints are often serious enough in face of the type of problems our earth is internally confronted with, for example, (1) the near certain probability of gradual exhaustion of non-renewable resources as the living standard is bound to rise for the ever-increasing population of the earth; (2) that the 'hot-house effect' of the earth is enhanced in the process of oxygen decrease coupled with increase of CO_2 in the atmosphere; and (3) the radioactive pollution which still remains with us as nuclear testing is continued by some countries. Be it noted that these problems are not endemic to a particular institutional characteristic of nation states but are types of physical phenomena *internal* to the earth as a whole, and that they demonstrate to us dramatically as examples of 'our capacity to intrude on the environment far outstripping our knowledge of the consequences.'[8] Although it is normally the case that each of the viable economic activity units has capability to control its 'internal' affairs, the spaceship earth, having no master pilot at present, is only remotely capable of unified systematic control of its 'internal' matters of real or physical character.

CONCESSIONS TO THE PREVAILING POSITION OF THE
REAL-PHYSICAL ASPECT

The enemy of the market is not ideology but the engineer.

J.K. Galbraith, *The New Industrial State*,
Houghton Mifflin Co., 1967, p. 33

Some of the 'value in use,' in Adam Smith's terminology, which are not included in the category of 'value in exchange' have been termed 'inappropriable resources' in more recent years and cannot be priced in the 'internal' logic of the institutional aspect of a given society. Thus, their intrinsic value tends not to be evaluated sufficiently in the accounting in economics, with a result, in the case of Japan for example, that a large part of shore-lines with natural beauty have been reclaimed for factory sites with a prospect of monetary returns. 'A garden was encroached upon for the sake of expanding a kitchen' has been the metaphor used in critique of a policy slighting the 'value in use' that is inappropriable.

However, once we take a methodological stand of distinguishing the real-physical aspect and the value-institutional aspect, we realize immediately the importance of losing inappropriable resources and feel called upon to reflect over the habit of thinking which gives precedence to the value-institutional aspect. One of the clues for such reflection would be to look into the type of situations where conflicts arise because an inseparatively related phenomenon in its real aspect is split up in its value aspect.

Let me offer here a pedestrian example in this regard, that is the supplying of chicken eggs. Eighty years ago when I was a pupil in a primary school, our household used to keep a chicken-hut in the corner of our garden. It was my father's avocation; but for a child of my age it constituted a pleasant pastime to saunter about through a suburban field for chickenweed or to run to the hut, on hearing the typical note of clucking, for a fresh egg which was still slightly warm. From time to time, we took steps to hatching to increase the stock. We also made use of droppings as fertilizers for a little vegetable garden we had. In other words, the entire process of chicken-egg supply was conducted as 'closed circle' within our household with additional benefits on the side of giving taste of rural life to city dwellers. No doubt, even at that time there were commercially operated chicken farms. But their production process was typically of the type not very far different from the one in our household, except it was on a much larger scale. What changed this process in recent years has been the development of the factory-type egg-supplying establishment, where hens are kept in a group of three within a narrow wire basket arranged in rows in such a way that feeding as well as collecting of eggs can be done with greatest economy. Droppings are also gathered by a conveyer system to be slurried for further disposal. Through such a process of modern egg-supplying 'industry,' productivity has been no doubt enormously raised. But at the same time, 'industrializing' of chicken-egg production caused us to lose the seat of its erstwhile suburban spectacle, thus making us aware that at least in this regard the days are gone now when man's life and that of animals complemented each other harmoniously in the bosom of Mother Nature while the economy of mass production intruded into our environment as a priority principle.

A lesson we learn from this kind of example is that policy considerations should be oriented toward giving prevailing position to the real or physical aspect in such a way that those biases caused by the 'internal' logic of a particular institutional mechanism can be remedied. How this reminder could be applied to each of the major categories of economic activity unit might be mentioned briefly here.

In the first place, there is the economic activity unit of the 'household' (or an individual person). If we are to yield prevailing position to the real-physical aspect, the market (or value) principle of equating the contribution of a unit of labour power with the wage payment could be questioned, especially in the modern period of automation where 'the creation of real wealth depends less on the labor time and the quantity of labor expended than on the power of the instrumentalities set in motion during the labor time.'[9] In such a situation,

> the great pillar of production and wealth is no longer the immediate labor performed by man himself, nor his labor time, but the appropriation of his own universal productivity, i.e., his knowledge and his mastery of nature through his societal existence – in one word: the development of the societal individual.[9]

It is to be noted, however, that in a much earlier period of technological development, that is, in the nineteenth century, the principle of 'giving according to one's needs' was enunciated as a matter of human rights, notably by John Ruskin (1819–1900) whose best-selling booklet *Unto This Last* carried the implication of commanding to pay the same remuneration for the full day's work to the man who came belatedly to the work place as the last man. In the heyday of the commercial principle of the Victorian period Ruskin was a precursor of the modern principle of the welfare state which gives prevailing position to the real-physical aspect over the value-institutional one.

In regards to another major economic activity unit, that is, business firms, history reveals to us a rather typical course of development of the value-institutional over the real-physical aspect. Private enterprises under capitalism did develop, most typically in the case of Japan, by taking full advantage of the 'external' economies provided by the state while pursuing their 'internal' economies to the utmost and ignoring any 'external' diseconomies caused by them. Thus, in due course of such capitalistic development, not only the type of events exemplifying 'market failures' occurred frequently enough, but also some flagrant instances of environmental disruption arose, creating inevitably a realization that the 'Invisible Hand' of the market mechanism might be in need of emendation of some kind. The practice of refraining from detrimental 'spill-over effect' is one such consequence and the general agreement on the 'Polluters Pay Principle' (now accepted by the OECD countries) is a concession to the prevailing position of the real-physical aspect.

There is another important respect in which business firms have come to allow the value-institutional aspect to prevail over the real-physical one; and that is with respect to the contribution of the basic sciences to improvements in productivity. The very fact of cost reduction implies that there exists an agent of production whose contribution is greater than its market valuation. Scientific contribution belongs to this category. It is an openly available free good unless its application is patented.

However, in the current period of the 'scientific-industrial revolution,'[10] it has come to be realized by many of the business firms that basic science itself needs to be embraced as a factor of production in the form of privatized know-how. This constitutes a recognition that the real-physical aspect of the production process could have a prevailing position in the latest period of capitalistic development.

When we come to the third economic activity unit, i.e. nation states, the need to confer the prevailing position to the real-physical aspect has come to be accepted as a matter of common sense now-adays. Questions, for example, relating to the undeniable limitation of underground resources of the earth, or the warming of the earth's surface, not to speak of the pollution caused by nuclear-bomb experiments – all these involve the real-physical aspect of human activity which defies market-value accounting. In addition, from a yet longer standpoint, there is the question as to what, and how much of which, we are to bequeath as heritage to our posterity. This problem again can hardly be answered in terms of dollars and cents.

THE CONCEPT OF 'SOCIAL COSTS' REVIEWED

In the evolutionary process of the capitalistic system we can observe a development of the market economy gradually spreading its realm to cover practically all the produced goods and a large part of the endowed resources including land as well as human labour power. At the height of such development, however, there still remained a con-siderable portion of man's activities and nature's endowment which for one reason or another escaped a market valuation and thus arose the area called the 'external economy' and 'external diseconomy.' And it was characteristic of capitalistic development, as stated earl-ier, that individual private capital could make use of the 'external economy' freely while taking no responsibility for the 'external dis-economy' it caused. The latter involved a cost item, constituting a part of what in general terms has been called 'social costs,' of which environmental disruption is the most common example.

It has to be admitted that there is no unique definition of the term 'social costs' among economists. For example, the reputedly authori-tative *The New Palgrave Dictionary of Economics* defines 'social cost,' as written by J. de V. Graaff, in the following manner:

> The idea underlying the notion of social cost is a very simple one. A man initiating an action does not necessarily bear all the costs (or reap all the benefits) himself. Those that he does bear are *private* costs; those he does not are *external* costs. The sum of the two constitute the *social* cost.[11]

Contrasted to this is the definition given by K. William Kapp in his classical work: *The Social Costs of Private Enterprise*, as follows:

> The term social costs ... covers all direct and indirect losses suffered by third persons or the general public as a result of private economic

activities. These losses may be reflected in damages to human health; they may find their expression in the destruction or deterioration of property values and the premature depletion of natural wealth; they may also be evidenced in an impairment of less tangible values. As an instrument of analysis the concept carries no quantitative connotation; it will serve its purpose if it helps to trace and to reveal a substantial proportion of the social losses of production for which neither law nor custom has as yet established an adequate responsibility of the individual producer.[12]

The contrast in the above two definitions is most striking, coming from the same discipline of economic science. But it may be conceded that the latter definition by Kapp gives a more specific focus upon the type of problems calling for social concern, although even in the mind of Kapp the concept is understood to cover not only what we nowadays call 'external diseconomies' but also the possible social losses due to the failure to provide for certain public goods (such as a light house) which are essential and yet are not profitable for private enterprises to undertake. This latter component, of course, can be minimized by adequate provision by public bodies.

It may be instructive, however, to follow Kapp in reviewing the concept of 'social costs' as he understood it, in order to obtain a historical perspective in relation to the development of the capitalistic market economy.

Kapp starts with Adam Smith. Smith, the champion advocate of 'the invisible hand,' was fully aware of the fact that the market mechanism could be relied upon to secure the optimum solution of the economic problem only if at least three conditions were fulfilled: (1) that there would be free competition; (2) that the free competition were restrained in their action by 'sympathy' and 'moral sentiments'; and (3) that in addition to defence and the administration of justice,

> the sovereign or commonwealth erects or maintains those public institutions and those public works, which, though they may be in the highest degree advantageous to a great society, are, however, of such a nature, that the profit could never repay the expense to any individual or small number of individuals, and which it therefore cannot be expected that any individual or small number of individuals should erect or maintain.[13]

If these 'works' which Smith mentions were left to private enterprise, serious social losses would ensue; and in this sense we might say that here was an evidence of the recognition of social costs in Kapp's sense. But such awareness, it can be pointed out, was fairly prevalent among nineteenth century economists; and as Kapp suggests, Smith's theory of 'public works' was 'an early specimen of the classical realization of the social returns of public investments.'[14]

A much more forcible way in which the social cost element was decried historically, however, was in connection with the impact of technological improvements.

An economist who personified the transition from Adam Smith's liberalism to socialistic 'economic romanticism' was Simonde de Sismondi (1773–1842), who started his career by publishing an expository book on Smith's *The Wealth of Nations* (*De la Richesse Commerciale*, 1803) and subsequently developed into a systematic critique of the 'Invisible Hand' effect of market equilibrium (*Nouveaux Principes d'Economie Politique*, 1819). Without denying the existence of equilibrating tendencies of the market, Sismondi makes it clear that the attainment of a new equilibrium, for instance, *after technological innovations*, is usually achieved only at the price of extraordinary human costs and capital losses. 'Let us beware,' he wrote, 'of this dangerous theory of equilibrium which is supposed to reestablish itself automatically. . . . It is true a certain equilibrium is reestablished in the long run, but only after a frightful amount of suffering. It is a fact that capital is withdrawn from a particular industry only as a result of bankruptcy of the owner, and workers give up their occupations only when they die; indeed, laborers who find it easy to shift to other occupations and move to other places must be regarded as exceptions and not the rule.'[15]

From Sismondi on, there developed, especially among European socialist writers of the nineteenth century, a recognition of the general thesis that the social costs of technical change are inherent in the process of dynamic change. A typical instance in this trend was Justus von Liebig's empirical discussion of social costs in agriculture,[16] which obviously influenced Karl Marx to formulate the often-quoted statement that

> all progress in capitalistic agriculture is a progress in the art, not only of robbing the laborer, but of robbing the soil. . . . In other words, capitalist production develops technology, and the combining together of various processes into a social whole, only by sapping the original sources of all wealth – the soil and the laborer.[17]

The Marxian political economy was actually a most systematic analysis of 'the social costs of private enterprise,' emphasizing in particular the class antagonism between capital and labour and pointing towards the historical necessity of revolutionary struggle by labour to clear away such social costs.

It is noteworthy that Friedrich Engels, a close partner of Marx, conducted an early investigation into the 'human costs' of the industrial revolution in England[18] and called attention to another kind of social cost, the full magnitude of which was brought to light only in more recent times, namely, the damage caused by air pollution. Engels' indictment is quite concrete. He wrote:

> In London, two hundred fifty thousand fires crowded upon an area three to four miles square, consume an enormous amount of oxygen which is replaced with difficulty because the method of building cities in itself impedes ventilation. The carbonic acid gas, engendered by respiration and fire, remains in the streets by reason of its specific gravity and the chief air current passes over the roofs of the city. The lungs of the inhabitants fail to receive the due supply of oxygen and the consequence is mental and physical lassitude and low vitality.[19]

No less a person than William Morris (1834–96) whom Engels called 'a sentimental socialist' spoke more explicitly, even passionately, in critique of environmental disruptions in cities and country landscapes. In a lecture he gave in November 1883 in Oxford, he 'launched into a prophetic passage,' in Fiona MacCarthy's words, 'on the themes of great concern to modern environmentalists'[20] in the following manner:

> To keep the air and rivers clean, to take some pains to keep the meadows and tillage as pleasant as reasonable use will allow them to be; to allow peaceable citizens freedom to wander where they will, so they do no hurt to garden or cornfield; nay, even to leave here and there some piece of waste or mountain sacredly free from fence or tillage as a memory of man's ruder struggles with nature in his earlier days: is it too much to ask civilization to be so far thoughtful of man's pleasure and rest, and to help so far as this her children to whom she has most often set such heavy tasks of grinding labour? Surely not an unreasonable asking. But not a whit of it shall we get under the present system of society. That loss of the instinct for beauty which has involved us in the loss of popular art is also busy in depriving us of the only compensation possible for that loss, by surely and not slowly destroying the beauty of the very face of the earth.

William Morris, who is remembered better for his advocacy of 'the arts and crafts movement' and also as a leader of the Socialist

League in England in the 1880s, had an eye-opening experience during his visit (between summer 1875 and spring 1878) to Leek, a small industrial town in Staffordshire, where he tried to obtain an intensive course in the technique of textile dying. There, 'for the first time he was faced with the realities of things he had previously considered only in the abstract: industrial landscapes, commercial production, the pattern of loyalties within a small community, the man–master tradition, the innate conservatism of the British working class.'[21] According to J.W. Mackail, a son-in-law of Morris' close friend Burne-Jones, the experience in Leek apparently had altered Morris to become intensely concerned with the pollution problems. His friends remember him, perched on a stool at a street corner in the East End of London expostulating on the ruin of the landscape, in the oft-quoted words of his: 'God made the country, men made the town, and the devil made the suburb.'

If we are to broaden the concept of 'social costs' to include within it the social losses, or a kind of waste as ascertained against the normatively defined social welfare standard, as Kapp does, we can add another contribution by William Morris, in which he owed to John Ruskin for the importance of the problem, agreeing with him on 'the brutalizing cycles of contemporary commerce.' Fiona MacCarthy comments that 'Morris always insisted that Ruskin came at the right time and that he was the prime mover in the turning of the tide away from a blind faith in materialist progress and towards a perception of the damage to society this implied.'[22]

If Morris could be called a champion of the 'Love of Art in Daily Life,' Ruskin was undeniably a champion of the 'Humanization of Ordinary Labor.' Both men in these regards were pushed to the periphery of the orthodox camp of Victorian economic thinking. It was characteristic of Ruskin to write, while discussing Adam Smith's doctrine of the division of labour:

> It is not, truly speaking, the labor that is divided; but the men: – divided into mere segments of men – broken into small fragments and crumbs of life; so that all the little piece of intelligence that is left in man is not enough to make a pin, or a nail, but exhausts itself in making the point of a pin or the head of a nail.[23]

Ruskin was so critical of the contemporary orthodoxy of political economy that he characterized it as 'a science of gymnastics which assumed that men had no skeletons,'[24] and had an occasion to describe John Stuart Mill as 'a flat fish – one eyeless side of his always in the mud.'[25] Aside from these Ruskinian somewhat abusive slurs, his castigating remarks in critique of excessive commercialism, spoken in his lecture to manufacturers in 1859, have the relevance even 100 years later as bespeaking of the wasteful expenditures entailed in the competitive society of private enterprise. The remarks are so appropriate that they are worth quoting at length:

> You must remember always that your business, as manufacturers, is to form the market, as much as to supply it. If, in shortsighted and reckless eagerness for wealth, you catch at every humour of the populace as it shapes itself into momentary demand – if, in jealous rivalry with neighbouring States, or with other producers, you try to attract attention by singularities, novelties, and gaudinesses – to make every design an advertisement, and pilfer every idea of a successful neighbour's, that you may insidiously imitate it, or pompously eclipse – no good design will ever be possible to you, or perceived by you. You may, by accident, snatch the market; or, by energy, command it; you may obtain the confidence of the public, and cause the ruin of opponent houses; or you may, with equal justice of fortune, be ruined by them. But whatever happens to you, this, at least, is certain, that the whole of your life will have been spent in corrupting public taste and encouraging public extravagance. Every preference you have won by gaudiness must have been based on the purchaser's vanity; every demand you have created by novelty has fostered in the consumer a habit of discontent; and when you retire into inactive life, you may, as a subject of consolation for your declining years, reflect that precisely according to the extent of your past operations, your life has been successful in retarding the arts, tarnishing the virtues, and confusing the manners of your country.[26]

In reading this paragraph, one is reminded naturally of Vance Packard's *The Waste Makers*, 1960, which reminded us of the waste involved in the latest stage of capitalistic prosperity and also of the critical analysis of business enterprise by that unique American economist Thorstein Veblen (1857–1929), who wrote:

> The absorption of goods and services by extra-industrial expenditures, expenditures which as seen from the standpoint of industry are pure waste, would have to go on in an increasing volume. If the wasteful expenditure slackens, the logical outcome should be a considerable perturbation of business and industry, followed by depression; if the waste on war, colonization, provincial investment, and the like, comes to an

abrupt stop, the logical consequence, in the absence of other counteracting forces, should be a crisis of some severity.[27]

It may be mentioned in passing that William Morris did have some influence on the Fabian Socialists in Great Britain, particularly because G.B. Shaw (1856–1950) was a close family colleague. The Fabians, organized as a society in 1884, were in a sense pioneers in proposing the doctrine of the welfare state, devoting their analysis in large measure to the social costs in the industrial sphere.

A close associate of the Fabians in particular, that is, J.A. Hobson (1858–1940), calls for special attention not only as a broad-minded political economist but also as an advocate of the uniquely Victorian philosophy of net social welfare in the sense of social benefit exceeding social cost. His formulation was quite unique in terms of orthodox economics of his time, anticipating in fact what Kapp chose much later to frame the concept of social welfare as the difference between social benefits and social costs. As for Hobson, he represented

> economic activity diagrammatically as generating human utility and incurring human cost on both the production side and the consumption side. Human utility is generated not only by consumption, which satisfies needs or offers 'abundance,' but also by production, when it takes the form either of art and exercise or of 'labour,' that is to say of satisfying work, as opposed to 'toil.' Human cost is incurred not only by production which takes the form either of 'toil' or of 'malproduction,' the latter referring to work which is degrading, but also by consumption which involves either satiety or 'mal-consumption,' the latter referring to such 'base' modes of consumption as the taking of drugs. The aggregate excess of human utility over human cost measures ... 'organic welfare' or 'social welfare.'[28]

Hobson's reference to human cost in the form of 'mal-production' and 'mal-consumption' has the implication of social costs in the more modern definition by Kapp. But it is admitted by Hobson himself that many utilities and costs, as he visualized, are not reflected in the market and thus are difficult or impossible to measure. And this was a point of the neo-classical critique on Hobson's formulation. However, as Michael Schneider writes: 'Much of what modern theory has to say on external costs and benefits was anticipated by Hobson, in his discussion of the relationship between welfare and production.'[29] And as a matter of fact, A.C. Pigou, whose writings are the principal source of this aspect of modern welfare economics, may well have been influenced by Hobson, whose writings are cited five times in Pigou's *Wealth and Welfare*.[30]

It is generally agreed that A.C. Pigou was probably the first neoclassical economist who paid considerable attention to social costs. His analytical approach to this problem is phrased in terms of his discussion of the divergence of the 'marginal social net product' from the 'marginal private net product.' The former, which Pigou called 'the true net product' in his *Wealth and Welfare*, is defined as

> the total net product of *physical things or objective services* due to the marginal increment of resources in any given use or place, no matter to whom any part of this product may accrue. It might happen, for example, . . . that costs are thrown upon people, not directly concerned, through, say, uncompensated damage done to surrounding woods by sparks from railway engines.[31]

The marginal private net product, on the other hand, is defined as

> that part of the total net product of physical things or objective services due to the marginal increment of resources in any given use or place which accrues in the first instance – i.e. prior to sale – to the person responsible for investing resources there.[32]

It is quite characteristic of Pigou's discussion that both of these 'marginal net product' concepts are understood to be expressible in terms of *market value*. And within this limitation, he enumerates the cases where a divergence could occur between the two, such as:

(1) The over-running of a neighbour's land by rabbits originating from game preserves;
(2) the destruction of the amenities and lighting of neighbouring sites by the construction of a factory in residential districts;
(3) the wearing out of the surfaces of roads by motor cars;
(4) the increase in expenditures for police and prisons made necessary by the production and sale of intoxicants;
(5) the costs of diplomatic manoeuvres, military preparedness and actual war caused by foreign investments;
(6) the costs of competitive advertising;
(7) various negative effects of monopolistic practices;
(8) the social costs of technical improvements;

(9) the social losses resulting from unequal wage bargains between employers and unorganized labour, etc.

In all these instances of possible social losses, Pigou surmised that we might be confronted with evidences of 'the bankruptcy of capitalism' and a 'prima facie case for extending the range of public ownership and public operation to industries in which they have not yet been invoked.'[33]

Pigou's analysis of 'social losses' was essentially within the framework of neo-classical economics with the self-imposed constraint of conceptual operationality in terms of the market mechanism. And yet, the coverage of his concern with external diseconomies was quite broad, as can be seen from the examples cited above. However, when we come to W. Michalski, whose *Grundlegung eines operationalen Konzepts der 'Social Costs'*[34] provided a critical discussion of Kapp's formulation of 'social costs,' the constraint of operationality is made even more rigorous, and he limits the conceptual scope of 'social costs' to the following four categories only:

(1) Costs involved in the pollutions of air and water and also of noise.
(2) The damage to road surfaces caused by heavy motor vehicles and the congestion on roads caused by disabled cars.
(3) Forest fires caused by sparks from railway engines.
(4) The conglomeration of manufacturing industries and their unplanned construction.

Michalski's major concern was to deal with these phenomena consistently within the framework of traditional economic theory, thus requiring no introduction of a new paradigm. Kapp had an occasion to offer a lengthy rebuttal to this approach.[35]

Among the several experts who have dealt with the concept of 'social costs' in its broad sense in recent years, Roefie Hueting of the Netherlands Central Bureau of Statistics could be singled out as a somewhat unique, systematic, discussant of the subject.[36] Hueting's central thesis is:

(1) The environment (its major components being water, soil and air) provides certain possible uses for man, which can be called 'functions.'
(2) 'A conflict is being waged between the growth of production

and population on the one hand and the environment on the other.' (p x)

(3) Through such conflict, increasing calls are made on the 'functions' of the environment, causing its deterioration or the occurrence of losses of function, which may be regarded as costs.

(4) 'An environmental component always has three aspects, a quantitative one (the amount of matter), a qualitative one (the degree of pollution) and a spatial aspect.' (p 98)

(5) 'Human activities are leading to increasingly violent competition between the functions of the environment, [which] . . . means that the limits of the qualitative, quantitative and spatial possibilities of using our environment have been reached or already exceeded.' (pp 186–7)

(6) 'This amounts to the fact that our level of consumption is most probably at the expense of the consumption by, and indeed the very possibilities of life of, our children and grandchildren.' (p 187)

(7) Since environmental functions supply the essential needs of man, losses of function form an aspect of 'negative growth.' Therefore, 'for a correct insight into economic growth the losses of function, valued against the shadow prices, ought to be subtracted from the national income, [although] the shadow prices of these losses usually remain unknown because the preferences are expressed only partly in market quantities.' (p xii)

It is clear enough that Hueting is formulating in his own way the nature of 'social costs' in connection with the major components of the environment, in particular water and air; and it should be pointed out that he and his associates attempted to carry out a painstaking task of numerical evaluation based on the definitions given in his theoretical framework.

Hueting's analysis, which suggests the possibility of 'more welfare through less production,' poses essentially the problem of a trade-off between development and environment in the sense that if a community or a country prefers to incur cost in taking appropriate countermeasures against environmental disruptions, then development will have to be sacrificed in some measure, or conversely, if a higher rate of development of industries accompanied by a greater degree of social costs in the form of pollution of all kinds is preferred, such pollution will have to be tolerated. As a matter of fact, when the

Stockholm Conference on Human Environment was proposed for 1972, it was essential that practically all the countries in the world should be invited; and for this purpose it was considered necessary for there to be a unified philosophy of positive character to which developing countries no less than developed ones could subscribe. But many of the countries in the 'South' were taking the position at the time typically exemplified by the trade-off statement above, even saying that they would welcome some pollution for the sake of development. In addition, they raised a question of the responsibility for the presumably critical state of affairs as regards the environment, using the following metaphor:

> Suppose there is a lake fit for swimming and fishing. A small number of people first come to reside on the lakeside and enjoy the use of the lake for all kinds of purposes. After a while, the lake water begins to be dirtied through untreated sewerage and the fish population also declines. By that time, the early settlers have so exploited the surrounding nature that they have become wealthy enough to afford leisurely living of swimming and boating all day long. Then comes a group of new settlers, much larger in number, and they start building huts on the lake shore and working hard on fishing activities. Thereupon, the now affluent early settlers call upon all the settlers around the lake to hold a meeting and propose at that meeting that the fishing catch be limited, each hut should have a treatment facility for sewerage, and the lake water be kept clean enough for swimming. The still-poor late settlers protest that they can never improve their level of living if they have to abide by such restrictions. The early settlers say to them then that the proposed restrictions are for the good of all and if they don't like them they can always move to somewhere else.

Now, this of course is an extremely simplified representation of the relative position of the 'North' and the 'South' in regard to today's environmental problems. But it could not be denied that many of the developing countries had a psychological attitude somewhat similar to that of the late settlers above so far as the internationally imposed pollution controls were concerned.

In such context of historically conditioned differences among the countries in the world as regards the impact of the environment on them, it was not surprising that many people in the developing countries questioned the relevance of the new concern for environment in the light of their own compellingly urgent development priorities. In order somehow to bridge the gap in recognition of the urgency of the problem, the Secretary General of the United Nations

Conference on Human Environment took the initiative in organizing a meeting of experts in Founex, Switzerland, in June 1971. This panel brought out a report, entitled 'Development and Environment,' which subsequently served as a basic document for discussion at regional UN organizations and elsewhere. The philosophy which ran through this report can be summarized as follows:

> To a large extent, the current concern with environmental issues has emerged out of the problems experienced by the industrially advanced countries. With these problems, developing countries, too, will be increasingly concerned. But the major environmental problems of developing countries today are essentially of a different kind. They are predominantly problems that reflect the poverty and very lack of development of their societies. In other words, their environmental problems are those that can be overcome by the process of development itself. If we can say that in advanced countries development has been a *cause* of environmental problems, the contrasting expression we may use for developing countries will be that development is a *cure* for environmental problems.
>
> It should be added, however, that concern with human environment does provide new dimensions to the development concept in that a new emphasis is now to be placed on the attainment of social and cultural goals as part of the development process.

Stated succinctly, the basic position taken by the report is that for developing countries the 'environment' is an issue in mass poverty and 'development' is a cure for it whereas in advanced countries 'development' has been a cause of the 'environment.' In other words, by saying that 'development is a *cure* for environmental problems,' the Founex report chose to broaden the coverage of the term 'environment' so that the countries in the 'South' could be persuaded to participate in the UN Conference on Human Environment. This specific purpose of strategic expediency was successfully attained; and the 'environmental band-wagon,' so to speak, was in evidence in the sense that the current environmental concern on the international scale could be taken advantage of to load on to that concept as many problem areas as possible so that aid activities in such fields could be intensified. Broadening of the coverage of the 'environment' concept thus went so far as to include such matters as soil erosion, urban plight, public health problems, etc., all of which happen to be actually within the purview of Kapp's category of 'social losses.'

But a question remains if it might not be better to delineate more precisely the scope of environmental problems so that needed counter-measures could have a well-defined focus. In view of this consideration, I propose to take up next a somewhat narrower, but rather unique, concept used in Japan called '*kōgai*' which might be rendered in English as 'disamenities inflicted on the public.'

But before doing this, we may dwell upon another recent conceptual innovation which has become internationally popular in the field of environmental problems, namely, 'sustainable development' – an expression used in the 1987 'Brundland Commission' report. This was then defined as 'development that meets the needs of the present without imperiling the ability of future generations to meet their needs.'

This definition actually reminds us of Hueting's warning, mentioned earlier, to the effect that 'the present level of our consumption is most probably at the expense of the consumption of, and indeed the very possibilities of life of, our children and grandchildren.' Such inter-generational concern has now become an integral part of the environmental problem. But as a matter of fact, the concept of 'sustainable development,' which became a keyword in the so-called 'Earth Summit' at Rio de Janeiro, was broadened to entail, in the opinion of Maurice Strong, Secretary General of that UN Conference, the three basic normative criteria of 'social equity, ecological prudence and economic efficiency.'[37] 'Social equity' here implied the need for bridging the gap between the 'North' and the 'South,' as can be gleaned from the following explanatory statement by Strong:

> We know today that our civilization and even life on our planet will be doomed unless we shift to the only viable path for poor and rich alike. For that the North must dampen its consumption of resources and the South escape from the poverty. Development and environment are indissolubly linked and must be addressed by changing the modalities, the content and the uses of growth.[38]

Here again, Hueting's suggestion of 'more welfare through less production' is quite appropriate, calling for the rethinking on the nature of the social minimum standard against which we can speak of 'social costs.' One is led inevitably to recall Keynes's dictum in his lecture in 1930 at Madrid:

> The day may not be all that far off when everybody would be rich. .... We shall then be able to rid ourselves of many of the pseudomoral principles which have hag-ridden us for two hundred years, by which we have exalted

some of the most distasteful of human qualities into the position of the highest values. . . . [Then] we shall once more value ends above means and prefer the good to the useful.[39]

THE CONCEPT OF 'KŌGAI' DEFINED

As has been seen, the concept of 'social costs,' though useful, has become too polysemous for analytical purpose; and it is here suggested that a Japanese expression '*Kōgai*,' which came into use as early as in the 1870s, may enable us to focus more adequately on the type of phenomena which we now call environmental deterioration or disruption,[40] such as air pollution and water pollution, dating back several centuries in the history of man. As early as in 1273 England passed a Smoke Abatement Act in order to control the use of coal in a certain part of London; and the term 'nuisance' was commonly used in this connection. Germany preferred to focus on the legal aspects of the problem, using a legal term 'Immission.' Lately in France, a more descriptive expression, 'les pollusions et "nuisance" d'origine industrielle et urbaine', has been in use. But the Japanese word '*kōgai*' is probably the simplest and yet meaningful enough. In using this term, however, a more detailed definition may be called for, for which purpose I proposed as early as in 1968[41] the following particulars as constituting the essential aspects of *kōgai* phenomena:

(1) In the stage of economic development where technological progress heightens the social character of production more and more and thus strengthens the degree of dependence of an industrial economic unit upon external influences as well as the extent of its spill-over effects upon others;

(2) So long as we permit the atomistic cost-accounting to prevail in the decision-making process of individual enterprises;

(3) There will be a natural trend, on the one hand, for such individual economic units to take full advantage of external economies, often bringing about the condition of excessive agglomeration;

(4) On the other hand, undesirable external effects, for which minimum compensatory action is taken, accumulate in the neighbourhood, and become aggravated through the process of 'quantity transforming itself into quality.'

(5) But each individual economic unit escapes responsibility for the consequences of such a process inasmuch as it is usually very difficult to establish a causal connection between a particular economic unit and the overall consequences;

(6) Thus there result damages or disamenities which are suffered usually by an indefinite number of individuals and/or enterprises.

How I came to define *kōgai* problems in this manner may be explained in some detail.

The *kōgai* phenomena have three distinct stages for each of which an institutional dimension has some relevance. The three stages are: (A) the technical or engineering aspect of pollution *sources*, (B) the objectively ascertainable *phenomena* of environmental pollution, and (C) the *damage* or disamenities inflicted upon human beings and/or valuable objects.

Stage (A): Sources

As was mentioned earlier (in the section on 'Concessions to the Prevailing Position of the Real-Physical Aspect' in this chapter), in the modern period of 'scientific–industrial revolution,' basic science itself is embraced as a factor of production in the form of privatized know-how. In this process, 'pollution tends to become intensified,' as Barry Commoner has written, 'by the displacement of older productive techniques by new, ecologically faulty, but more profitable technologies.' In other words, 'pollution is an unintended concomitant of the natural drive of the economic system to introduce new technologies that increase productivity.'[42] It is true, of course, that the degree of pollution caused can be mitigated by the individual economic unit concerned through the installation of anti-pollution measures. Thus, technically, there is no inevitability as to the quantitative magnitude of the pollution spoken of. However, given the institutional system of atomistic cost-accounting of private capital, unfavourable external effects are generally disregarded.

Stage (B): Phenomena

Pollution phenomena, whether of air or of water, can be quantitatively measured both in intensity and duration. Ecological significance of such quantitative magnitude depends greatly on the nature of the milieu where it occurs. Allowable limits for effluent discharge naturally become more severe in the milieu where the affected population is concentrated, with consideration being given to the fact that there is a characteristic tendency of 'quantity transforming into quality' in the case of polluting effluents.

Stage (C): Damage
This last point in stage (B), i.e. 'quantity transforms into quality,' is quite relevant in bridging the stages from (B) to (C), in the sense, for example, that doubling the quantity may cause more than doubling of the effect, thus bringing about qualitatively a new dimension. Furthermore, it is generally observed that a physically identical discharge of polluting effluents can be reflected in different degrees of damage depending on various circumstances such as the location of offending plants, the density of population in the area, climatic conditions, etc. An additional problem that has to be kept in mind is the synergy effect of two or more types of effluent discharges, as was exemplified by the so-called 'London Incident' of December 1952, when the extent of smog damage was far beyond what could be inferred from the then maximum density of 0.4 ppm in sulphurous acid gas. The concurrence of heavy smoke at the time was to blame for the 'Incident.'

We can follow a causal chain abstractly from (A) pollution sources to (B) ascertainable pollution phenomena and to (C) actual occurrence of damage. But in a large number of cases, specific damage that has occurred is very difficult to trace to a specific offending source. Even when a specific offender is identified, it may turn out only to be an intermediary, as in the case, in the 1960s, of the Miyé Thermal Plant in Japan, which drained its cooling water at the mouth of the river near a fishing village, causing stench damage on fish. The plant was simply pumping up the harbour water for its cooling use and the water was already polluted and dirtied by the effluents from *other* factories facing the harbour. Difficulties of this kind in identifying the specific offender abound in victims' attempts to confirm specific responsibility in *kōgai* problems.

CHAPTER TWO

Historical analysis – the prewar period

THE INITIAL STAGE OF JAPAN'S INDUSTRIALIZATION

It is commonly agreed that the bench-mark year for the emergence of modern Japan was 1868, the year Imperial rule was restored more or less peacefully, following the power decline of the feudal Tokugawa shogunate. Then, the circumstance was such that the new leaders of Meiji Japan, keenly aware of the consequence of the Opium War in China and also feeling pressure from Commodore Perry's visit to Shimoda in 1853, were determined to resist any encroachment by foreign powers on Japan's independent attempt for modernization. For this purpose, dependence on foreign capital import had to be shunned; and furthermore, it was clear enough that the treaty constraint earlier of the maximum of 5 per cent *ad valorem* tariff limitation was hardly enough to protect Japan's infant industries at the time. These handicaps forced the country to search for the only other device of enabling the country's viable capitalism to evolve, which was to exploit the native working class to the utmost. In particular, producers in the agricultural sector constituted the Atlas on which the severest burden fell. And the continuing plight of poor peasants was a contributing factor to the extremely low supply price for the factory labour force, especially the type of labour which the leading manufacturing industry of the time – cotton textiles – required. Young girls were recruited from destitute farm areas usually in the form of contract labour in which parents were paid a lump sum. Even in cases where supplying labour for factory work was 'voluntary,' the supply price hinged largely on the consideration of *supplementing* the family income and not much more. Furthermore, working conditions in manufacturing plants in general were of the type least mindful of public health considerations. It was only in this way that Japanese capitalism managed to develop what Rostow calls 'a leading industry' for the take-off in the period roughly around the 1890s.

A most energetic import-substitution effort was made in the cotton textile industry;[1] and this gained momentum between 1886 and 1890 at the end of which Japan started exporting cotton yarns for the first time. Then in 1891, the domestic production of yarns overtook imports; and by 1897 exports of this product were exceeding imports.

Along with such progress in the 'leading industry' for the take-off the decade of 1890s saw a number of path-breaking events, such as: (1) the victory in the Sino-Japanese War (1894–5) yielding an indemnity of the magnitude (364 million yen) roughly equal to one-half of Japan's national income at that time; (2) Japan's joining the camp of gold standard countries in 1897; (3) the establishment of a major iron-works in Yawata in 1896, etc. Thus, confidence in the future both on the side of government and private capital at that time was patently reflected in their routine utterances and deeds. It is in this light that we can make allowances for the proud tone with which the municipal anthem was sung in Yawata – the city for a major iron-works. Its refrain went as follows:

> Blazing flames scorching the waves,
> Billows of smoke overspread the sky:
> This iron works of ours,
> A grandeur unmatched of the Empire.
> Yawata, Yawata, our proud city of Yawata!

The Yawata Iron Works evolved in subsequent years as the biggest steel manufacturing company in Japan.

Given such a background in the sphere of industrial workshops, it can easily be understood that whatever industrial pollution that might have been caused in the factory towns could be considered by the townspeople as of no more damaging character than within the workshops. Nevertheless, it is significant to record that there was on the other hand some evidence of far-sighted awareness of environmental problems in the post-Restoration period of Meiji Japan. As early as in 1877, that is even before the Matsukata Deflation of 1881–5, which is likened to the English Restriction Period of 1815–21 'in providing a secure frame for entrepreneurial activity,'[2] and which prepared for the establishment of industrial capitalism in Japan around 1890, the Osaka Prefectural Office issued a set of regulations controlling the establishment of iron and steel works, smitheries and public bath houses.[3] The regulations were quite concrete, specifying that:

(1) All those manufacturing plants, employing 50 or more workers, which make use of motors or fireworks, or which discharge poisonous gas or offensive odour or noise, are requested to obtain specific permission in advance of their establishment, the same prescript applying to those manufacturing plants, other than the ones cited above, which are apt to cause material harm or injury to health.

(2) In principle, all the manufacturing plants should be located at an appropriate enough distance from neighbouring residential quarters.

(3) Even after permission is granted for setting up of the plant, it might be rescinded in cases when damage occurs or is threatened to occur.

During the Tokugawa shogunate period Osaka prospered as the foremost commercial centre in Japan. But as a new vista came to be opened after the Meiji Restoration, Osaka became a bustling city for manufacturing development, even likened as 'a Manchester in East Asia.' It is understandable that the sudden mushrooming of workshops called for a type of municipal regulations like those cited above, especially the prescript specifying 'appropriate enough distance' between the projected plant location and neighbouring residential quarters. This prescript, however, could not be enforced strictly in the face of a dynamic march of private profit-seeking enterprises. And when a more comprehensive 'Manufactories Control Regulation' was promulgated in 1896 by the Osaka Prefecture, an extenuating condition was allowed for the proximity rule in those cases 'where *kōgai* is likely to be negligible.'[4] In fact, a tug-of-war over the question of *kōgai* control continued in Osaka between environmentalists and business groups in the subsequent decades mainly in the form of forensic battles without any substantive gain for the anti-*kōgai* camp. One example was a proposal made for the promulgation of 'Smoke Prevention Ordinance' in 1913 by a study group organized by some prominent citizens (headed by Chikaaki Takasaki, a former governor of the Osaka prefecture) and a couple of leading local newspapers (the Osaka *Jiji Shimpō* and the Fuji *Shimbun*). The proposal went as far as the Osaka Prefectural Police Department which drafted concrete articles for the ordinance, submitting them for comments in July 1913 to the Osaka Chamber of Commerce as well as to the study group referred to above. The latter replied within nine days, supporting the draft with a few suggestions for minor revision. The Chamber of Commerce, on the other hand, took more than one year to respond, with a concluding remark to the effect that:

> Having made an intensive research, we have come to the conclusion that a faultless device for the purpose is not available at present and that relatively effective devices would be too expensive for factory owners to bear. If the proposed ordinance were to be enforced, an inevitable consequence would be the closing down of many of the factories which would strike a deathblow to the vital sinews of the city of Osaka.[5]

Toshitaka Okubo, the then Governor of Osaka Prefecture, accepted the conclusion of the Chamber of Commerce – this was in November 1914 – and decided to shelve the draft ordinance for smoke prevention.

It is pertinent to recall that the First World War began in July 1914 and it is reasonable to surmise that Japanese business groups, being in the position of fishing in the troubled waters, became sanguine in their new investment activities, ignoring entirely attendant consequences on the environment. Thus it was also in November 1914 that the Osaka Association of Manufacturing Industries met in their general assembly to pass a resolution in critique of the Manufactories Control Regulation which was still in force at the time. The upshot was an enactment in 1920 of the Factory Control Regulation by the Osaka Prefecture in place of the earlier Manufactories Control Regulation, substituting the notification for the licensing on such matters as the construction, enlargement and reconstruction of factories. Priority was clearly given to the dictate of capital.

Although the general trend was in the direction of favouring 'the development over the environment' in those days, it was a source of encouragement for environmentalists to learn that a number of prominent opinion leaders of the time sided with them in public. Shimpei Goto (1857–1929), for example, who started as a medical expert, later to become Mayor of Tokyo, wrote in 1888:

> The present condition of our country Japan is doubtless far behind that of England or Germany. However, some people seem to rejoice idly the increase in the number of smoke-stacks, showing no resistance to the increasing installation of them in the heart of our cities, believing apparently that the spectacle is thereby enhanced. Such a situation evokes grave apprehension for the country's future.[6]

Another well-known public figure, Toyohiko Kagawa (1888–1960), a Christian evangelist, wrote in his satirical novel *Mastering the Sky* (1922), in which he feigned himself to be Mayor of Osaka and spoke to citizens in his hypothetical inaugural address as follows:

> Dear fellow citizens! There are many things I will have to do as Mayor of this city. But the first task above all is the mastering of Osaka's sky. If we continue to be beset by the sky like the present one with those smoke-stacks pouring out smoke as you see them, I believe that Osaka citizens will not be able to maintain their health during the coming half century. . . . It is estimated that the quantity of carbon acid gas in the city of Osaka exceeds five per cent [sic] at all times, with the quantity of smoke discharged being the gravest in the world. If the present Osaka has to admit that our infant death rate as well as the incidence of lung disease will be the highest in the world, that is, our city will top the world as an unhealthy urban area, my duty as Mayor of the city, I believe, is to devote the primary task for guaranteeing the health of you citizens.

Actually, studies were made in 1922 onwards on the degree of air pollution in Osaka by the Municipal Research Institute on Public Health, confirming the extent of environmental deterioration at the time.[7] Also, records show that the Osaka Prefectural Assembly adopted by majority in 1902 'The Proposal regarding the Prevention of Smoke' to be presented to the Governor, in which the details were given of the estimated number of smoke-stacks in the city and also of the induced damages on citizens' health and other objects.

In spite of these indications of fairly serious concern over the environmental conditions by public opinion leaders and the regional legislative body, city dwellers in general in Osaka were not stirred up into a major protest movement against offenders, except in an isolated case like a petition signed by several thousand citizens in 1912 to the Prime Minister and the Minister of Interior over the nuisance caused by sulphurous acid gas emitted by the Osaka Coal-gas Company.[8]

Incongruity one feels in this connection can be clearly explained by the circumstance, referred to at the beginning of this section, that working conditions in urban workshops themselves were of such censurable character that the point of criticism was naturally directed more strongly against the labour management inside the workshops than to the environmental conditions outside. Characteristic incidents of mass movement by *kōgai* victims, thus, could be

32   *The Political Economy of the Environment*

seen in the initial stage of Japan's industrialization mainly among the agricultural class suffering from pollution caused particularly by mining industries – a topic we shall take up in the next section.

REPRESENTATIVE INCIDENTS OF KŌGAI – THE CASE OF THE COPPER MINING INDUSTRY

There was a good enough reason for the urban pollution to be tolerated inasmuch as the working conditions in factories were, if at all, relatively worse than outside them. But when the pollution struck agricultural areas with unmistakable damage to the products, there was no extenuating consideration as in the case of *kōgai* in factory towns. Notable in this respect was the impact of copper mining on the farm land.

The copper mining industry, when uncontrolled, caused pollution of multiple character. In their initial stage of development, copper mines discharge untreated sulphurous acid gases and arsenious acid from copper digging and refining, and large volumes of mine sediment containing copper, lead, bismuth, zinc and other toxic heavy metals, into the air and water. And the sulphurous acid gas and toxic heavy metal particulates emitted from smelter smoke-stacks inhibit crop growth and destroy woods and forests. Dead forests, then, lose their ability to retain water and lead to a higher probability of heavy flood damage in downstream areas. When the fine ore, tailings and debris, with their content of arsenic and harmful heavy metals, flow down with the acidic discharge water into rivers, into irrigation canals and then into paddies and fields, enormous damage is caused to farming, particularly to rice – a most important Japanese agricultural crop. Further damage could occur, not only to species of fish in the river, but even to the health of residents in the vicinity.

In other words, it could not be doubted that copper mining was one of the most glaring examples of the *kōgai*-generating industries. And yet, it happened that Japan had to depend heavily on copper as one of the major export items in the post-Restoration period, as can be confirmed in Table 2.1. Cotton fabrics' role as a major export item came only after 1900; and other than copper and coal, which were the mining products, Japanese exports depended heavily on silk, tea and rice in the last decade and half of the nineteenth century. It was the irony of fate that copper was the *kōgai*-generating industry and

(in 1000 yen)		
1886–90	1891–5	1896–1900
Raw silk	20,599 (I)	30,202 (I)	46,759 (I)
Green tea	6,544 (II)	7,482 (II)	7,423 (V)
Silk fabrics	460	5,782 (III)	13,226 (III)
Coal	3,375 (IV)	5,665 (IV)	13,915 (II)
Copper	3,217 (V)	4,906 (VI)	8,645 (IV)
Rice	4,347 (III)	5,635 (V)	6,774 (VI)

Table 2.1 *Japan's major exports by commodities: five-year averages, 1886–1900*

Source: Compiled from *Nippon Bōeki Seiran* (Detail Statistics of Japan's Foreign Trade), Tōyō Keizai Shimpo Sha, 1935.

Note: Roman numerals indicate the ranks in value for each quinquennial period. The sixth in position for the period 1886–90 was waste silk.

rice-farming the victim. We shall see next how three major copper-refining centers in Japan tackled, or failed to tackle, the *kōgai* problems which were inevitably generated.

THE ASHIO COPPER MINE[9]

There is a story of Ducktown, often related in connection with the Tennessee Valley Authority in the United States, that tells of a transformation of a beautiful village perched on the western slope of the Appalachians and surrounded by stately hardwood trees into a prosperous copper-refining centre just before the First World War and subsequently into a place of desolation with surrounding forest land denuded, the river water contaminated and no longer serving as a habitat for fish and the erstwhile green pastures made bare and eroded.

Historically prior to Ducktown, however, there is a story of Ashio which is usually cited as a classical example of *kōgai* in Japan. Ashio is situated along the upstream of the River Watarasé, a major tributary of the Toné, 100 kilometres directly north of Tokyo and 20 kilometres southwest of Nikko, a popular tourist spot for foreign visitors as well. Copper was discovered there as early as in 1610, and though with some vicissitudes the Ashio mine remained as a top supplier of copper for two and a half centuries under the direct management of the central feudal government of Tokugawa. After the Meiji Restoration, the mine was transferred (in 1871) to a private firm; and from 1877 on, under the ruthless entrepreneurship of Ichibei Furukawa, it was made into a modern copper-refining centre. With this modernization and prosperity of the copper-refining activities there emerged inevitably spillover effects of a harmful kind, first (around 1880) in the form of damage to fish in the River Watarasé, then (from 1888 on) affecting the rice crops which depended on the river for irrigation, and thereafter causing ill effects on the health of the people residing along the river.

A major difference between the case of Ducktown and that of Ashio was that whereas the former was located in a sparsely populated area in any case, the latter was quite close to a river which within 50 kilometres affected directly 200,000 hectares of cultivated and densely inhabited land. The protest movement against the Ashio copper-refining began at first in a somewhat timid fashion and, naturally, did not make a dent to the composure of a rising capitalist firm. The Furukawa firm took a superior attitude by denying any causal connection between their operation and the woes of the farmers along the river. It is noteworthy that the government at the time, by ostensibly taking an attitude of non-interference, actually sided with the copper interest, for it would have been easy enough for the government to launch an investigation on the spillover effects of copper refining and to establish firmly the causal connection which the protesting farmers contended as existing.

The protest movement, however, went on intermittently and gained momentum after Shōzō Tanaka, a Diet member from the region, made it his cause and took its leadership from about 1891. Although Tanaka chose to keep himself quiet during the Sino-Japanese War of 1894–5, his energetic activities, now dramatizing the issue in the Diet, now spending days and nights with farmers in the region for solidifying of the protest organization, and now making a direct appeal to the Emperor (1901), were instrumental in wresting some concessions from the copper-refining firm and also in causing the government to establish an *ad hoc* committee for investigation. But the concessions by the firm were in the form of (1) the payment of solatium calculated more to bribe village elders than in proportion to damages suffered, and (2) the announcement that 'a filtering device' would be imported from Germany and installed. This turned out to be a device for recovering of reusable waste (called the 'locked particle collectors' and did not have the ameliorating effect which the protesting farmers were led to expect.

The protest movement went on, if at all, in a more acrimonious form than before, reminiscent of tenants' riots in the past. What was then locally called 'oshidashi' (push out), meaning a mass mobilization for marching to the capital, was organized repeatedly for five times, starting in 1897, in an attempt to petition directly to the central government. A most memorable 'oshidashi' occurred in February 1900 when upward of 4000 farmers clashed with the military and civil police at Kawamata on the way to Tokyo, resulting in the arrest of more than 70 protesting farmers, who were subsequently indicted under the hastily enacted 'Fomenting Rebellion Act.' The incident, which came to be long remembered as 'the Kawamata Incident,' occasioned the setting up in 1902 by the government of the Second Mine Poisonings Survey Committee composed largely of élite bureaucrats who were prone to side with the copper-refining company. This Committee, in effect, recommended that flood prevention work be done on the ground that the flow slope of the Watarasé being gentler than that of the Toné, the water from the Toné reverses into the Watarasé causing mine poisons to accumulate in the lower reaches of the Watarasé, and therefore, the plan to construct a poisons catchment basin would be effective for the disposal of these poisons where they are at their highest concentration. The Committee's recommendation in other words was to substitute the construction of a catchment basin for more direct steps to eliminate the cause of mine poisons flowing into the Watarasé river. Thus in consequence, the government struck a fatal blow upon the Ashio protest movement by designating the Yanaka area as a reserve land for emergency overflow of the Toné river. Farmers were forced to give up cultivating the land there, and, with a pittance as compensation, had to disperse. Shōzō Tanaka fought as hard as ever against this move, even going as far as to build a hut to live there with the driftwood left in the village, but could not turn back the tide any more. And with this episode of defeat, the Ashio protest movement turned into a rapid eclipse. Tanaka himself died in September 1913.

It is characteristic of the story of Ashio that the *kōgai* problem was fought mainly as a political issue and did not even become a legal issue. One would have expected that the incident as glaring as the Ashio *kōgai*, with the source of spillover so clearly identifiable, should at least serve as a stimulus to developing a new legal framework to contain the kind of strife that was inevitable. But even to this obvious challenge there was no response from the side of legal specialists of the day. The spirit of the times was such that the engine of economic growth and prosperity should have no muffling impediment to weaken its function.

It happens that the most critical stage for the Ashio protest movement coincided with the age of imperialism[10] when the fledgling Japanese capitalism no less than other advanced capitalist countries was intent on not to be left behind in the race. Japan's expansionist ambition towards Korea was acquiesced by England at the time on the grounds (1) that weakening of China will make it easier for Britain to obtain further concessions from her and (2) that Japan's thrust towards the northwest would be a desirable buffer against Russian ambition to move southward. Thus, Japan was emboldened to start a surprise attack in Korea on 23 July 1894, followed one week later by the declaration of war against China. Even Yukichi Fukuzawa, a liberal-minded publicist, applauded this as 'the righteous war for the cause of progress of civilization.'[11] The war ended in March 1895. But the so-called Tripartite Intervention (of Russia, Germany and France), which enjoined Japan to give up the Liantung Peninsula – a part of the war prizes – triggered a new wave of expansionist public opinion in support of a war against Russia. After obtaining moral support from Britain through the Anglo-Japanese Alliance of 1902, Japan again was emboldened to start the war against Russia with a surprise attack on Port Arthur on 8 February 1904. In a sense, it was characteristic that a strong statement was issued by 'The Seven Professors of Tokyo Imperial University' in support of this war. Such being the social atmosphere at the time that there was no incongruity in the official order issued (on 25 January 1901) by the President of the Tokyo Imperial University, Kenjiro Yamakawa, prohibing the students of the university from visiting Ashio for inspection of the *kōgai* there on the ground that such an action would be 'unworthy of the university students.' He was prompted to issue the statement on account of the *kōgai*-critical publicity caused by some students who had gone to Ashio on their own initiative. In Yamakawa's mind there apparently was an inveterate conviction that the Tokyo Imperial University after all was the top-flight training institution for the élite bureaucracy of Imperial Japan.

THE BESSHI COPPER MINE

The Ashio Copper Mine was under the direct management of the central feudal government of Tokugawa and was acquired by Ichibei

Furukawa in 1877 after the Meiji Restoration and later became a core enterprise of the Furukawa *zaibatsu* (industrial and financial combine) controlling some 84 companies at one time – still, however, ranking clearly below the major *zaibatsu* like Mitsui, Mitsubishi and Sumitomo. The Besshi Copper Mine, on the other hand, was under the management of the Sumitomo interest ever since 1690 with an exclusive licence granted by the Tokugawa shogunate. Sumitomo had learned the processing method for copper and silver from Dutch specialists in the late sixteenth century, and the Besshi Mine actually was the primary source of copper exports at the time of the Restoration. Although the new Meiji government rescinded the shogunate licence to Sumitomo at first, the latter mobilized various connections with the new regime including Tomomi Iwakura and succeeded in regaining the development rights of the Besshi. It was characteristic of this period in Japanese business history that Sumitomo's strategy to approach closer to the 'establishment' was to bring in as an adopted son a younger brother of Kinmochi Saionji, a distinguished court noble. The social atmosphere created by the nobility as head of the family enterprise was important, and the *de facto* managers of the Besshi Mine like Tadahira Hirose and Sadanori Iba were in many ways motivated to behave in a relatively creditable manner. Thus, the contrast in managerial countermoves between the two major copper mines of the same period, the Ashio and the Besshi, is quite notable, as we shall see.

The Besshi Copper Mine was no exception in causing smoke damage even during the pre-Restoration period. But the sulphurous acid gas pollution became a social problem of some proportion only after the smelting plant was established in Niihama in 1883 and a protest movement by farmers of the region exploded in 1893. At first, The Sumitomo and the police suppressed the movement, arresting a large number of farmers, and it appeared that they succeeded in quieting the protesting farmers. But when the wheat crop in the following year (1894) visibly failed and the farmers' protest erupted with renewed vehemence, Sumitomo decided to buy up the pollution-affected area (some 800 hectares) from the farmers, proposing to make that area a buffer zone. To the farmers who sold the land to Sumitomo, an additional concession was given in the form of gratuitous permission to use the land for cultivation if they so wished. Since, however, the *source* of *kōgai* was left untouched, the pollution *phenomena* continued and the ensuing *damage* occurred elsewhere, this time to vegetable fields and mulberry trees, and also in the form of lung diseases to nearby village residents. Inevitably, the protest movement became escalated to the extent of a 40-member delegation of protesting farmers travelling to Osaka in order to negotiate directly with Sumitomo's main office. By this time (it was in 1895) Sumitomo had become aware of the seriousness of the situation in their own way and planned a drastic step of moving the entire Niihama smelting plant to a no-man's island, Shizakajima, in the Seto Inland Sea – some 20 kilometres distance from the shore. The purchase of the island itself was consummated in November 1895 at the cost of 9,373 yen, but the cost of the plant transfer and expenses for the minimum infrastructure needed amounted altogether to more than 1,700,000 yen – close to twice the sum of the annual copper sales by Sumitomo at the time. The entire planning was directed by Monnosuke Shiono, an engineer, who received a *carte blanche* on the cost involved by the managing director of Sumitomo, Sadanori Iba. And this huge operation of transferring the source plant of *kōgai* to a distant location with less possibility of causing actual damage was certainly one of the basic anti-*kōgai* steps that could be recommended. Thus, the credit it is due to Iba and Shiono for their hold decision in this regard.

It happened, however, that the transferring of the smelter plant to Shizakajima did not solve the smoke damage problem. Soon after the start of operation at the new plant in 1904, it was observed in Miyakubo village on the opposite shore side, 20 kilometres from the island plant, blighting of young buds in the wheat field – a phenomenon which resembled closely what used to be observed in Niihama village before the transfer of the smelter plant from there. This was a most unexpected occurrence for both Shiono and Iba. But the engineers of the Agricultural Experiment Station commissioned by the prefectural office confirmed that the damage was entirely different from insect blight, and furthermore in the following year (1905) damage of an identical kind spread to other nearby villages as well. Thus, suspicion about the Shizakajima smelter plant could no longer be assuaged. The mood of protest by farmers happened to be dampened in the year 1905 most likely on account of the sizable contribution Sumitomo made to several villages including Niihama in commemoration of the new smelter plant construction in Shizakajima. But when the blighting damage continued on a wider area from 1907 to 1908, the prefectural office itself could no longer stand aloof and appointed a special investigation team in order to ascertain the cause-and-effect relation. The conclusion arrived at by the experts in this team was that in the special atmospheric conditions of high temperature with clear sky and soft wind blowing only in one direction the sulphurous acid gas emitted from Shizakajima would be carried, as if wrapped by the air, as far as 20 kilometres southward in its original density. Upon hearing this conclusion, the farmers' protest movement was renewed in a much stronger form than before. They became united in demanding the following three basic concessions from Sumitomo:

(1) Stoppage of smelting operation during the season of flowering and coming into ear of rice.
(2) Restriction of smelting quantity and putting into practice of fundamental removal measures of the source of smoke damage.
(3) Compensation for the damage suffered by the farmers.

At this point, the issue became a national one and finally resulted in 1910 in a mediation by the Minister of Agriculture and Commerce to which ten representatives from the farmers's organization and three board directors of Sumitomo assembled. A compromise agreement as a result of mediation contained the following particulars:

(1) The annual smelting quantity shall be limited to 55,000,000 *kan* (206,250 tons).
(2) Production shall be restricted during 40 days in the critical season of growth of rice and wheat, and the operation shall be suspended for 10 days.
(3) The annual sum of compensation to be paid to each of the farmers shall be 77,000 yen.

No doubt, the agreement arrived at was far severer for Sumitomo than expected by them. For example, the sum of compensation offered by Sumitomo was 7,692 yen against the figure demanded by the farmers of 112,895 yen. We can imagine Sumitomo's displeasure from an account they gave in the company document, which, referring to the incident, wrote: 'Frankly speaking, this contractual agreement imposes such a heavy burden to a mining enterprise as unheard of even in the world, let alone in this country. The burden meant a severe fetter for the operation of our smelting plant.'[12]

Even after such innovative countermeasures, the smoke damage

problem of the Besshi Copper Mine continued, until finally in 1939
Sumitomo decided to construct a neutralization plant for sulphurous
acid gas and more or less succeeded in settling the problem for the
time being. According to a report issued by Sumitomo, the emitted
sulphur quantity declined by 1934 to the index level of 8 against the
base year figure of 100 in 1916, and the density of sulphurous acid
gas emitted decreased to the 0.19 per cent level by 1934 compared
with 1 per cent in 1916.[13] The fact that this last figure of 0.19 per cent
is actually lower than the control standard in the 1962 'Smoke Regulation Act' means that Sumitomo's effort was at least pioneering in
this respect.

   The contrast that can be found between the Ashio and the Besshi
is quite revealing of the distinctly different attitudes taken by the
entrepreneurial leaders in coping with the copper mine *kōgai* problem, and also of the basically different strategies taken by the victimized farmers. Sadanori Iba of Sumitomo was quoted to have
remarked that he 'would not resort to the indulgence with money
while letting the smoke damage continue unmitigated.'[14] Furukawa
of the Ashio, on the other hand, tried to settle the strife with
farmers either by the payment of solatium calculated to bribe village elders or by mobilizing central government support to suppress the farmers' protest movement. Shōzō Tanaka, an activist
against the Ashio *kōgai*, appreciated the difference and had an
occasion to comment: 'Sumitomo has a sense of social justice and
has stuck to moral principles. The Besshi is a model of mining
places.'[15]

   On the side of protesting farmers also, the difference between the
Ashio and the Besshi in their basic orientation *vis-à-vis kōgai* phenomena was noteworthy. Whereas in the former case the farmers
placed a greater emphasis on such matters as the appeal to government to reduce the land tax on the ground of the depreciation of
land values through pollution damage,[16] the farmers in the Besshi
area fought from the beginning for the curtailment if not the
elimination of the *source* of *kōgai* itself.

THE CASE OF THE HITACHI MINE

If we can refer to the Besshi Copper Mine under Sumitomo as
pioneering in the *kōgai* countermeasures in the form of locational
transfer of the *source* factor itself and mandatory limitation of production in a critical season for farm products, we may refer to the

Hitachi Mine of Nippon Kōgyo-sho as pioneering in the adoption of an effective form of diffusion of *kōgai sources*.

Hitachi comes later than Ashio or Besshi in its place as a major copper producer. The Hitachi Mine began only in the early 1880s, then called the Akazawa Mine, and it quickly became one of the top four copper producers by 1910 after Fusanosuke Kuhara (1869–1965), a unique entrepreneur–politician, acquired it in 1905.[17] Kuhara's long-sighted decisiveness was no doubt a positive factor in coping with the *kōgai* problem in Hitachi. But it happened that there were two singular players in the drama: Tokuji Kaburagi on the mine-operating side and Tenshū Seki on the *kōgai* victims side. Kaburagi, born in a poor family in 1883, worked his way through college by writing articles for pay on the subject of smoke damage, to which Kuhara's attention was drawn and which became the basis for Kaburagi's joining the Hitachi Company in 1909. The smoke damage had already been reported in the nearby farm and forest regions in 1906, and Kaburagi's first step upon joining the company was to suggest the construction of a meteorological observatory on the Kaminé mountain, convinced as he was that air pollution had a close relation with the meteorological conditions. Collection of data on temperature, humidity, wind direction, etc was carried on at 12 observation points on the nearby mountains, and the correlative relations of such data with the smoke damage were studied. Kaburagi made further experimental researches on high-atmospheric conditions around the clock by the use of balloons and on the effectiveness of chimneys for diffusion of smoke, and also on the cultivation of *kōgai*-resistant vegetation.

Tenshū Seki on the opposite side, born in 1888 of an old respectable family of the region, interrupted his promising career as a diplomat and returned to his native place with an intention of devoting himself to activities for the betterment of the material and cultural conditions of the farming population in the region. His involvement in the smoke-damage problem lasted actually for 35 years since the time he was chosen by the victim farmers to become chairman of an anti-smoke-damage committee in 1911. In this capacity Seki devised a unique plan of quantifying the density of smoke damage by the index number of 1 to 10, believing as he did that a scientific approach was essential in such matters. Differentiating criteria for this purpose were specified by Seki in the following manner:

A. A density index of 10 be given when the throat is irritated immediately upon inhaling smoke, causing repeated coughing and pain in breathing.
B. A density index of 5 be given when the effect is no worse than unpleasantness in breathing.
C. A density index of 1 be given when scanty smoke can be recognized by the naked eye but no unpleasantness is felt.
D. Density indices of 2, 3, 4, 6, 7, 8 and 9 are to be judged by common sense in comparison with the conditions for the indices of 1, 5 and 10.

With these criteria in mind, Seki took upon himself the task of recording the particulars of smoke occurrences, such as the time of the day, the indexed duration, and the effect observed on various kinds of vegetation. For example, this entry appears in his notes:

> When the index is 9 or higher, leaves of leguminous plants are bleached in ten to twenty minutes; but when the index is identified as 5, the damage begins to show itself only after six hours.

Engaged in this task day after day, often even in the middle of the night, Seki was fully aware of the effect of acclimation upon himself and tried to take that into consideration, too.

In a number of ways, the Hitachi did take positive steps in aid of farmers and general residents in the region, such as setting up of experimental farm and forest stations to develop *kōgai*-resistant products and the improvement of waterworks, the construction of school buildings and shrines, etc. Seki appreciated these matters and had an occasion to comment in praise of Kaburagi's efforts inside the Hitachi company. However, as the production of copper increased markedly in the 1910s, smoke damage was seen over a wider area than was first expected by the company, especially in a farm community of Irishiken where even a serious discussion of mass transfer to a safer region began among the residents. Thereupon, the central government became concerned with possible consequences and suggested to the Hitachi company, on the strength of the recommendation by the Third Copper Mine Poisoning Survey Commission, to install a low-standing smoke dispersion system equipped with fans to vent out the smoke. Hitachi took up this suggestion and rushed the construction work of a low-standing stack of 18 metres diameter and started to operate it from June 1913.

But the consequence was disastrous: the stack forced sulphurous acid gas back into the refinery and contaminated the air inside, affecting even the workers' health. 'A Moronic Chimney' was the opprobrium fastened upon it in the locality at the time. The governing body of Hitachi, headed by Kuhara, was made to realize the impracticability of the government advice and decided, barely within ten months after the setting in motion of the low-standing stack, to consider the construction of a high-standing one. But the Copper Mine Poisoning Survey Commission was unrepentant. As late as in 1915, it recommended to the Besshi mine the construction of a low-standing stack rarefaction system, to which Sumitomo acceded and spent 350,000 yen to shorten the then existing 48-metre-high stack to the height of 33 metres. Here again, the consequence was quite similar to what happened in Hitachi a few years earlier. The incident is an eloquent testimony to the irresponsibility of a bureaucratically chosen anti-*kōgai* commission at the time.

Hitachi's plan to rely on a high-standing stack, on the other hand, was an entirely self-reliant attempt. The company engineers, who studied foreign documents on the subject, were not confident of success for a projected stack of 156 metres high, especially as regards standing up to the contingency of earthquakes and typhoons. But it was Kuhara himself who made the final decision by saying that 'smoke tends to rise up straight; therefore, when a smoke stack is high-standing, the smoke is given a momentum to rise into the upper air currents and dissipated there. The smoke damage, it is certain, will be reduced thereby.'[18] Thus, the construction of a 156-metre-high smoke-stack on the top of a 325-metre-high hill was begun on 13 March 1914. It took nine months for the completion, incurring the total cost of 152,218 yen and using 36,840 man-days and 32,000 logs for scaffolding work. These logs were carefully tied with hemp palm cords to guard against typhoons. And yet, working near the top of the scaffolding was considered to be so dangerous that workmen often kept themselves from their duty when even a small happening of bad omen, such as dropping of a rice bowl at breakfast, occurred in the morning. Still, there were reported some casualities in the process of construction. Local people called it 'The Monster Chimney' in contrast to the earlier 'Moronic' one. We can well imagine the risk involved in pioneering such a project in the conditions which characterized Japan nearly 100 years ago.

Thanks to this high-standing stack (500 metres above sea level), the smoke emitted from the smelter plant was vented up into the upper air currents, blown subsequently towards the Pacific ocean. And it was estimated that 80 per cent of the smoke damage problem was thus solved. Kaburagi, who suffered from insomnia with apprehension during the months of construction, was flushed with joy when he noticed fresh twigs on the nearby cedar forest for the first time since he came to Hitachi in 1909. Nevertheless, a remark has to be added here that the emission of sulphurous acid gas from the refinery continued to some extent even after the high-standing stack was built and the payment of annual compensation for the smoke damage had to be continued to the local farmers to the amount of some 40,000 yen. That is why Tenshū Seki continued to serve as chairman of the anti-smoke-damage committee for another 30 years.

There is a significant sequel to the story of 'The Monster Chimney' in connection with another *kōgai* incident a few years later. It was the case of the Osaka Alkali Company sued by the local farmers for the damage caused by the company's emitting of sulphurous acid gas. A lawsuit began in 1907, and the Osaka Court of Appeals handed down a decision in 1915 in favour of the plaintiff, whereupon the Osaka Alkali appealed against the ruling to the Supreme Court. It was typical at the time that the Supreme Court would take a position dictated more by political considerations than on strictly legalistic judgement, and its decision in this case was that the development of the chemical industry, then championed by the Osaka Alkali Company, was so important that whatever damage they may have caused should be tolerated in the light of the 'adequate enough equipment' they had installed in the conduct of their operation. Based on such judgement, the Supreme Court referred the case back to the original court in 1919. Thus the Osaka Court of Appeals had to reconsider the case, but it did not challenge the basic reasoning adopted by the Supreme Court excepting the concrete interpretation of the 'adequate enough equipment.' An example cited in this connection was 'The Monster Chimney' of Hitachi. The Court argued that compared with the 156-metre-high 'Monster Chimney' the Osaka Alkali chimney was only 33 metres high, which could not be considered as 'adequate enough.' Thus, the final decision was in favour of the plaintiff. It should be noted that this was the first time that a victim plaintiff of *kōgai* litigation won in the final court decision after the opposite judgement had been handed down by the Supreme Court.

SUMMARY

It is reported that at just about the time of the Meiji Restoration in Japan, that is the year 1868, there was a visitor from England who travelled extensively in the Orient staying in both Siam (present-day Thailand) and Japan and wrote that these two countries were remarkably similar, having an Emperor system with a Buddhistic tradition and never been colonized by a foreign power and enjoying about exactly the same standard of living, and further that most probably Siam would in the coming decades outstrip Japan in the process of modernization.

History's verdict, however, was otherwise. Driven by a strong sense of 'reactive nationalism,'[19] the Meiji leaders of Japan guided the country's economy with the singular determination of catching up with the Western advanced nations and in fact succeeded in doing so in a manner characteristically helped along by successive and successful wars. In chronological order, the earliest expansionist move after the Restoration was the cabinet decision for the 'Take Over Korea Policy' of 1873, followed by sending of troops to Formosa in 1874 and then of a warship ('Un-yo') to the Korean coast in 1875, succeeding to obtaining extra-territorial rights in Pusan in 1877. The policy and conduct of the Japanese military advisers sent to Korea in 1881 provoked a mutiny by traditionalist Korean troops in 1882 (the so-called 'Imo Mutiny'), which set the stage for the Chinese and Japanese rivalry in Korea that culminated in the Sino-Japanese War of 1894–5. Of the 45,000 foreign troops sent to China on the occasion of the Boxer Rebellion of 1900, one half was from Japan, and the after-effects, coupled with Russia's refusal to withdraw troops from Manchuria, intensified Japan's determination to fight against Russia,[20] which actually took place in 1904–5. Then, the First World War of 1914–18, in which Japan participated, mainly to 'fish in troubled waters', so to speak. The Russian Revolution of 1917 gave an occasion for Japan to send troops to Siberia, the intervention lasting until 1925. Emboldened further in an expansionist state of mind, Japan started in June 1928 a flagrant, undisguised step on the way to aggression in China by killing Chang Tso-Lin, followed by the so-called 'Fifteen-year War' which covered the period from the Manchurian Incident of 1931 to the unconditional surrender to the US and allied powers in 1945.

This brief chronology of consecutive war-like activities is a striking enough reminder of the unique character of Japan's modernization process since the time of the Meiji Restoration – the process which was associated quite significantly with a higher than average rate of economic growth among senior capitalist countries. A mainstream economist's judgement in this regard is that of J.M. Keynes who wrote that 'past experience shows that a greater cumulative increment than one per cent per annum in the standard of life has seldom proved practicable.'[21] In actual fact, for example in the United States, the average rate of growth of real net product per capita *per decade* was 9.7 per cent over the almost 80-year period of 1869 to 1948, which meant that per annum cumulative growth rate was clearly less than 1 per cent.[22] On the other hand, Japan's performance, expressed in a similar fashion for the period of 1874 to 1929 was 27.8 per cent,[23] corroborated by another study which found the per capita *annual* growth rate of GNP in real terms to have been 1.52 per cent between 1887 and 1917 and 2.33 per cent between 1917 and 1937.[24]

Keynes' prediction notwithstanding, such a creditable performance of the Japanese economy in its developmental process inevitably was accompanied by frequent occurrences of environmental problems, of which only a few major ones have been discussed in this chapter.[25] Significantly enough, there is a certain consistency in the manner in which a local *kōgai* problem was reflected in a nation-wide public discussion. For one thing, the mass media would not publicize an issue unless it becomes an 'incident' involving violence of some sort. Secondly, in a chauvinistic social atmosphere of war time, which prevailed frequently enough in Japan in those decades after the Meiji Restoration protesting victims of *kōgai* would feel constrained to keep quiet at least for a while. As mentioned earlier, even a consistently most active anti-*kōgai* fighter, Shōzō Tanaka, chose to lie low during the Sino-Japanese War of 1894–5.

In spite of all such evidence of 'the development' winning over 'the environment' in the tug-of-war between the two, it is highly significant that through the experience of some notable instances which created conflict of interests, such as the Ashio case, Japanese capitalism did learn in the pre-WWII period, though gropingly, some basic elements of anti-*kōgai* principles and put them into practice. They are:

(1) The suitable choice of industrial sites and, if necessary, even

the transfer of a *kōgai*-generating plant to a new place with less damaging environmental consequences.

(2) Controls designed effectively to eliminate pollutants at their source.

(3) The providing of diffusion structures, as exemplified by the high-standing 'Monster Chimney' of Hitachi.

(4) Emergency measures such as the cut-back of production in *kōgai*-generating plants at the critical season for cultivation in the neighbourhood.

(5) Compensation of victims.

These were the lessons learned locally in most cases by the time the Taisho era ended (1926), but they were conveniently shunted aside in the period subsequent to Japan's militaristic adventures beginning in the late 1920s and it will be noted that they were almost completely forgotten in the postwar reconstruction period.

CHAPTER THREE

Historical analysis – the postwar period I

'CREATIVE DEFEAT'

In reviewing Japan's environmental problems in the post-WWII period, it will be pertinent to give a summary account of the impact of the defeat in a major war on the country's economy.[1]

Joseph Schumpeter, an economist who coined the expression 'creative destruction,' made a typical comment of his at the time of the Great Kanto Earthquake of Japan in 1923 to the effect that 'paradoxical though it may sound, a disaster of this kind will redound under capitalism to a blessing in the form of business prosperity.' He did not err in this judgement. But would he have confirmed his unique theoretical insight when confronted with a cataclysmic dislocation of the entire economy in Japan at the end of the Pacific War? With hindsight we can say that he would have been vindicated. And hence the heading, 'creative defeat', of this section.

There were two main kinds of loss suffered by Japan in the war. Firstly those which occurred in the process of conducting the war, and secondly those which were imposed on the country because of the defeat in the war. As for the former, it is estimated in the category of *material* goods that of the total national man-made material wealth which would have been in existence in 1945 in the absence of wartime damage, roughly *one-quarter* was lost. Among several categories of material wealth, most severely hit were commercial ships. 8.6 million tons of them were sunk in the war, leaving approximately 1.5 million tons of which two-thirds required considerable repairs. The major damage, other than plant and equipment closely related to war activities, was in residential houses, most of which in Japan, being of wooden construction, were highly vulnerable to incendiary bombs during air attack. Then, in a number of industries, what is called 'indirect damage' has to be taken into account, that is to say, the loss of capacity performance due to insufficient repairs and up-keep caused by lack of component materials and speed-up production. The extent of the loss in this regard, however, is not easy to estimate in quantitative terms of stocks.

The overall effect of the war on manpower supply is rather complex. The number of those who died in battle or from diseases contracted at the front is officially estimated to have been about one and a half million, to which we have to add, as casualties in the war, (1) those who were 'missing,' (2) the heavily wounded persons who subsequently died, (3) those who died on non-official duties in battle areas, (4) the number of civilian deaths through bombing (including atomic bombs), and (5) the civilian casualties in Okinawa. Thus, the total fatal war casualties could be estimated to be anywhere around two and a half million. Against this negative population effect, however, we have to take into account the positive addition to the *domestic* population in the form of compulsory returnees from mainland China and other Asiatic regions after the end of the war, numbering some six million, many of whom were technically qualified personnel. And most of such returnees entered the employment market, willing to work at lower wage-rates than their qualifications warranted. Thus, the net effect of the defeat in the war upon the manpower situation could be considered as positive from the standpoint of needed economic reconstruction within the shrunken territory of defeated Japan.

Organizationally, the consequences of the defeat in war were considerable. The normal distribution system was naturally slow to recover after commandeering for military purposes was terminated and the dire shortage of basic consumers' goods continued in the atmosphere of popular resistance against war-time rationing. An inevitable consequence was the hoarding of any stock that promised price rise on the one hand and the mushroom growth of black market dealers on the other. The lid was lifted by natural force, so to speak, from sundry restraints that had been imposed by the wartime government. The obvious, overall consequence was the general price rise which was further stimulated by the wanton disbursement of the budgetary war fund, immediately subsequent to the unconditional surrender, for the liquidation of wartime contracts and for lump-sum retirement grants to the military personnel. A good enough indication of the general price rise was the trend of the official producers' price of rice, which was raised six times between September 1941 and March 1946.

There is another realm in which the wartime isolation inevitably meant a negative factor: that is, the missing of the opportunity to learn from new developments in science and technology abroad. Usually, this factor is not sufficiently appreciated in the wartime cost accounting.

As for the punitive losses of Japan in her defeat, the most important was the territorial partition of the erstwhile Japanese empire. By the terms of the Cairo Declaration of December 1943, the

> stripping of all the islands in the Pacific which Japan has seized or occupied since the beginning of the First World War in 1914, and restoring to the Republic of China all the territories Japan had stolen from the Chinese, such as Manchuria, Formosa, and the Pescadores

was prescribed. Then, secondly, by the terms of the Yalta Agreement of February 1945, the cession to the Soviet Union of the southern half of Sakhalien (Karafuto) and the Kurile Islands was dictated. In other words, Japan at the end of the war was shrunk essentially to the four main islands of Hokkaido, Honshu, Shikoku and Kyushu. Related to such loss of territories was the severe restriction of fishing grounds imposed by the Allied Powers. Before the war, Japan was the world's foremost fishing country, with an annual catch of almost one-million tons. But the catch declined to 360,000 tons by 1950.

The second major punitive loss item could have been reparations. The Pauley Reparation Mission in November 1945 stated to the effect that the Allied Powers 'should take no action to assist Japan in maintaining a standard of living *higher than* that of neighboring Asiatic countries injured by Japanese aggression.' (Our italics.) The initial reparation statement by Mr Pauley was released on 7 December 1945, starting in a tone thick with dramatic effect, to wit: 'Four years ago today Japan attacked Pearl Harbor. America will never forget the attack. Japan will never forget the consequences.' The statement went on to recommend 'an interim program of removals' of various categories of plant and equipment, including among other things 'half the capacity for the manufacture of machine tools' and 'all steel working capacity in excess of 2,500,000 tons per year of the existing capacity of 11,000,000 tons.' It was also suggested to 'deprive all Japanese, including the Japanese Government, the Emperor and the Imperial household, and the *zaibatsu*, of the ownership or control of any assets located outside Japan proper.'

However, the fact of the matter is that in the end an almost complete about-face took place on the reparation question and the Treaty of Peace with Japan, signed on 8 September 1951, specified:

(1) The allies in general will be satisfied with the taking of those assets which were held in their countries by the Japanese state and Japanese nationals.
(2) Those allies which had been occupied by Japan will obtain, in addition to (1) above, service reparations in the form of producing activities and of salvaging sunken vessels.
(3) Other allies are to forfeit any claims for reparations.

Thus, the final aggregate obligations for Japan at the closing of accounts in 1958 turned out to be 1,012 million US dollars, which sum meant, in terms of annual instalments, a mere 0.4 per cent of Japan's national income in the relevant years and was actually about one-half of the US aid to Japan for relief and rehabilitation ($2,118 million) over the period from September 1945 to December 1951. In other words, the reparation question turned out to be rather insignificant as a punitive measure.

The third major punitive step designed by the occupation authorities was the dissolution of the *zaibatsu* and concurrently the purge orders against wartime business leaders. Pauley's formulation on this matter at the initial occupation stage was eloquent enough, namely:

> Japan's Zaibatsu are the comparatively small group of persons, closely integrated both as families and in their corporate organizations, who throughout the modern history of Japan have controlled not only finance, industry and commerce, but also the government. They are the greatest war potential of Japan. It was they who made possible all Japan's conquests and aggressions. . . . Not only were the Zaibatsu as responsible for Japan's militarism as the militarists themselves, but they profited immensely by it. Even now, in defeat, they have actually strengthened their monopoly position. . . . Unless the Zaibatsu are broken up, the Japanese have little prospect of ever being able to govern themselves as free men.[2]

Presumably in this spirit the so-called 'Directive 230' was submitted by the US government to the Far Eastern Commission in June 1947, which was treated as a unilateral order to the Japanese government. Thus, the Law for Elimination of Excessive Concentration of Economic Power was pushed through the Diet in December 1947, giving the Holding Company Liquidation Commission (HCLC) the authority to designate 'excessive economic concentrations' and to reorganize such combines into independent companies to ensure a reasonable degree of competition and freedom of enterprise. In February 1948, the HCLC designated 325 companies as chargeable under the Law and issued orders for their deconcentration.

It did not take long, however, for the US state managers to become concerned over the possibility of strengthening pro-Soviet tendencies in Japan as a result of these somewhat drastic deconcentration measures[3] and appointed William Draper to organize the Deconcentration Review Board (DRB) to reconsider the entire procedure. The final result was the formal withdrawal of the 'Directive 230' in December 1948 and the elimination by the DRB of all but *nine* companies from the original 325 list subject to deconcentration.

The last but not the least of the punitive measures was the constraint on foreign trade in general. This was an extremely severe retribution for a country like Japan with its customary dependence on import and export transactions for viability. Partial freedom for foreign trade was granted finally to Japan two years after the end of the war.

Against such background as regards the wartime losses and the postwar constraints, it was probably quite natural that Dr Edward Ackerman, who made an intensive investigation of Japan's natural resources as a special adviser to the Occupation authorities in the immediate postwar years, was rather pessimistic, as can be seen from the following concluding remarks in his Report to General Headquarters in 1948:

> In the light of an analysis of its resources, the Japan of the next three decades appears likely to have one of two aspects if its population continues to grow to 100 million or more. (1) It may have a standard of living equivalent to that of 1930–34 if foreign financial assistance is continued indefinitely. (2) It may be 'self-supporting,' but with internal political, economic and social distress and a standard of living gradually approaching the bare subsistence level. Either of these alternatives seems more likely than that of a Japan which will have made itself self-supporting at a 1930–34 standard through foreign trade and improved resources utilization.[4]

Again, history's verdict was otherwise. Only a decade later after Ackerman made such a prediction, the Japanese economy was already eulogized as 'the rise of the Phoenix', and by 1973, that is within less than the 'three decades period' Ackerman spoke of, the soaring performance of the growth rate of labour productivity in manufacturing in Japan registered the index number of 1,412 with the 1950 level at 100, contrasted to 210 for the United States and 411 for West Germany. How this dramatic mutation came about requires a special study outside our subject matter here. But at least a brief expatiation is called for.

It can hardly be doubted that Japan's road to recovery after the debacle in defeat was paved by the coincidental developments on the international scene. With the heightening of the cold-war psychology from about the time of the announcement of the Truman Doctrine (March 1947), reinforced by the demonstrably successful march of communists in China in 1948 onwards, the US government apparently became determined to make Japan 'a bulwark against communism.' The consequence was a major shift in the US policy in Japan towards expediting the latter's economic recovery. The initiatives of occupation policies came to be taken directly by Washington itself, firstly backsliding on reparations and *zaibatsu* dissolution programmes while voting sizable aid for relief and rehabilitation, then advising strong-armed measures for the arresting of the inflationary trend and setting a single exchange rate, and lastly, hastening the steps for a separate peace with Japan. What put the finishing touch on the US determination was the outbreak of the Korean War in June 1950. This, incidentally, constituted a most significant watershed in the recovery of Japan's postwar economy, with impetus given by materials acquisition in Japan by the 'United Nations Army' for the prosecution of the war. The tragedy of war in a neighbouring country turned out to be a windfall boon for the Japanese economy. This category of extraordinary dollar receipts for Japan, called 'special procurements,' lingered on until 1955, by which time the aggregate amount was estimated to have reached $3.56 billion. If we take fiscal 1952 as an example, such dollar receipts accounted for 62 per cent of the total dollar intake of Japan's international payments.

Even before the Korean War, John Foster Dulles, an architect of 'a separate peace with Japan' drafted his first memorandum on Japan, in which the guiding principle was stated as: 'Japan should be part of the free world and friendly to the United States and should set an example to the rest of Asia by thriving in the free world, thus contributing to a general will to resist communism.'[5] It was clear enough that the basic orientation of US policy at the time was to bring up

Japan as a 'show-piece in the free world.' And Japan honourably responded and lived up to this expectation.

When the record of West German growth in real GNP was reported as 9.3 per cent per annum in the first half of the 1950s, publicists in general did not hesitate to characterize that attainment as a 'miracle.' The West German economy kept on growing, albeit at a decelerating pace, at the quinquennial average of 6.6 per cent for 1955–60, 5.0 per cent for 1960–5, 4.7 per cent for 1965–70, and 3.0 per cent for 1970–4 – still far surpassing the 'common sense' rate of improvement suggested by Keynes. All the more was it a source of surprise for the economics profession when Japan came to show, shortly after West Germany, firstly the quinquennial average growth rate in real GNP of 7.0 per cent for 1954–8, followed by 10.8 per cent for 1959–63, 10.9 per cent for 1964–8, and 9.6 per cent for 1969–73, only to have her sustained expansion stalled by the first oil shock of 1973.

Hence, Kenneth Boulding's apposite remark: 'Japan is an example of a fantastically creative reaction to defeat'.[6]

EARLIER LESSONS FORGOTTEN

Ackerman's prediction of 1948 turned out to be woefully pessimistic. Japan regained the prewar (1934–6) standard of living by 1953–4, attaining at the same time the status of 'self-supporting' economy without any 'internal political, economic and social distress' to speak of, and went on to bask soon afterwards in the rapid growth period of 1955–7 which was referred to as the 'Jimmu Boom', with the implication that it was unprecedented since the days of Emperor Jimmu, the first of Japan's mythological emperors. When the high growth rate continued in 1959 and 1960 (8.9 per cent and 13.3 per cent), reference had to be made to a still earlier myth of the Sun-Goddess coming out of the Gate of the Celestial Rock Cave, which could briefly be rendered as 'Iwato' – hence the 'Iwato Boom.' By 1960 then, the stage was set, as a matter of political slogan under the Ikeda cabinet, for the proposal of 'Plan for Doubling Income' in ten years. This Plan, though criticized initially as over-ambitious, was in fact over-achieved. And riding on the bandwagon of high-growth posture there appeared in 1972 'The Plan for Remodeling of the Japanese Archipelago' championed by the then Prime Minister,

Kakuei Tanaka. The general philosophy enunciated in the Plan was in a sense quite timely, emphasizing that it sought 'to usher in a new era for the "Restoration of Human Rights" where humans, the sun and greens, instead of big cities and industries, become masters of our society.'[7] In order apparently to be consistent with this philosophy, the Plan proposed the dispersing of industrial centres throughout the country, for which purpose vast networks of transportation and communications were to be developed. It was no joke for Tanaka to suggest that as much as one-fifth of the plane area of Japan would be required as highway space by the year 2000 and that by 1985 27 million trucks would have to be active for the transporting of 600 billion ton-kilometres of freight.[8] The annual rate of growth of real GNP during 1970–85 was projected to be 'potentially 10 per cent' attaining a GNP level of one trillion dollars (in 1970 prices) by 1985.

Another aspect of the macroeconomic management of the Japanese society which was savouring the animal-spirited stampede for high rate of growth in the 1960s in particular was the reclamation planning of coastline areas for factory sites.

Compared with the availability of capital and labour, that of land for manufacturing-factory sites used to be taken for granted, possibly because what might be called 'land productivity' in manufacturing is incomparably greater than in agriculture. For example, in 1970 in Japan, some 5,740,000 hectares of agricultural land produced 4,579 billion yen worth of gross product (about 800,000 yen per hectare) whereas 108,566 hectares of factory-site land produced 57,815 billion yen worth of gross product (about 532 million yen per hectare), the comparative ratio per hectare being 1 to 665. Thus it may appear that a slight transfer, of let us say 2 per cent, from agricultural use to manufacturing use could immediately double the land space for factories. Since there appeared to be a chronic over-supply of domestic rice production in 1970, it was actually proposed by the then Minister of Agriculture to transfer permanently 200,000 hectares of rice land to other uses. Arithmetically, this would mean a possibility of tripling the factory-site land without much difficulty.

But the problem is not quite as simple as this. Factory-site land has to meet a number of requirements if it is to satisfy the efficiency conditions, such as availability of adequate industrial water, convenience from the standpoint of transportation, proximity to the source of labor supply, etc. Even if by happy coincidence what used to be rice land, now to be fallowed or given up, satisfied these conditions, a crucial hurdle is the price of transfer which would satisfy both the sellers and the buyers. Cost accounting for reclamation of shallow coastline at the time confirmed that it would be cheaper than the selling price demanded by agricultural land owners, even if additional cost is incurred concurrently for the compensation of the loss of fishing rights. There was obviously an added advantage to the reclaimed land in that with the remarkable technological improvements in the facilities related to ocean transportation (such as automated warehouses, roll-on/roll-off facilities for transferring supplies to and from giant purpose-built vessels, etc.), the siting of plants by the sea with adequate enough ports nearby would mean substantial cost reduction for those industries where bulky cargo is involved, such as the steel industry.

Although reclamation had been going on here and there with good enough reason as explained above as manufacturing industries and public utilities expanded in the postwar period, a fresh rationalizing ground to support the nationwide plan to expand the reclamation area came to be accepted by the government towards the end of the 1960s; and a new plan was drafted in 1969 based on the assumption that the annual growth rate of real GNP during 1969–75 would be 10.6 per cent. In order to accommodate the economy's expansion of this scale within the limited land area of the country, it was suggested that 'green gardens had to be sacrificed for the needed expansion of the kitchen,' so to speak. The plan mapped out was to reclaim a total of 38,270 hectares of coastline area throughout Japan during five years (1971–5), as contrasted to the reclamation of 27,184 hectares during 15 years up to 1970. At the same time when this plan was drafted it was estimated that the cost of reclaiming would be on average 45 million yen per hectare – a figure which was in most places less than one-half the price of farm land in the vicinity.

In the end, however, actual reclamation completed during 1971–5 turned out to be 12,512 hectares or about one-third of the original plan. For one thing, as will be noted later, environmental concern became notably acute around 1970, putting a brake on the transformation of scenic beaches into factory sites. But rethinking was forced anyway by the fact that the actual annual growth rate (in real GNP) for the five years of 1971 to 1975 turned out to be 4.4 per cent on average, compared with the 10.6 per cent rate that had been assumed in the prospective reclamation plan of 1969. Although the growthmanship of the earlier decades was visibly blunted especially after the first oil shock year of 1973, the reclamation for industrial purposes which had proceeded for a decade or more in the Seto Inland Sea, for example, caused a flagrant transformation of this national park area. The Act for the Environmental Conservation of the Seto Inland Sea (1973) described the area as 'not only a natural endowment of incomparable beauty of Japan and the world but also a treasure-house of valuable marine resources for the nation.' But along the coast of this sea, with an expanse of 22,000 km^2 surrounded by three major islands of Japan and connected with the Pacific Ocean and the East China Sea via three straits, are now concentrated 53 per cent of the total steel-making capacity of Japan, 40 per cent of oil-refining and 76 per cent of lead-refining industries of Japan. All told, the industrial capacities of the region are bigger than the total of similar capacities of the whole of the United Kingdom, and over 500 kilometres of the coast has now become artificially filled in by concrete walls. What was once the pride of Japan's natural beauty has become a problem area of the first order from the environmental viewpoint and, in spite of strenuous counter-measures, the condition keeps on deteriorating. The average measure of transparency at representative points in the region, for example, declined from 9.3 metres in 1953 to 6.3 metres in 1972 and the concentration of ammonia and phosphoric acid increased from 1.5 ppm to 3.6 ppm and from 0.33 ppm to 0.54 ppm, respectively, during the same period. Red tide or the abnormal proliferation of marine flora was reported to have occurred 298 times in 1974, compared with 79 times in 1970 and only four times in 1950.

What has happened to the Seto Inland Sea area was more or less typical of the manner in which the animal-spirited stampede for high rate of growth went on with little regard for environmental amenities in the first few decades after the end of the war. This was the period when there occurred (1) an extremely rapid *relative* expansion of heavy and chemical industries which are generally more polluting than other industries, (2) progress in the degree of urbanization far in excess of demographic changes,[9] and (3) the explosive character of boom in mass consumption markets, notably private cars.[10] Thus, although the impact was slow to impress itself upon general public, there did occur a number of early harbingers of the latter-day concern over the environmental disruption even before the year 1970, which is called 'Kōgai Gannen' in Japan as the year initiating the era of environmental challenge. This was the year when the awareness of aggravating incidence of *kōgai* finally gripped the establishment circles to introduce legislative reforms in this regard. In the next section we shall give a summary review on what might be called 'the other side of affluence' up to the period around the 'Kōgai Gannen' year.

At any rate, it is important to point out that in the social atmosphere of the forward stampede of the 1950s and 1960s the importance of environmental problems was appreciated only by a small minority of concerned scientists and scattered local citizens' groups. More important, perhaps, the lessons learned by Japanese capitalism in the prewar years as regards some basic elements of anti-*kōgai* principles (which were itemized at the end of the last chapter) were almost completely forgotten, thereby delaying the effective action that could have been taken and actually aggravating the disruptive consequences unnecessarily. Typical in this connection – reflecting such politico-economic atmosphere of the period – was a statement by a prominent businessman, Hōsai Hyūga, then the president of Sumitomo Metal Processing Corporation (later to become the head of Japan's Western Federation of Economic Organizations during 1977–87). On the occasion of stressing the importance of off-shore reclamation for siting of steel plants, he spoke to a citizens' group, which deplored the loss of natural sea-shores of the Seto Inland Sea, asking them: 'Which do you prefer – the conservation of an attractive environment or an improvement in your standard of living?' Here was an implication, stated quite categorically, that the environment and the standard of living are generally a kind of trade-off objectives. And in effect, Mr Hyūga was proposing that priority should be given to policies for improving 'people's standard of living' (as defined by him) with much less emphasis on the matter of tackling environmental problems.

THE OTHER SIDE OF AFFLUENCE

While Japan of 1945 to 1970 was displaying outwardly what Kenneth Boulding called 'an example of a fantastically creative reaction to defeat,' the much less recognized, nevertheless quite important, events were taking place in the country at the same time, as has been noted briefly towards the end of the last section.

Ackerman's pessimistic prediction, which was quoted earlier, was fully appreciated by the Japanese themselves, and as early as in April 1947 a few officials in the Economic Stabilization Board took an initiative, with encouragement of Ackerman, in establishing the Resources Committee (*Shigen Iinkai*) 'to make it play the role as a central organ for drafting concrete plans of applying science and technology to the effective use of resources in general, but particularly those which are indigenous in Japan.' The Committee was to be composed mainly of scientists and was authorized to be quite discretionary in proposing its independent ideas on the relevant problems. The actual establishment of the Committee was in December 1947, with four subcommittees under it on 'water,' 'land,' 'energy' and 'underground resources.' Quite energetic researches by the Committee went on, expanding the scope of its competence further to cover matters like 'substitute fibres,' 'regional planning' and 'disaster prevention.' Within two years, however, that is, by June 1949, administrative reorganization took place and the Committee was renamed as the Resources Research Council (*Shigen Chōsa Kai*) and a new emphasis in its competence was given on the problems of forest conservation and flood control. It was on this account that the Council members made a field trip to the notorious Ashio copper mine area and subsequently drafted a report on 'Actual Conditions of Water Quality in the Watarasé River,' calling attention to the lingering remnants of copper smelting pollution of the prewar years.

While the Resources Research Council was concerned more with the positive potentiality of resources utilization in the period when the urgency of such matters was on the mind of almost every one in Japan, the negative aspect of resource use, or the *kōgai* phenomena, though locally reported often prominently in each case, did not attract much nationwide attention. After all, that was the period when the dominant ideology of growthmanship prevailed over the concern for environmental amenities. The decade of the 1950s, however, did witness already a number of typical *kōgai* incidents which portended blustery events later on. Three of them in particular may be mentioned here:

(1) The reporting of the convulsive deaths of cats and crows in the Minamata area in 1953, followed by the first filing of a report in May 1956 by the Chisso Company to the local health office on 'the incident of inexplicable disease' among some residents of Minamata.

(2) Citizens' complaints reaching the municipal office of Yokkai-chi (a site of the earliest petrochemical complexes in Japan) in 1959, citing a sudden increase in bronchial ailments.

(3) Reporting in 1955 at the 17th Conference of Surgical Specialists on the existence of a peculiar disease in a certain region along the Jintsū River, locally known as the 'itai-itai disease.'

All these cases, already serious enough in the 1950s as local *kōgai* problems, erupted some years later into nationwide disputes of major proportion. Therefore, we shall discuss them in greater detail in the next chapter.

Other than these three *kōgai* instances which subsequently acquired international fame (or rebuke), there occurred in the period under discussion a fairly large number of *kōgai* instances which involved local occupational group like fishermen or citizens in general. When *kōgai* causes clear enough damage to an occupational sector, there operates a logic of necessary response in varied measures depending on the social strength of that sector. In any case, the reaction may entail a demand for compensation and, often enough, a resistance and/or protest movement leading up to a legislative innovation. A typical instance of this kind happened in 1958 when a group of fishermen descended upon the Edogawa plant of the Honshū Paper Manufacturing Company, protesting against the damage to their fisheries through the river pollution caused by the plant's effluents in the process of manufacturing chemical pulp from wooden material. The fishermen's association had sent a delegate earlier to the company giving details of the damage to their livelihood and asking for appropriate restitution measures. But the company's response was far from satisfactory, and thus inevitably a violent intrusion into the company's plant by a crowd of fishermen occurred on 11 June 1958. And this incident consequently touched off in December of the same year legislative innovations in the form of the 'Water Quality Conservation Act' and the 'Law for the Regulation of Factory Effluents,' and in February 1959 an agreement by the Company to pay 19 million yen as an indemnification to cover the 1958 damages caused by the effluents.

Contrasted to this type of incident where damage is inflicted upon a socially defined occupational sector is the case where general public or local citizens in general happen to be either actually or potentially victimized. As was remarked by one commentator that 'private enterprises have a cold-blooded aspect of making advances while treading upon humble welfare of the locality where they operate,'[11] it is not easy for citizens in general to organize themselves to bring out effective steps against offending polluters. Why is it that such things are so difficult? Basically the reason is that the first principle for the capitalist system is the normative character of the market. The idea that 'whatever answer that comes from the market is the most impartial' is the apologue which has been fostered during an extended process of the capitalistic development, and in that process a tendency of not recognizing any value unless priced in the market was clothed with authority. Therefore, in the environs where the basic character of the economic system itself rests on the normative view of the market, the very task of organizing a movement toward throwing an objective light on those phenomena which are not captured by the net of the market (*kōgai* is one of them) and bringing the issue into focus for practical action requires not only an untried type of initiative on the part of contestants but also is likely to involve decision costs of no small amount. The difficulty encountered there can be likened to the one of those swimming against the stream challenging those who are flowing with the stream.

In spite of such handicaps, there do exist a number of instances in which citizens' movements contending in favour of the environment succeeded in attaining an objective. A memorable example in the 1960s is the case where the citizens of two cities (Mishima and Numazu) and one town (Shimizu) in the Shizuoka Prefecture succeeded in thwarting in 1964 the setting up of the plants by Tokyo Electric Generation, Fuji Petroleum and Sumitomo Chemical. What was characteristic of this citizens' movement was firstly that they made an inspection field trip to Yokkaichi, the city already notorious as a *kōgai* city, in order to be well armed with the knowledge on *kōgai*, and secondly that they began, in opposition to the governmental Kurokawa Study Group which was sent on the request of the Shizuoka Prefectural Office for the purpose of muffling the voice of opposition, to organize their own research corps with Dr Matsumura of the National Heredity Research Institute in Mishima City as their leader, supported by a large number of high school teachers and medical experts of the region and conducted their own imaginative field researches. One of them was to set up observation points at 11 places of from 3 to 200 metres above sea level where the atmospheric conditions in the winter season of Numazu were automatically recorded around the clock, and another was to make use of all the carp streamers available to hoist them for 10 days in order to survey the strength and direction of the wind in the region. This idea of mobilizing carp streamers owned by the citizens for the purpose of wind survey reminds us of a story of St Louis citizens who cooperated with the research people by collecting 200,000 baby teeth in over a period of seven years in testing (in 1958) the hypothesis that radioactive fall-out strontium-90 can best be analysed by measuring the degree of its residue in the children's bones which are replaced within a definite period. This St Louis episode also confirms a singular characteristic of citizens' movement which often attains its objective through quiet persevering mass efforts to scrutinize the problem on an empirical basis. At any rate, on the occasion of confrontation between the governmental Kurokawa Study Group and the citizen-sponsored Matsumura Research Corps, it transpired that there was a serious flaw in the former's report, and as a consequence, the plan for setting up of a multi-firm *kombinat* turned out to be stillborn.

The success of the citizens' movement in the Mishima–Numazu–Shimizu area apparently brought a considerable shock to the government and the business world, and thereafter the administration reflected over the earlier unqualified policy of plant-siting and issued a statement to the effect that they were ready to enact a basic anti-*kōgai* law and to pursue a 'rational' policy of industrial location. The first step taken by the government in this connection was to appoint in 1965 a commission composed of experts (The *Kōgai* Commission, so-called) to deliberate on the subject of 'environmental pollution control.'

This Commission submitted their interim report in August 1966 in which for the first time in Japan a systematic philosophy dealing with the *kōgai* problem was spelled out officially. Its highlights could be summarized as follows:

(1) The responsibility for *kōgai* in the light of the civil law resides, in principle, on the source-agents.
(2) This responsibility is not affected by the question of intention or negligence.
(3) The cost of prevention and elimination of *kōgai* shall be borne by the source-agents concerned.

(4) The setting up, for example, of a buffer zone for the purpose of preventing the effect of *kōgai* should be an integral part of any urban planning and the responsibility for such zoning arrangement, including the shouldering of its cost, should be shared by the central government and local autonomous bodies.

(5) Pollution control should be in terms of ambient quality standards rather than in terms of specific effluence limitation.

(6) Compensation for damage should be based on offensive excess beyond the tolerance limit as commonly understood.

The practical consequences of these ideas could be quite far-reaching, and some of the members of the Commission representing industries put up a strong resistance against a number of specific points. But when the Commission submitted its final report to the government in October 1966, the basic philosophy remained more or less intact and became the basis for a new legislation – The Basic Law for Environmental Pollution Control (*Kōgai Taisaku Kihon Hō*) – which was passed by the Diet in July 1967.

The Basic Law is a kind of charter which sets out a general programme of action but leaves the matter of concrete application of that programme to specific legislation and administrative actions. These latter, therefore, might be said to be more important for the parties concerned – such as enterprises, inhabitants, etc. – who are affected by the *kōgai* problem. But an explicit phrase in the Basic Law can always be appealed to for the justification of a certain line of action, and for this reason it is quite significant that the final wording in the Basic Law contained a compromise with the interests of private industries. There are two places in the Law where consideration for 'harmoney with sound economic development' is indicated: firstly in Article I where the purpose of the Law is spelled out, and secondly in Article IX where the prescribing of ambient quality standard is specified. In both places the unmistakable implication is that the need for environmental pollution control is not absolute but might, in certain cases, yield to the interest of promoting economic activities. This compromise, which was the product of the 'growthmanship' atmosphere of the decade of 1960s in Japan, nevertheless, invited a great deal of criticism from various quarters; and the Diet, in passing the Law, was constrained to supplement it with a rider, in the form of a resolution of the Diet, in which the major purpose of the legislation was reiterated to be that of 'protecting the health of the nation.'[12]

The first major attempt at implementing the specific clauses of the Basic Law was in connection with Article IX which provided that 'National Government shall prescribe, with respect to air pollution, water pollution and noise, the ambient quality standards that are deemed desirable to be maintained for the protection of people's health and the conservation of their living environment.' The procedure for this was for the Minister of Welfare to request deliberation on the subject by the Commission of Living Environment, a consultative body to the Minister, and, on the basis of a recommendation by this Committee, for the Environmental Pollution Control Council (specified in the Basic Law Article XXV) to review the question and to propose a particular set of standards to the Cabinet meeting for the final decision. But when the matter was finally placed on the table for deliberation by the Commission on Living Environment after several months' discussion by its technical subcommittee, some members of the Committee representing industries succeeded in having the point on 'harmony with sound development of the economy' put on record as one of the basic principles guiding the decision on ambient quality standards and thus in modifying the draft recommendations significantly to weaken them. The Cabinet decision, incorporating such extenuating provisos, was handed down on 12 February 1969. Although this decision had no force of law by itself and the enforcement had to rely on the legal provisions of the Air Pollution Control Act which could regulate specific effluence limitations on each plant, at least it was the first time in Japan that an ambient quality standard was specified on a national scale as regards air pollutants, namely sulphur oxides.

However, this Cabinet decision of February 1969, which incidentally contained a provision for years of grace for those areas where the pollution at that time was known to be excessive (e.g. 10 years for Tokyo and Osaka), was criticized for being too lenient; and some of the local autonomous bodies, such as the Tokyo Metropolitan government, proceeded on their own to work out a plan of air-pollution control – a plan that was severer than the one proposed by the central government. Thus arose a controversy at that time over the question of 'administrative priority.'

At any rate, it was only in the summer of 1967 that the Basic Law for Environmental Pollution Control was promulgated in Japan. Although there existed a number of legislations before that time that could be applied for controlling of environmental pollutions, a new era of legislative programs on *kōgai* was ushered in after the promulgation of the Basic law. Thus, the old Smoke and Soot Control Act of 1962 was replaced in 1968 by the new Air Pollution Control Act, and also in the same year the Noise Abatement Act was newly enacted. The old laws on water pollution, which were enacted in 1958 after the Honshū Paper incident, were also replaced by a stronger law in 1970. The process of rounding out related legislation was clearly on the horizon as the decade of the 1960s was ending.

The time was ripe around then for environmental issues to become of worldwide concern, converging in particular on several UN organizations in 1968, first in the Economic and Social Council in May, then in the UNESCO's Intergovernmental Conference in September, and finally in the General Assembly in December. In each of these, the question of convening an international conference on the problems of the human environment was raised. Above all, an appeal made by Ambassador Aström of Sweden in the General Assembly meeting was particularly eloquent and comprehensive. It opened up a gateway, so to speak, to the holding of the 1972 Stockholm Conference on Human Environment, and his address at the time still remains, after 30 years, so remarkably *au courant* in taking stock of the urgent problems humanity faces environmentally that it may be worth quoting here some of the passages at length:

(1) [On the risks inherent in the uncontrolled application of modern technology] The first and obvious answer is that all efforts should be encouraged which are designed to reduce or to eliminate the harmful side-effects of the large-scale application of modern technology. . . . The achievements of science and technology are the prerequisites of rapid economic development, just as they form the material basis for the armaments race. . . . Let me say in passing that if only a fraction of those resources in the form of brain-power, technical know-how, equipment and capital which are now devoted to the perfection of the means of mass destruction were released to be utilized for social purposes, for the rational planning of the human environment in urban and rural areas, then the total gain in terms of human happiness and of social justice would be enormous.

(2) [On the greenhouse effect] One well-known example of pollution is the rise in the concentration of atmospheric carbon

dioxide produced by the intensive combustion of fossil fuels during the past few decades. The buffering action of the oceans has not been able to keep pace with the increased rate of production and we now find the carbon dioxide content increased by 10 per cent and still rising. . . . A four-engined jet passenger aircraft in normal flight emits about two and two-thirds tons of carbon dioxide and one and a third ton of water vapour every ten minutes. The increase in the proportion of carbon dioxide may have certain effects on the radiation balance of the earth and thus on the world's climate. Carbon dioxide and water vapour are more transparent to short-wave solar radiation than to the long-wave heat radiation from the earth to space. The increased proportions of those substances in the atmosphere tend to bring about a rise in the earth's surface temperature – the so-called green-house effect. . . . What is evident is that man has already rendered the temperature equilibrium of the globe more unstable.

(3) [On the pollution caused in oceans] It has been reported that DDT has been found in penguins in the Antarctic. . . . According to a scientific report issued in the spring of 1968, 1/1000 of a gram of DDT in 1,000 kg of water may lower the metabolism of the algae by 75 per cent. This would be a direct threat to the life of the algae, since hundreds of thousands of tons of DDT are spread over the continents every year, of which a major part ultimately finds its way to the oceans. Global oxygen production depends largely on photosynthesis of oceanic plancton and algae. We may thus endanger even the critically important oxygen content of the air. Finally, the algae also constitute the basic food for all marine organisms. If the existence of the algae is threatened, then all life of the kind we know is also threatened.

(4) [On the noise pollution] If and when supersonic aircraft are introduced also for civilian use, hundreds of millions of people may be exposed to intense noise without being able to protect themselves – in order, may I add, to allow relatively few people to reach their destinations a few hours earlier.

Ambassador Aström also spoke briefly on the 'eutrophication' problem, saying that 'certain wastes from homes and industries – for instance, synthetic detergents – may fertilize lakes and rivers to such an extent that, ironically, they ultimately die.' Commenting on this passage, Mr Kaplan, the Canadian delegate, spoke on the conditions in Lake Erie, which was quite revealing, as follows:

> At least one startling example of how the delicate balance of nature can be upset is provided in the Great Lakes region of North America. Lake Erie is, or was, one of the largest fresh-water lakes in the world. Through persistent neglect and inadequate remedial measures that great lake has been converted from a source of food, fresh water and recreation into a chemical tank, in which pleasure boating, let alone swimming, is done at peril. For example, if a man falls from a boat into Lake Erie he is advised to have a tetanus injection. As for food from the lake, it should suffice to say that the blue pike fish catch, which was 6,900,000 pounds in 1956, had by 1963 dwindled to less than 200 pounds.

In conclusion, Ambassador Aström referred to a number of collaborative works in progress among several international organizations such as WHO, UNESCO, FAG, etc., and also to the fact that the Council of Europe had designated the year 1970 as the 'Nature Conservation Year'; and he proposed that the United Nations should hold a conference in 1972 'in order to provide a framework for a comprehensive consideration of all the problems of human environment within the United Nations.'

It happened that the International Social Science Council was holding its executive committee meeting in Paris a week after the UN General Assembly meeting of December 1968 and promptly responded to Ambassador Aström's appeal, creating a Standing Committee on Environmental Disruption. This Committee subsequently organized an international symposium in March 1970 in Tokyo with the title, 'Environmental Disruption in the Modern World – A Field of Action for the Social Scientists,' where prominent experts in the field such as K. William Kapp, Allen V. Kneese, Wassily Leontief, Ignacy Sachs and Joseph L. Sax assembled. Besides producing a number of most fruitful discussion papers on this occasion, the symposium adopted in the closing session what came to be known as the Tokyo Resolution, which proclaimed in part:

> Above all, it is important. that we urge the adoption in law of the principle that every person is entitled by right to the environment free of elements which infringe human health and well-being and the nature's endowment, including its beauty, which shall be the heritage of the present to the future generations.

In view of the above, and considering that further change in technology and economic and population growth may create further deterioration in man's environment, social scientists in particular are called upon to multiply their efforts on:

(1) Thorough-going research on the impact of environmental disruption and of its direct physical and biological effects upon social, psychological, cultural and economic conditions of man's life in present societies;

(2) Analysis of the institutional mechanism of our societies relevant to the emergence of environmental disruption and also to the successful continuing management of this problem; and

(3) Appropriate legal, political and economic steps aimed at reversing the present trend towards increased environmental disruption and also at establishing effective measures of environmental quality management.

The proceedings of the symposium were made public expeditiously four months later[13] and were circulated widely outside Japan, too. But more important, the symposium itself had a strong impact on Japanese public opinion and on the bureaucracy, too; and the Tokyo Resolution, in particular, served as a springboard for a basic reorientation in the matters concerning the environmental rights of citizens.

One of the significant effects was the revision in the wording of the 1967 Basic Law. This Law, as was explained earlier, contained a compromise with the interests of private business. The compromise consisted in adding a paragraph in Article I which spelled out the purpose of the Law; namely: 'In conservation of the living environment provided in the preceding paragraph, harmony with sound economic development should be considered." The implication of this so-called 'Harmony Clause' was that the need for environmental pollution control was not absolute but might, in certain cases, yield to the claims of promoting economic activities. This clause generated a great deal of criticism at the time of the enactment and developed into a focus of heated controversy in the subsequent years. Thus the government finally decided to propose a revision in the Law to strike off the paragraph in question. The 1970 Diet Session passed this revision, and the purpose enunciated in paragraph one of Article I – that of 'protecting the health of nation and conserving their living environment' – became less qualified, one might say, than before. This Diet Session, which took place in December 1970, came to be called in later years the '*Kōgai* Session,' because aside from the revision of the Basic Law it passed and/or revised 14 other acts of law, all related to the matter of environmental protection. It also called for the setting up of a new Ministry, the Environment Agency, charged with the task of formulating and promoting basic principles with regard to the conservation of the environment and of coordinating the activities of other administrative agencies in this field. The Environment Agency of the Japanese government came into being in July 1971.

CHAPTER FOUR

Historical analysis – the postwar period II: major kōgai incidents

Ill fairs the land,
to hastening ills a prey,
Where wealth accumulates
and men decay.

Oliver Goldsmith (1730–74)
The Deserted Village

POLLUTIONS COMPOUNDED IN THE CITY OF YOKKAICHI[1]

In the process of Japan's economic rehabilitation in the early postwar period the development of a modern petrochemical industry was one of the essential requirements. And geographically favourable conditions for this development were spotted in the city of Yokkaichi as early as in the first half of the 1950s. Thus, a fateful transformation of the city began to take place.

The city of Yokkaichi faces the Bay of Isé not far from the city of Nagoya in the central part of Japan. It started out as a port city in the modern Japan, combined with a scenic bathing beach studded with a row of wind-twisted pine trees. It was in 1938 that the Japanese Imperial Navy decided to set up a fuel depot there and reclaimed a portion of the bay. The city was bombed because of this during the war and was heavily damaged by the spreading fire. In the immediate postwar decade rehabilitation went on more or less after the prewar pattern of industrial and residential locations. But when in 1955 the Mitsubishi–Shell interest bought the former site of the Naval fuel depot and began constructing a modern oil-refining and petrochemical complex, the city authorities were awakened to the possibility of transforming Yokkaichi into a great industrial center. A group of 'regional development experts' was commissioned to draft 'The Yokkaichi Master Plan' and a gigantic piece of reclamation was commenced along the scenic seashore. 'The Plan' spoke of 'a birth of a new industrial city with abundant sunlight and greens'; but clearly foresight was lacking. For there was no suggestion of moving either the residential section along the seashore or the congested urban centre near the port facilities. The result was – to give only one example – that one of the best residential sections, in fact the one constructed by Yokkaichi municipality, came to lose the scenic view of the bay and found itself separated from a huge thermal electric plant only by a narrow strip of road. So innocently unaware were the authorities concerned at the time of the inevitable spillover effects of crowding modern plants near the places people were living.

The first group of petrochemical complexes (in the Shiohama area) was completed in 1961; and the second group (in the Umaokoshi area), which started their construction activities in 1961, began their regular operation in 1963. So confident were the municipal authorities at the time about the future of the city as that of 'an industrial centre with abundant sunlight and greens' that they took an initiative, and succeeded, in becoming a sister city with Long Beach, California. The ceremony for this friendly association took place in September 1963. Industrial production in the city, naturally, grew by leaps and bounds, as can be seen from the values of manufacturing products shipped, contrasting Yokkaichi with the country as a whole in the index form, as shown in Table 4.1. It is quite clear from the table that whereas manufacturing in Yokkaichi grew more

	Yokkaichi	Japan as a whole
1956	57	56
1960	100	100
1961	123	122
1962	150	134
1963	174	153
1964	207	167
1965	218	179
1966	262	206

Table 4.1 *Value of manufacturing products shipped –*
Index with 1960 as 100

Source: *Kōgyō Tōkei Hyō*, Ministry of International Trade and Industry.

or less *pari passu* with the national trend until 1961, the trend suddenly started diverging from 1962 on, and within five years the shipment more than doubled in Yokkaichi while the national total showed a respectable enough growth rate of 70 per cent in half a decade.

At the same time, however, the spillover effects of industrial operation, particularly in the form of air pollution, became gradually noticeable in Yokkaichi. In 1959 already, that is one year after the first petrochemical plant on the old site of the Naval fuel depot started its operation, asthmatic complaints were heard of in unusual frequency in the Shiohama area and actually in that year the death rate of aged females suddenly soared. Soon the bronchial ailment which became common in the city came to be known as 'Yokkaichi asthma' and started to attract wide attention. Citizens' woes were not of respiratory trouble only. Indeed, Yokkaichi presented an 'ideal' (!) classroom case of *kōgai* in a multiple form, for almost everyone of the latter-day *kōgai* phenomena – the pollution of air by sulphur oxides, smoke and various dust particles; noise and vibration; water pollution; and offensive odour – began to plague the citizens almost at the same time from around 1960. The Municipal Health Centre has kept a record of complaints received that can be tabulated as in Table 4.2. The frequency of the complaints shows a marked rising trend, and it is especially to be noted that complaints about offensive odour soared suddenly after 1963. For these latter complaints the sources could be identified in most cases as coming from volatile organic matter (such as butadiene, naphtha, acrylic esters, etc.) contained in the factory drainage.

In addition to these complaints by ordinary citizens, there also occurred in Yokkaichi a spillover effect damaging an industry, namely, that of fishing. At the mouth of Suzuka River, south of the Shiohama industrial area, there has long been a small fishing village for which the Bay of Isé provided good fishing grounds. From about 1960 complaints were heard occasionally that the fish caught near the bay had a peculiar odour, and soon the accusing finger was directed by fishermen to the Miyé Thermal Plant nearby which drained its cooling water at the mouth of the river near the fishing village. The Electric Generating Company, however, would not take any action on the matter while the stench damage to fish kept on increasing and the fishermen became desperate, and finally in June 1963 they resorted to direct action by throwing sandbags into the drain

	'Poisonous' gas*	Smoke	Dust particles	Noise and vibration	Contaminated water	Others	Sub-total	Offensive odour	Total
1960	8	4	6	0	0	11	29	7	36
1961	8	6	7	5	2	5	33	12	45
1962	11	9	9	1	2	11	43	10	53
1963	9	28	8	15	11	3	74	103	177
1964	29	15	15	37	13	4	146	221	367
1965	27	30	30	36	6	17	148	439	587
1966	72	51	51	31	4	9	218	452	670

Table 4.2 *Kōgai complaints received*

* Apparently, this is the laymen's way of identifying the invisible but oppressive condition of air affecting the respiratory function of those who are especially sensitive for one reason or other.

pipe. This riotous action provided an occasion for the prefectural Governor to intervene and led to the settlement by compensation. At the same time it was made clear that the Miyé Thermal Plant was only an intermediary of the stench damage since they simply pumped up the harbour water from one end for the purpose of cooling boilers and drained it at the other end without adding anything or otherwise changing the quality of the water. The harbour water itself was polluted and dirtied by effluents from other factories alongside the harbour.

At any rate, the stench fish incident in the summer of 1963 attracted so much publicity throughout the country and added gasolene to the fire on other more widespread complaints by citizens over *kōgai* in general that the central government finally decided in the autumn of that year to appoint a special committee (the so-called Kurokawa Investigation Team) to look into the whole range of *kōgai* phenomena in Yokkaichi. The Committee began its investigation in November 1963 and submitted to the government their 'Final Report with Recommendations' in March 1964. Nationwide concern was naturally heightened with the intervention by Tokyo and was further aroused by the coincidental death, in early April that year, of a certain Mr Furukawa, aged 63, who had been known as one of the victims of air pollution in Yokkaichi. Pathological autopsy of Mr Furukawa's body revealed a great deal and became a focus of more than purely scientific interest. The Kurokawa Committee's recommendation was, belatedly, to designate Yokkaichi as one of the specially appointed areas under the Smoke and Soot Control Act of 1962 for specific effluence regulations as regards sulphurous acid gas, allowing, however, a two years' grace for implementation.

From around this time, that is in 1963 and 1964, Yokkaichi came to be known throughout the country as 'a city of *kōgai*', a reputation which led to a tour of inspection by the *Kōgai* Research Committee, an interdisciplinary group of experts, in June 1964. One of the pieces of practical advice of this group was for the victim citizens to go to court against the offending petrochemical and other companies, especially in view of the death of Mr Furukawa in April 1964. The local organization which was expected to mobilize the anti-*kōgai* interest of citizens was Yokkaichi *Kōgai Taisaku Kyōgikai* (The Council for *Kōgai* Countermeasures in Yokkaichi) composed of progressive parties, local trade unions, etc. But quite significantly, the most important union organization of workers in the *kombinat* companies began to back away from the idea of a law-suit, apparently on the ground of apprehension of their employing masters becoming defendants in the court.

A symptomatic episode in this connection happened to occur in January 1964 in one of the *kombinat* companies, Shōwa Yokkaichi Petroleum. It is a story of Yasushi Hasegawa, an employee in the transport section of that company, who was given an operation order from above to switch the use of crude oil to the lower sulphur content variety for the occasion of an inspection visit to Yokkaichi by the Welfare Minister Takeharu Kobayashi. Hasegawa complied with this order at the time; but he brought up this incident openly at a subsequent union meeting, commenting on that occasion to the effect that the union should be concerned more with *kōgai* problems in the future. At that time, however, the union leadership did not support Hasegawa's proposal; instead, they let the company management know of the incident. The consequence was an abrupt transfer of Hasegawa's position to the ground duty for shipment. While in this capacity in 1966, Hasegawa was elected as an executive officer of the union, whereupon the company transferred him to a branch office in Nagoya. Hasegawa protested this as an unfair transfer; but the majority of the union executive officers supported the company decision, keeping their consistent record as an accomplice against any complaint of the Company's environmental malpractice.

Eiji Ono, who reported on this episode in his book, wrote in his summary comment[2] that 'the reason we write critically of the workers in Yokkaichi is, though it may sound paradoxical, for no other reason but a strongest call for solidarity from us to them.' He wrote further to the effect: 'The mistake perpetrated by the labour movement in Yokkaichi was not only that they turned their back on the citizens' movement but had the consequence of obstructing such a movement.'[3]

Though with such a handicap in an attempt to organize a united front for bringing about the law-suit, the citizens' group finally succeeded in filing a complaint with the court on 1 September 1967 against six *kombinat* companies. While preparation was going on for this decisive step, it sounds incongruous, but nevertheless true, that in 1966 the city of Yokkaichi started planning the development of a third *kombinat* area further north in the Bay; and the first stage of reclamation for this (1,267,000 m²) began in 1970, with a promise of siting the Shin-Daikyōwa petrochemical naphtha centre.

On the other hand, the court deliberation took five years to come to a decision on 24 July 1972. The main bone of contention, above all, was the question of the causal connection between the operations of the companies and the damage to plaintiff victims. The former persisted in requiring the proof that a particular asthma ailment was caused by a specific company's effluent. But the court decision was otherwise, stating that 'the legal proof of causation' did not require such 'natural scientific' causal proof, and that in this case not only were the defendant firms 'collectively responsible' for the pollution damage but also the epidemiological data were sufficient for indictment in the case. In addition, the court pointed out that the defendant firms 'were obligated to pay attention, in advance of their plant location, to their relative position vis à vis the residential quarters in the light of their own expected effluents and the neighbourhood meteorological conditions.' This statement, it should be noted, was a most far-reaching general premonition for which the Yokkaichi court decision was credited as pioneering. There was, however, one point which remained inadequate in the decision, namely, the judgement that the defendants' polluting action could not be construed as 'intentional' inasmuch as their effluents were within the threshold values prescribed by the administration. As a matter of fact, there was no guarantee that these administratively prescribed values at the time were adequate enough for the anti-*kōgai* purpose; and the defendant firms themselves could have been able to foresee the consequences of their emitting of the effluents if they really wanted to do so.

Although the civil law-suit in Yokkaichi was of a somewhat limited scope in the sense that only nine air-pollution patients in the Isozu district were sueing for damage compensation against six companies in the so-called First *Kombinat* area, the judgements by the district court in arriving at its July 1972 decision actually contained three path-breaking judicial innovations, namely: (1) the effective application of the joint-tort principle, (2) the adoption of epidemiological data for the 'legal proof of causation,' and (3) the indictment on the negligence in locational propriety itself. The verdict was a victory for the plaintiff side in the sense that the payment of 88,210,823 yen by the six defending companies was ordered as damage compensation. The monetary loss incurred on these companies was a trifling amount for them, and they desisted from appealing the case to a higher court. But the repercussions of the arguments wielded by the court on public opinion at the time were far-reaching, most likely beyond what the parochial capitalists of Yokkaichi could have realized. Otherwise, it is difficult to explain why during the very period of the court sessions on the air-pollution case (that is between 1967 and 1972) one of the defendant companies in the case – Ishihara Sangyō Company – saw nothing wrong in draining 200,000 tons of sulphuric acid waste water per day in the Bay of Isé.

Thus, the city of Yokkaichi was to witness another *kōgai* trial case on the heels of the asthma victims' case. Behind the effectuation of indictment in this additional case, however, there was an episodic contribution by a single man – none other than the late Muneaki Tajiri (1928–90), who came to Yokkaichi in 1968 as head of the Guard and Rescue Section of the Maritime Safety Agency. On his arrival to this Isé Bay region, Tajiri's immediate responsibility was to pick up poaching boats in the bay. Poaching consisted of going outside the assigned fishing zone for each unit of the fishermen's association. But the bay had been polluted and dirtied by effluents from factories facing the harbour for some time, and as was mentioned earlier in this section, the stench fish incident had already erupted in 1963. In these circumstances, the zoning regulation could not be enforced too strictly. On one occasion, an old fisherman arrested by Tajiri said in protest:

> You must know why I have to poach. Years ago the Bay of Isé was a treasure house of fish; but the *kombinat* came over and dirtied the sea, annihilating our treasured fish. They are the culprits. They are the ones who killed the fish by breaking the law which is designed to protect the marine resources. Instead of indicting them, you arrest us for poaching. Am I wrong in thinking that you are an agent for those culprits?[4]

This was an eye-opener for Tajiri. Then and there he made up his mind to do his utmost to investigate the nature and quantity of waste drains by the harbour-facing factories and to use the relevant legislation which could regulate them. The story of the up-hill battle he fought in this task is in fact a memorable drama reminiscent of historical pioneers in many of the path-breaking works.[5] For one thing, none of the offending companies would cooperate in any way even on divulging information as to the waste drains, insisting that what they were doing was perfectly in accordance with the legal prescriptions in the Water Quality Conservation Act and the Law for the Regulation of Factory Effluents. Furthermore, the administrative supervisory office regarding this last-mentioned law, that is, the Ministry of International Trade and Industry itself, was on the side of the effluents-draining factories when Tajiri attempted to confirm if in fact the factories were adhering to the law.

Thus, when he was thinking that he had come to the end of his tether, he received a telephone call one day from a person who remained anonymous, informing him that the Ishihara Sangyō Company was discharging some 200,000 tons of waste sulphuric acid water every day into the Bay of Isé. Upon hearing this, a thought struck on him that uncommon materials of such magnitude in the bay could constitute a serious hindrance to the safe navigation of ships in the harbour and that such discharging act can be indicted as a violation of the Harbour Regulation Act of 1948. This was the revelation which emboldened Tajiri to work for the criminal law suit against the Ishihara Sangyō, which law-suit began in June 1970 as the first of the kind in which *kōgai* was tried as a crime. It was significant that in this case no damage to humans was involved and further that a corporate entity as a structure rather than any particular mismanaging individuals was being indicted in violation of the Harbour Regulation Act. At first, the district public prosecutor was hesitant in pursuing the case, openly commenting that '*kōgai* is propaganda by "reds". I don't like them. So I will not concern myself with a *kōgai* problem.'[6] Resistance by the company concerned was also elaborately strenuous. Thus, the trial of the case took 10 years and finally ended in March 1980 with the criminal charge upheld against the Ishihara Sangyō. 'A Quiet victory for Kōgai-G-men Tajiri' was a newspaper headline at the time. But Tajiri himself wrote:

> Discharged sulphurous acid waste water amounted to 100 million tons altogether, which transformed the Yokkaichi harbour into a chemical pond where no fish could any longer live. And yet the penalty on the culprit company is a mere three months imprisonment (with suspension) for the factory manager and only a fine of 80 thousand yen to be paid by the company. With such a nominal penalty for the discharging of 100 million tons of sulphurous acid waste water, I doubt if we can really cope with the *kōgai* problem in this country.[7]

Although prosecution of the Ishihara Sangyō under the harbour Regulation Act was in a way successful, it was a sour victory for

Tajiri. Furthermore, his frequent visits for inspection inside the Ishihara plant itself made him realize the shameful negligence for safety by the factory management in handling the sulphurous acid inside the factory ground. So long as the human rights of workers inside are slighted in such a manner, Tajiri thought, it was difficult to expect them to join up with fishermen outside in the anti-*kōgai* movement before they could successfully improve their own work environment. One of the lessons he recounted repeatedly later on was to the effect that *kōgai* in Japan would not be eradicated until the basic human rights of workers inside manufacturing plant were ensured.[8] It was only in 1972 that a comprehensive law on labour safety and sanitation was promulgated in Japan.

THE TRAGEDY OF MINAMATA[9]

In contrast to the pollution compounded by multiple *kōgai* sources in Yokkaichi, the case of the Minamata disease involved just one firm, the Nippon Chisso Company.[10] It started in 1906 as a small firm producing carbide, used mainly as a lighting source in dark-night fishing. The founder was Shitagau Noguchi (1873–1944), a young college-educated electrical engineer, who came to Minamata village, rather hesitantly, mainly in response to accommodating offers by village leaders in the provision of almost free land space that had been used for salt production which became a government monopoly and was about to lose its viability as a profitable enterprise. Manpower resource was also available at low wages coincidentally on account of the closing of coal mines nearby which were defeated by the introduction of electricity. From the beginning, Noguchi, as an innovative entrepreneur, had a distinctive philosophy of business, attaching special importance to hiring as his subordinates top graduates of the electric-engineering department of Tokyo Imperial University. And by 1915, Chisso began using carbide as a material to produce calcium cyanamide which was then used to produce metamorphic ammonium sulphate for agricultural fertilizers. The success in this enterprise came only with the advent of the First World War which halted the importation of fertilizers from abroad. Chisso as a corporation began with capital assets of one million yen; but by 1920, its assets expanded to 22 million yen and within the ensuing half-year period it was paying dividends at the 104 per cent level. Immediately after the First World War, Noguchi visited Europe and purchased (for one million yen) the new Casale ammonia synthesis technology which was still at the pilot-plant stage. This constituted an epoch-making innovation for the Japanese chemical industry, enabling Chisso to construct in 1922 the ammonium sulphate plant in Minamata with an annual production capacity of 60,000 tons.

The inevitable direction in which Noguchi's attention was drawn was the westward expansion into Korea and Manchuria where the imperialistic Japan was already spreading its wings. Without a *zaibatsu* financial base, however, Noguchi had some difficulties until he was able to obtain warm assistance from a wing of the military clique, in particular from General Kazushige Ugaki, and also from two state-policy oriented banks, namely the Industrial Bank of Japan and the Bank of Chosen (Korea). Noguchi's penetration into Korea started in 1924, that is 14 years after its annexation by Japan, first obtaining the right to develop hydroelectric generation on a Yalu River tributary and then acquiring a piece of land of 320 acres for the construction of the Hungnum plant – the largest electrochemical compound production facility in Asia at that time. Then, closely following the militarists' march into Manchuria, Noguchi's imaginative ambition caught the hydroelectric development of the main stream of the Yalu River itself as a possibility and he succeeded in setting up a special company for this purpose in 1937 to construct the Sup'ungho dam with a generating capacity of 700,000 kilowatts. It was a logical consequence from this for him to expand his sphere of activities beyond the chemical fertilizer production into other electrochemical sectors including military supplies. Thus by 1941 Chisso came to be identified as a major-size chemical *kombinat* of a semi-*zaibatsu* character, with scores of subsidiary companies widely spread in the East-Asian region as a whole.

Meanwhile, the decade of 1930s in Japan was the period when the chemical industry turned its attention to organic chemical compounds derived from calcium carbide-generated acetylene. It was known at the time that acetaldehyde could be produced from acetylene though its industrial production was late in coming. At this juncture in time, Chisso developed its own techniques of producing not only acetic acid, which is a direct derivative of acetaldehyde, but also, on an experimental basis, sundry downstream products such as ethyl acetate, butanol, isooctane, etc. It was in 1938 that I.G. Farben, one of Germany's monopoly firms, announced the production of a vinyl chloride plasticizer; but the Minamata plant of Chisso successfully produced the same material in 1941. There was no doubt that by the time the Pacific War started in 1941, Chisso could be considered as at the top level in Japan in the organic chemistry field[11] and the town of Minamata in particular grew into 'a company castle town' in the sense that its economic prosperity depended on the Chisso plant and major infrastructures were constructed mainly for the convenience of Chisso.

The founder of Chisso, Noguchi, died in 1944; and Japan's defeat in 1945 caused the loss of all the overseas assets of Chisso and the disbanding of its *zaibatsu* structure by the occupation order while the Minamata complex, the only surviving asset, had been destroyed by bombing. But it did not take long for Chisso to resuscitate itself as a company with a high-level capacity for chemical synthesis. The immediate postwar food shortage in the country was a propitious condition for the production and sale of ammonium sulphate fertilizer for which Chisso had a comparative advantage. Besides, one of the typical consumer products imported at the time was polyvinyl chloride plastic, and the only installation in all Japan that could then produce polyvinyl chloride was the Chisso Minamata complex. This advantage too was quickly capitalized on. In both of these matters, the government gave generous enough assistance to Chisso. Then, in addition, the staff of the company, on their traditionally acquired knowledge of acetylene-derived acetaldehyde, succeeded in 1952 in producing for the first time in Japan the raw material (octanol) for an essential plasticizer in the making of polyvinyl chloride. Thus in the 1950s, the Minamata complex was able again to increase its capacity for the production of acetaldehyde and polyvinyl chloride, for which purpose large amounts of mercury compounds were made use of as reaction catalysts. Discharging of the production wastes without any treatment into Minamata Bay resulted in the extraordinary human tragedy we now know.

As we review the history of the Minamata disease, we realize that on so many occasions there were reflections of two singular features of the incident, namely: (1) the elitist pride with which the Chisso company conducted their affairs from the early days of Noguchi's fostering of top science graduates of Tokyo Imperial University; and (2) the 'company castle town' character of Minamata where even the Mayor of the city was a former factory manager of Chisso. In both these respects we discern somewhat typical traits of the Japanese society.

The rising of the curtain on the Minamata disease drama was the reporting of convulsive deaths of cats and crows in the Minamata area in 1953, followed by the first filing of a report in May 1956 by Chisso to the local health office about 'an incident of inexplicable disease' among some residents of Minamata.[12] This story was reported in *Kumamoto Nichi-Nichi Shimbun* on 16 May 1956, which turned out to be the first concrete public information on the Minamata disease through a local mass media.. More than 40 years have passed since that time, and what now impresses us most is the fact that the scope of what are called environmental problems and the concern therewith have expanded enormously during these two score years. For example, the first time *The Asahi Yearbook* (*Asahi Nenkan*) devoted space to *kōgai* was in its 1960 edition, and even that for only about one-third of a page, commenting briefly, in connection with the Minamata case, that 'a controversy is continuing as to the cause of the disease since both the Chisso Company and the experts of the Tokyo Institute of Technology are strongly opposed to a suggestion that the peculiar disease could be tracked back to the Chisso factory effluents.' By that time, however, that is in July 1959, it had already been confirmed by a research group in the medical faculty of Kumamoto University that the factory effluents containing methyl-mercury were most likely to have been the direct cause of the peculiar disease.

Retrospectively, the above comment by *The Asahi Yearbook* has to be judged as rather naive, if not deliberately misleading, on the tragic event which has caused the 'officially certified deaths' of 1,196 persons by the end of 1995 and upward of more than 10,000 patients who are enduring agonizing impairment of central nervous systems. It is proposed, therefore, to review first the records of two important professional sectors in their involvement in the Minamata case: the academia circles and the realm of mass media.

As for the involvement of scholars and research people, we have to point out the following sequence of honourable and dishonourable records:

(a) Dr Hajime Hosokawa, head of the factory hospital of the Chisso Company, suspected already in 1956, at the time he heard of a report about a peculiar disease called 'dancing-cat disease' (neko-odori byō), that it might have been caused by fish and shellfish in the Minamata Bay and attempted in July 1959 an experiment of giving to a cat the feed mixed with the factory drainage. The cat, which later came to be known as 'Cat Number 400,' was observed within some three months time to manifest the typical mercury-toxic symptoms of severe-acute type, whereupon Dr Hosokawa proposed to an executive officer of the factory technical division on 10 October of the same year that he be allowed to continue a similar experiment in order to ascertain whether the 'Cat Number 400' case was atypical or not. However, the factory executive would not permit any further extraction of the factory drainage for the proposed experiment, and in addition, Dr Hosokawa was enjoined from making the 'Cat Number 400' experiment public. He repented later of the fact that he did not have courage to make the result of his experiment widely known, recalling a story in Ibsen's *An Enemy of the People* which he had repeatedly read in his youth – a story of a medical expert whose motto was: 'The strongest man in this world is a person who stands alone.' By 1962, however, Dr Hosokawa retired from the Chisso Company, and suffering from a lung disease, he was hospitalized in the Affiliated Hospital of the Cancer Research Institute in Tokyo, where, in July 1970, he testified in the bedside questioning by Kumamoto District Court about the experiment he conducted 11 years earlier which showed an unmistakable causal connection between the factory effluent and the Minamata disease symptoms. This testimony of his provided an important clue for the court argument in favour of the disease victims. He died three months after the testimony at the age of 69. In *The Minamata Disease – Its Fifteen Years Record*, published by the Chisso company in 1970, there is recorded a personal recollection by Dr Hosokawa spoken to a colleague in the Company some years after the 'Cat Number 400' experiment, saying:

> I am a medical expert. The command of this calling comes before my association with the Company. My appointed lot as a medical expert transcends my loyalty to the employing company. In other words, to do my best in delving into the cause-and-effect relation is my appointed lot; and for me to state frankly whatever the scientific result I obtain is my responsibility as a medical expert hired by the Company.[13]

It is truly unfortunate that in spite of such conviction of Dr Hosokawa's, his deference to the company superior at the time of the 'Cat Number 400' experiment helped miss the opportunity of *officially* identifying the true cause of the Minamata disease at least several years sooner than actually was the case.

(b) Just about the time Dr Hosokawa was obtaining concrete evidence on the causal connection between the factory effluent and the 'peculiar disease,' the 'Research Group on the Peculiar Minamata Disease' organized in August 1956 by the Medical Faculty of Kumamoto University was making some progress in its research, though with a serious handicap of non-cooperation by the company in the form of being checked by guardsmen from obtaining mud near the factory drain ditch. In July 1959, however, the Research Group made a report in their discussion meeting to say that 'the Minamata disease is a type of nervous disorder most likely to have been caused by mercury.'

(c) Upon hearing about this report of the Medical Faculty of Kumamoto University, the Chisso Company apparently felt that a rebuttal was called for and consulted with the Ministry of International Trade and Industry (MITI) and also with the Japan Association of Chemical Industries, resulting in the appointment of Professor Raisaku Kiyoura of the Tokyo Institute of Technology as an expert consultant. Within a few months Professor Kiyoura came to the conclusion that the amine contained in the seafood was likely to have turned toxic due to one reason or another, and he submitted this report to the MITI on 11 November 1959 followed by a press conference. (The earlier reference to an account in the 1960 *Asahi Yearbook* on the cause of the Minamata disease was strongly influenced by the Kiyoura report.) This November the 11th happened to be the day immediately after Minamata fishermen thronged the factory and had a clash with the riot police force. Only a few days later, there occurred a heated discussion in the ministerial Fisheries Agency between the Agency's section chief on fisheries development and Mr Eiichi Nishida, a Minamata factory chief. Part of the conversation went on as follows:[14]

> *Section chief*: It is our suggestion that you suspend the factory operation temporarily, so that there will be no effluents during that time.
> *Nishida*: There is no scientific proof yet as to the causal connection between the Minamata disease and the factory effluents.

Section chief: But a number of people are dying. That is why we as administrative organization in charge are making an appeal to you on this matter.

Nishida: We believe that the cause of the disease can be traced to agricultural chemicals. If you ask me, I shall be glad to take a drink from our factory effluents every day.

It is evident that the confident manner the factory chief spoke was bolstered by the sense of authority associated with the professorship in the Tokyo Institute of Technology. In fairness, however, we must report that professor Kiyoura, after seeing in the post-1965 period a report on the experimental results by Professor Keigai Watanabe, formerly of Kumamoto University, took back his earlier judgement, saying: 'From now on, I shall quit making any counter-statement.' In any case, we have to admit that the academia circle has a mixed record on environmental problems in the postwar period.

As for the involvement of the realm of the mass media in the Minamata case, we cannot do full justice to all the aspects of the realm since it ranges quite widely both in the depth of treatment and the points of view taken.

The role played by the mass media in connection with *kōgai* problems is doubtless very important. And yet, the manner in which the reporting of the Minamata disease was handled was on the whole not quite satisfactory as we review the case with hindsight and in fact it is even recounted as a matter of self-reproach by the journalist concerned. An example taken here is from the *Asahi Shimbun*, reputedly a liberal-minded newspaper with nationwide circulation. We have earlier referred to the manner in which *The Asahi Yearbook* in its 1960 edition gave a brief and prejudiced treatment of the Minamata disease with an implication that the Kiyoura hypothesis denying the causal connection with the mercury effluents might be warranted. *The Asahi* is constituted of four main offices – Tokyo, Osaka, Nagoya and Fukuoka – each one with somewhat independent responsibility over the local news. Minamata is in the Kumamoto Prefecture and thus is under the jurisdiction of the Western Main Office with headquarters in Fukuoka. The *Asahi Shimbun* dated 25 August 1956 issued by the Western Main Office reported as a top news item a big story with the headline saying: 'Peculiar Disease in the Minamata Region – With a Fairly High Death-rate – But its Cause Unknown – Kumamoto University Hard at Probing.' Eleven

deaths were reported then. The Asahi Western Main Office considered this to be an unusually important incident and sent the
news item immediately to 'Three Main Offices in the East.' But the
Asahi Shimbun issued by the Tokyo Main Office did not consider it
worth printing. Once the initial reporting is neglected, subsequent
follow-up news also tends to be ignored. Thus, when the Western
Asahi reported in early 1957 on the investigation which strengthened
the suspicion that heavy-metal poisoning via intermediary of fish
and shell-fish might be the cause of the 'peculiar disease,' the Tokyo
Asahi preferred to overlook this news, and instead printed in April
1957 a brief item of news gathered in Tokyo to the effect that the
Ministry of Welfare was investigating the peculiar disease in
Kumamoto.

Further on, when the Medical Faculty of Kumamoto University,
after three years of arduous research surmounting all kinds of
obstructions set up by the Chisso Company, found their way at last
in July 1959 to the hypothesis that the cause of the Minamata disease
could be the organic mercury, this news, though highlighted by the
Western *Asahi* as a big scoop, did not appear at all in the Tokyo
Asahi. Not only the weighty import of the fact that the cause of the
strange disease – rare in the world at the time, killing already more
than 20 persons by then – was scientifically detected, but also the
serious implication of the possibility that the factory effluents could
be identified as the cause – both of these matters were passed over as
not worth reporting in Tokyo.

The occasion which prompted big reporting in Tokyo on the
Minamata disease was when in November 1959 the irate fishermen
thronged the Minamata plant of Chisso and clashed with the police
force as they started wrecking the interior of the building. The
report was a feature item on the human-interest page with a headline: 'Fishermen in a Row on the Minamata Disease, Thronging the
Chisso Plant – 72 Policemen Wounded.' It was well said at the time
that 'newspapers would not take up the matter, however important,
as a news item unless an uproar occurs.' At any rate, those people in
the Tokyo area who depended on the *Asahi Shimbun* for daily news
could not have any more knowledge on the Minamata disease than
as an incident where a large number of policemen were wounded in a
clash with the riotous fishermen; and as for the officials in central
government who often tend to judge the gravity of a problem
through the impression they obtain from its treatment in the major

newspapers in the metropolitan area, it may be surmised that they could not but slight the importance of the Minamata disease problem in the early 1960s. In spite of the fact that that period was already after the elucidation of the cause of the disease by the Medical Faculty of Kumamoto University, the mass media was unable to 'see through the manoeuvering by the Chisso side to prolong the ascertainment of the cause', and when the Kiyoura 'amine hypothesis' was propounded in detail in April 1960 at the interministerial research conference (MITI, Ministry of Welfare, Ministry of Agriculture and Forestry, and Economic Planning Agency participating) and the briefing to the press was done in advance, the evening paper on the same day reported in large printing type, saying: 'the mercury hypothesis of the Minamata disease is now denied.' For the government to come to accepting the mercury hypothesis took nine years (i.e. only in 1968) after the Kumamoto University advanced the hypothesis of organic mercury as the cause.[15]

The mass media has an important check function in society by providing unbiased, accurate news. But in the case of the Minamata disease it cannot be denied that that function was not adequately fulfilled, providing a valuable lesson for the future.

For an event like the Minamata disease case, there are three kinds of responsibility: (1) that of the sources agent, which in this case is unmistakably Chisso itself; (2) that of the authorities with executive power at least to mitigate the damaging consequences, which in this case are central and local governments; and (3) that of institutions or organizations which contributed in delaying of the relief work for the victims, which in this case is somewhat complex but is at least partly to be shared by government offices. In such matters of responsibility, it may be agreed that the academia and the mass-media sectors are not directly involved, although they do have significant enough influences on the decisions which the responsible sectors make.

Thus we come to the reviewing of the record of the central administrative office in its coping with the Minamata disease case. First of all, it must be pointed out, as mentioned earlier, that it was only in September 1968 that the Ministry of Welfare announced officially that the Minamata disease was 'caused by the methyl-mercury compound contained in the factory effluents of the Chisso Minamata factory.' This was nine years after the Kumamoto University research group made public their experimental conclusion to the same effect. It may be recalled that the first filing of a report by Chisso to the local health office on 'the incident of an inexplicable disease' was in May 1956, and soon after this, that is in August 1957, the Kumamoto Prefectural Office proposed to prohibit at least temporarily fishing activities in the Minamata Bay on the ground of the Food Sanitation Act of 1947 which enjoined the collection and sale of poisonous foodstuffs.[16] In response to this proposal by a local government office, the Ministry of Welfare made a reply on 11 September 1957, saying:

> Inasmuch as there is no discernible ground for the thesis that *all* the fish and shell-fish in the specific region of Minamata Bay are contaminated with poisonous materials, the Article IV of the Food Sanitation Act cannot be applied to *all* the fish-catch from that region. (Italics added.)

This was an infallible point in defence of Chisso since it would have been impossible to prove that *all* the fish and shell-fish in the Minamata Bay were poisoned. The official in charge in the Kumamoto Prefectural Office was far from persuaded by the Welfare Ministry response, but he had to accede to it.

There was another occasion when the then existing statutes could be applied for the purpose of arresting the spread of fish contamination by the mercury effluents of Chisso. That was in 1958 when, as was mentioned earlier (in Chapter Three), two new laws relating to water quality were promulgated, namely: the Water Quality Conservation Act and the Law for the Regulation of Factory Effluents. The former provided the need for designation by the Economic Planning Agency of those areas where water pollution is suspected and for establishing 'the water quality standard' as permissive threshold value for such 'designated areas.' The latter called for the application of the water quality standard concretely to each factory with a view to prescribing regulatory measures for those cases where the standard is found to be exceeded. It was clear enough to every one at the time that the two new laws of 1958 could and should be applied to the Minamata case. In fact, the Director of the Fisheries Agency in the central government officially asked for this application to the Economic Planning Agency in November 1959 but was turned down on the ground that the water quality standard could not be determined at the time on account of 'the inexactness of quantitative analysis used for the confirmation of the polluting source material.'[17] Thus, the opportunity for the mitigation of the damage was missed for the second time by the deliberate intervention of central government. It was only in 1969 that the government decided to apply the two laws mentioned above to the Minamata case. By this time, however, Chisso had carried off the transfer to a more modern petrochemical complex and had discontinued the production of acetaldehyde in Minamata. One cannot but interprete this chain of events as revealing the collusive tie-up between the central government and Chisso for the purpose of nursing along the development of the viable petrochemical industry in Japan.[18]

The source of the polluting damage was Chisso; the failure to regulate such pollution was on the part of the central government, and there remains the question of the responsibility for relief and therapeutic measures for the victims of the pollution. This last question had to be carried in the end to the trial in courts along with the matter of compensation. But the peculiar difficulties were inherent in the case of the Minamata disease as was fittingly expressed in Dr Masuzumi Harada's remark to the effect that there is a material difference between 'the Minamata disease problem' and 'the Minamata disease victims problem.' This discrepancy is rooted on two grounds, namely: (1) the lack of agreement among the relevant parties in dispute on the specific symptom or symptom group which delineates the Minamata disease; and (2) the dominating influence of the 'company castle town' character of Minamata City on its residents.

Common sense suggests that the question of identifying the Minamata disease should strictly be a scientific one of diagnosing a characteristic symptom or symptom group, allowing of course for a range of symptoms depending on the degree of severity of contamination. Disagreement on the identifying judgement was bound to occur when the question of the 'sympathy payment' by Chisso or the governmental compensation to the disease victims arose. The initial criteria adopted for the victim-identifying purpose was what is known as the 'Hunter–Russell' syndrome which summarizes the acute–severe case of mercury poisoning. But it was soon confirmed that the symptom group was of a pyramid shape, so to speak, where the 'Hunter–Russell' syndrome could be placed at the top whereas the much broader bottom part is characterized by non-specific symptoms like sense impairment of peripheral limbs. Many of the victims who in the course of time developed severer symptoms in the pyramid scale had been disqualified in the early stage of the dispute from the category of the Minamata disease patients. Some of them were even the target of malicious gossip and slandered as 'bogus patients who are seeking compensation money.'

The influence which the 'company castle town' character of the city of Minamata exerted on its residents was a sociological one. It was only at the time of the first law-suit, that is in 1972, that the workers employed in the Chisso factory agreed to testify in court, revealing the perfunctory manner in which mercury was used within the factory.[19] It was also at the end of the first law-suit in 1973 that the NHK (Japan's national broadcasting system) conducted a public opinion poll of the residents of Minamata City on the decision reached by the court and found that the majority of them were either quite indifferent or more sympathetic to Chisso than to the victims.[20] In the social atmosphere of Minamata City at the time there was a strong tendency to regard the Minamata disease as an anathema either exploited as a pretext for refusing marital proposal or interpreted as a deliberate instrument of those people who wanted to discredit the fishing industry in the region. There was also, as mentioned earlier, the slander of 'bogus patients.' In such circumstances, many of the unmistakable victims of the Minamata disease were more or less forced to remain as 'patients in hiding.' Such were the peculiar aspects of the 'Minamata disease victims problem' as distinguished from the 'Minamata disease problem.'

In any case, however, the victims in general, without a prospect of cure and lacking sustenance through loss of their jobs, had to appeal to Chisso for compensation. And for this purpose, some 78 of them, through their organization called the Mutual Help Association of the Minamata Disease Families, requested Chisso on 25 November 1957 that 3 million yen should be paid by Chisso to each one of the 78 victims as compensation. Chisso, however, turned down this request flatly on the ground that their factory effluents had nothing to do with the alleged disease. Whereupon, the members of the Mutual Help Association decided to sit down in protest at the front gate of the Chisso factory and kept on this protest move for one month. Finally, the Governor of Kumamoto Prefecture intervened and the official arbitration committee persuaded Chisso to accept a conciliatory plan of paying 'sympathy' money of 300,000 yen for each death and an annual pension of 100,000 yen for each surviving adult patient and 30,000 yen for a juvenile patient. The Mutual Help Association, though dissatisfied with these sums, had to accede to the plan, agreeing at the same time with a binding condition that the Association would not ask for any augmentation of the 'sympathy' payment even when the cause of the Minamata disease were to be determined in the future to lie in the Chisso effluents. The contract was signed on 30 December 1959, by which time, be it noted, the Kumamoto University research group had made public the research confirmation that the Minamata disease was caused by organic mercury in the fish eaten by the victims.

Once the contract was signed, both Chisso and the governmental office concerned started a big campaign heralding that the Minamata disease problem has been settled, and the atmosphere created in the city of Minamata was such that the disease victims, which were actually increasing in number at the time, felt obliged to remain anonymous. But, as will be discussed later, a second major Minamata disease case occurred in 1965 in the Niigata Prefecture and this case was expeditiously brought to court in June 1967. It is also pertinent to mention again that on 26 September 1968 the Ministry of Welfare finally announced officially that the Minamata disease was 'caused by the methyl-mercury compound contained in the factory effluents of the Chisso Minamata Factory.' And several days after this official announcement, Mr Yutaka Egashira, president of Chisso, visited each of the patient families extending his apology. Encouraged by these developments, the Mutual Help Association became inclined to cancel the earlier contract with Chisso but found themselves split as to the advisability of bringing the question of compensation to court. Chisso attempted to sway the Association in the direction of accepting a revised contract to be drafted by a third party committee the members of which would be decided by the Ministry of Welfare. Some of the members of the Association agreed to this idea and they were called the 'mandating group.' Others, numbering 29 households, decided to sue Chisso for damage compensation in the Kumamoto District Court on 14 June 1969. Thus began the first of the law-suits on the Minamata case, which continued for more than 20 years in three consecutive series, as summarized in Table 4.3.

The major issues contested in the court were: (1) the question of certifying the status of the Minamata disease patient; (2) the compensation to be paid by Chisso; and (3) the responsibility, in particular, of central government. In all of these, the court decisions were generally in favour of the claims of the victim-plaintiffs.[21]

	The First Series	The Second Series	The Third Series
Institution of the Suit	June 1969	January 1973	May 1980
Date of decision by the Court	March 1973	March 1979	March 1987
Plaintiffs	Early acute patients and 29 families	13 uncertified patients and one who died	1,197 patients either uncertified or in reserve
Defendants	Chisso	Chisso	National and Prefectural Governments and Chisso
The issues in dispute	Responsibility of Chisso, the causal relation and compensation	Confirmation as Minamata disease patients	Joint responsibility of the three defendants
Decision by the court	Plaintiffs win, Compensation: 16 to 18 million yen, Chisso does not appeal	12 out of 14 patients confirmed Chisso appealed	Responsibility validated Defendants appealed
High Court decision		August 1985 further confirmation on patients	March 1993 responsibility reaffirmed

Table 4.3 *Three Series of Law-Suits on Minamata Disease 1969–1993*

It is germane to recall that the years immediately following the institution of the first series of law-suits, that is from 1969 to 1972, coincided with the period of a worldwide awakening to environ‑ mental problems in general and were characterized in Japan by an extensive codification of the *kōgai*-related laws and the establish‑ ment of a new Environment Agency in central government. The Stockholm Conference on Human Environment was held in June 1972, which provided an opportunity for four of the Minamata disease patients to have personal contact with a large number of the non-Japanese participants there.

Now it was the time for central government to make a reply to the proposal of the High Court in Fukuoka[22] in January 1993, which suggested for the second time that the administration should agree to sit down for 'amicable settlement' with the patients on the basic understanding that those having lived in the region for some time and suffering from sense impairment of peripheral limbs could qualify as Minamata disease patients. To this suggestion, the Environment Agency, as before,[23] replied flatly in the negative, saying that 'there was no responsibility on the part of the administration and also the disease-certifying procedure requires no emendation.' The basic position taken by the administration was that 'the administrative keystone would be at stake' if it were to retract the commitment made on the basis of the recommendations by the officially appointed committee of experts.[24]

The administration, still obstinately maintaining such a position in the early 1990s, caused all kinds of protest movement in Tokyo and elsewhere, such as the surrounding of the Environment Agency building by a 'human ring' of 3,000 protesting citizens in October 1991, the presenting the of a list of one million signatures to the Diet and the United Nations in November 1992 appealing for the early settlement of the Minamata disease problem, the sit down protest in front of the Environment Agency in December 1992 and again in November 1994, at both of which the disease patients participated, and the holding of a 'Minamata Three-day Talk' in front of the Environment Agency on 23–5 May 1995 where altogether 158 persons appealed on a sound truck for the prompt solution of the Minamata disease problem.

It was soon after this 'Three-day Talk' that an agreement was reached on 21 June 1995 among the three political parties in the then coalition government, headed by Tomiichi Murayama of the Social Democratic Party – an agreement to exert maximum efforts in solving completely the Minamata disease problem as soon as possible. However, the executive branch of government was still unrepentant especially as regards the criteria for certifying the disease patient, and it took half a year until 15 December 1995 for the cabinet decision to break through a number of earlier bureaucratic obstacles and to propose substantive reorienting policy measures, as follows:

(1) Until then, the qualification for receiving relief as Minamata disease patients under the provisions of the Law relating to

the Compensation, etc., for Health Damages due to *Kōgai* was restricted only to those persons defined as such in the said Law, but hence forth, even those outside this category could be regarded as having suffered from 'the effects of methyl-mercury,' thus making the coverage broader.

(2) Claimants for relief are to be determined by a 'Status Judgement Council' attached to the Overall Medical Countermeasure Service operated by the administration, where the diagnosis by a patient's personal physician shall be respected.

(3) The Overall Medical Countermeasure Service will share the burden of paying medical expenses (the patient's share in medical insurance and the monthly treatment allowance) for those claimants who are still alive.

(4) Chisso shall pay the lump sum of 2,600,000 yen to each claimant for relief and a specified sum to the organization of the patients (3.8 billion yen for the National Association of the Minamata Disease Patients). Chisso is to receive financial assistance by the state for this purpose.

(5) For the purpose of regional development in the Minamata area, 4 billion yen is to be voted by the central government.

Thus in consequence, the total number of recipients of the lump-sum assistance through the new executive decision was at least 11,100 of which 1,900 were the plaintiff patients and 9,200 were the patients who had not sued.

The cabinet decision of 15 December 1995 was clearly a turning point. The Environment Agency's insistence on the theme of 'the administrative keystone at stake' was finally overcome, and the gateway to 'amicable settlements' suggested earlier by a number of the relevant courts was opened. After some wrangling negotiations on details between Chisso and the lawyers' group in defence of the patients, agreement on 'amicable settlement' was finally concluded on 19 May 1996. The agreement was essentially based on the recommendations contained in the cabinet decision of 15 December 1995 and was signed by the president of Chisso on the one hand and each representative of the five plaintiff groups (Kumamoto, Tokyo, Kagoshima, Kyoto and Fukuoka) on the other. And a ceremony for the 'amicable settlement' in the Fukuoka High Court took place at 9 a.m. of 22 May 1996, followed by similar ceremonies in other relevant courts later on the same day and also on the following day.

The occasion was clearly a historic moment for the Minamata disease litigation studded with 40–year-long human dramas of unique character. Yet, the central government would not participate in these ceremonies, apparently on the ground that 'recommendations for amicable settlement by the six courts since 1990 are of the nature which would place the administrative keystone at stake.'[25] Also for a similar reason perhaps, the reference to the May 22nd ceremony for 'amicable settlement' in the chronological account in the *Environment White Paper* is in the form: 'The Kumamoto third-series law-suit on the Minamata disease terminated due to the withdrawal by the plaintiffs' side.' An amazing distortion of the historic event, indeed!

Such grudging and apathetic posture of central government showed little change by the time the Governor of Kumamoto Prefecture made a declaration of safety of Minamata Bay on 29 July 1997. The occasion was the decision to remove the partition fish-nets separating the Bay from the sea outside. The net was installed 18 years after the first public confirmation of the Minamata disease in 1956, ostensibly to prevent the fish from coming into the Bay until the mercury contamination was reasonably well cleared in the bay water. Many of the patient-fishermen had felt the nets to have been mainly symbolic and continued to be sceptical as to the complete safety of the marine products in the Bay for human consumption. In fact, the *Asahi Shimbun's* editorial on 31 July 1997, with a title of 'The Minamata disease has not yet come to an end,' called the attention of public to the fact that 'even by now, both the state and the prefecture have not yet admitted their responsibility for the occurrence of the Minamata disease.' And it pointed out further a number of urgently needed assistance measures and research projects before we can truthfully say that the Minamata disease problem has come to an end.

It was on 1 May 1997 that the cabinet minister heading the Environment Agency visited the Minamata area and made a suggestion in public that 'we should propagate the lesson of Minamata to the world at large.' The idea itself is well-taken. But to hear it said by the person, head of a government office with its past record, gave 'a vain impression' to those who were present there, as was reported by one journalist.[26] In actual practice, many of the experts on the *kōgai* problem were aware of the importance of sharing the experience in Minamata with foreign countries and had made clinical and sociological research visits on their own, to such places as the Indian reservation in Canada ('Grassy Narrows' and 'White Dog' areas in Ontario), to Itaituba on the Tapajos (a tributary of the Amazon) in Brazil, to Alamogordo in the State of New Mexico in the USA, to the Hämeekyrö Kyrösjärvi region near Lake Kyrösjärvi in Finland, etc., and conducted effective interchange of experiences on the question of mercury poisoning.[27] The need for exchange of information on the actual experiences and for cooperation in the diagnostic and clinical attestation of methyl-mercury poisoning symptoms still remains as a continuing agenda for the future. In this sense too, we must say that the Minamata disease problem has not yet come to an end.

THE SECOND MINAMATA DISEASE IN NIIGATA

Were it not for the shameful negligence on the part of the central government in dealing with the Minamata disease in Kumamoto, the second of a similar tragic event in Niigata might have been forestalled before it became aggravated, since the first concrete public information on the Minamata disease was given in May 1956 and the initial public announcement on the occurrence of organic-mercury poisoning in Niigata was made in June 1965 by the Director of the Public Health Section of the Niigata Prefecture jointly with Professor Tadao Tsubaki of the Medical Faculty of Niigata University. The announcement suggested that the poisoning was likely to have been caused by eating of fresh-water fish of the river Agano. The pollution damage to humans was unmistakable, and the cause of the pollution was also fairly well confirmed. The question remained as to the source agent, for which the most likely candidate was the Kanosé factory of the Showa Denkō Corporation located some 65 kilometres upstream of the river Agano. Thus began the story of the Niigata 'Minamata disease' problem which dragged on for 30 years until 1995.

The Kanosé factory was the second biggest one in Japan after the Chisso Minamata factory in the production of acetaldehyde using mercury as a catalyst. And Showa Denkō Corporation was an arm of the so-called 'Mori *Konzern*' (financial and industrial combine) originally founded by Nobuteru Mori (1884–1941), who began his business career with a small family venture of iodine production.

Soon there developed bitter competition with Ajinomoto's Suzuki, which paradoxically enough ended in close cooperation between the two, culminating in the joint establishment of the Showa Hiryō (Fertilizer) Corporation. From then on, Mori took his own initiative in expanding his enterprise into the mining of nickel and the production of aluminium, etc., and finally amalgamated in 1939 his original iodine producing company with Showa Hiryō and created a new company called Showa Denkō. With a holding company Showa Kōgyō, Mori controlled 14 subsidiaries under him. The Kanosé plant had been in existence since the time of Showa Hiryō.

The Agano used to be one of the most beautiful of the big rivers in Japan, 'aga' meaning 'crystal clear' in *Ainu* dialect. Nature was bountiful in this region with abundant fish-catch in the river ranging from salmon and trout to lamprey and dace, and irrigating the surrounding paddy fields which harvested the choice brand of rice – 'koshi-hikari' – every year. The first mishap, however, befell the river when in January 1959 the storage building for carbide remnants of the Kanosé plant collapsed into the river with the consequence of annihilating a large portion of fish resources immediately. Just when the river was about to recover to its normal condition, a reversal of fortune occurred with a continuing impact, namely: eruption of the second Minamata disease, for which the river fish were apparently responsible.

The official announcement of the occurrence of organic-mercury-poisoned patients along the Agano basin was made on 12 June 1965, revealing that 'seven patients were confirmed as such and two of them had already died.' The announcement was significant in stating clearly that the pollution cause was organic mercury in the fish eaten by the patients. It did not say whence that organic mercury came. But in September 1965 the 'Special Research Group on the Niigata Mercury Poisoning Incident' set up by the Welfare Ministry went over to collect some mud near the drain ditch of the Kanosé plant and, after examining the mercury density there, made its report public in which Showa Denkō's culpability was affirmed. Whereupon the factory chief of the Kanosé plant went to visit the head of the public health section of the Niigata Prefectural Office protesting that they were not making any use of organic mercury and that the accusation of the Research Group was entirely unfounded. Thus began the controversy between Showa Denkō and the research scientists, which continued at least into September 1968 when the central government admitted finally the specific pollution cause of both the Kumamoto Minamata disease and the Niigata one. At first, Showa Denkō advanced a hypothesis that the Niigata earthquake of 16 June 1964 might have caused the spillage of agricultural chemicals from the warehouse near the Niigata wharf, thereby polluting the fish in the river Agano. When this was disproved, Showa Denkō's next tactic was to say that there was no proof that the inorganic mercury which they used as catalyst could have turned into the methyl-mercury found in the fish of the river. On this point also, the research scientists succeeded in upsetting Showa Denkō's assertion through constructing a model plant similar to the Kanosé's process of producing acetaldehyde. A decisive conclusion was reached by the research scientists' group by April 1967 and their report was submitted to the Ministry of Welfare, which agreed to have it made public on 18 April 1967. The concluding paragraph of the report went as follows:

> The methyl-mercury compound produced in the production process of acetaldehyde in the Kanosé plant of Showa Denkō was allowed to flow into the river Agano and was accumulated in the body of river fish. The so-called second Minamata disease of Niigata is *diagnosed* to have been caused through the toxic effect of the methyl-mercury compound accumulated in the human body in the course of eating such fish repeatedly. (Italics added.)

The italicized word in the above quotation was a concessionary expression suggested by the head of the Environmental Sanitation Bureau of the Ministry of Welfare on the ground that the more decisive expression in the original draft ('concluded') might drive Showa Denkō into a prolonged law-suit at their pace.

The official central-government admission on the cause of the methyl-mercury disease in Niigata, which came more than a year later in September 1968, was couched in some ambiguity, influenced perhaps by the inconclusive tone of the above report but more definitely as a result of pressure from the Ministry of International Trade and Industry, and it permitted President Masao Anzai of Showa Denkō to feel sufficiently self-assured to say: 'We shall decide our attitude after we will have given a close scrutiny over the government statement; we are still confident that our factory effluent is not the cause of the disease under discussion.'[28]

Even before the government admission in 1968 on the causal relation of the methyl-mercury poisoning along the river Agano, three patient families with 14 members joined in bringing the matter to court on 12 June 1967, sueing Showa Denkō for the damage, compensation amounting altogether to 44,500,000 yen. This turned out to be the first *kōgai* law-suit in the postwar period, taking place even before the first series law-suit of the Minamata disease in Kumamoto, which started in 1969. The plaintiffs in the suit were supported by 'the Niigata Organic-mercury Victims Association' (organized in December 1965 with 47 members) and 'the Democratic Groups Council for Anti-Minamata Disease' (briefly called 'Minsuitai,' organized in June 1965, significantly enough immediately after the first official announcement on the occurrence of organic-mercury poisoning along the river Agano). A second group of patients, numbering 16 families with 21 members, joined in the law-suit as the plaintiff in July 1968, and by August 1970 the total number of victims sueing Showa Denkō increased to 34 families with 76 members. The supporting 'Minsuitai' too was reorganized in January 1970 to become composed of 15 groups including trade unions, lawyers, etc., and came to be called 'Kyōtō Kaigi' (the Joint Action Council), playing the central role in assisting the victim-patients through their court battles against Showa Denkō and the state.

During the trial discussion in the Niigata District Court, which lasted from 1967 to September 1971, Showa Denkō persisted in claiming the causal relation between the mercury poisoning and the spillage of agricultural chemicals due to the earthquake, but in vain. The final judgement of the Court dismissed this earthquake hypothesis and stated in part:

> When there is a possible danger of causing damage to human lives and bodies even while employing equipment of the highest technology, firms are called for to consider a reduction in their operation, if not its total suspension, for the duration ... Showa Denkō did cause the so-called 'Niigata Minamata disease' through the utter indifference to the precedent example of the Minamata disease in Kumamoto which could have been known to them if they had listened with modesty to the findings of the Kumamoto University Research Group.

The Court also affirmed on this occasion the principle that the burden of proof should be placed on the defendant enterprise rather than on the accuser. Then the Court ordered Showa Denkō to agree to pay the appropriate amount of damage reparation to the victims. The time was again that period of rising tide in the environmental concern of 1969 to 1972, and Showa Denkō finally, but grudgingly, agreed on 21 June 1973 to sign 'the compensation agreement' with the Niigata Organic-mercury Victims Association and the Joint Action Council. In this agreement, Showa Denkō took a rather self-effacing attitude for a change and not only apologized 'for having caused the second Minamata disease through polluting the natural environment of the Agano River' but also admitted that 'it was their duty as an offender in *kōgai* to continue compensating for all the damage suffered by the victims throughout their lives.'

However, in order for the victims to qualify for compensation in accordance with the Agreement, they had to be certified as 'the Minamata disease patients' by the state. Here it may be recalled that 1973 was the year when in Kumamoto the second series law-suit was started mainly to obtain official certifying decisions as 'the Minamata disease patients' for many of the victims in that region. The administrative criteria for this purpose were very strict, as explained before. Thus in Niigata also the number of patients who passed the barrier, so to speak, of the certifying process to receive compensation was no more than 690, while the victims numbering 1,064 were debarred from the category of 'the qualified Minamata disease patients.' These uncertified patients organized themselves in May 1982 as 'the Victims of Niigata Minamata Disease' and began a second-series law-suit with the support of 'Kyōtō Kaigi' against Showa Denkō. The outcome of this too was a success for the plaintiff side resulting in the conclusion on 11 December 1995 of another compensation agreement with Showa Denkō. In a foreword to the agreement was a statement, saying:

> Since the occurrence of the Minamata disease in Niigata, many years have passed, during which time the deaths of 41 patients out of 231 plaintiff members are counted and the average age of those who have survived is now 70. Given this situation, humanitarian considerations alone, if not for any other reason, permit no more delay in bringing to effect the early solution of the problems in dispute.

Further in the main text of the agreement was a sentence in which Showa Denkō admitted that they were responsible in having caused the methyl-mercury poisoning and that 'they express their deep sense of apology not only to the plaintiff members of the trial but also to the residents in the Agano basin and to the society at large.' By voting a donation of 250 million yen to the Niigata Prefecture for the purpose of making the most of the experience of the Niigata case of the Minamata disease, Showa Denkō put a finishing touch to the tragic incident.

THE ITAI-ITAI DISEASE OF CADMIUM POISONING

We speak of the 'Four Major *Kōgai* Litigations' in the postwar period in Japan, and we have dealt with three of them thus far. The last one we now take up is the *itai-itai* disease case of cadmium poisoning, which in fact resulted in the first trial decision of the four.

As for the occurrence of a fairly large number of patients in a particular region along the river Jintsū who complained of grinding pains all over the body, especially around the pubic bone, with the common symptom of vulnerability to fracture of bones anywhere including ribs, there was no uncertainty. The question was what the chain of causation for this peculiar ailment was, which because of the patients' imploring cry of 'itai itai' (exclamatory words expressing acute pain) has come to be called the 'itai-itai disease.' There were some isolated instances of this disease before the war as early as in 1912, but the fact of its common occurrence in the postwar period prompted a call for special attention.

A country doctor who was in a key position in dealing with the problem was Dr Noboru Hagino, whose office was located in the town of Fuchū of Mei County in the Toyama Prefecture where it happened that an unusual concentration of *itai-itai* patients could be observed. Hagino was demobilized from China in 1946, and on return he took over the general practitioner office of his father and was immediately confronted with a patient whose symptoms were such that he could not neatly classify. Thus began his persevering struggle for ascertaining the nature of the *itai-itai* disease, which task took him 20 years until December 1967 when he could testify in the House of Councillors on his diagnostic and research travail leading up to his conclusion that the *itai-itai* disease was caused by the cadmium discharged by the Kamioka mine upstream into the river Jintsū. In arriving at this conclusion, Hagino was especially indebted to the scientific cooperation he was able to obtain from Dr Jun Kobayashi of the Okayama University, who not only contributed to the quantitative research by spectrum analysis but also managed to obtain a research grant of $30,000 from the NIH of the United States for the purpose of animal experiments on cadmium intake.

The chain of causation in the *itai-itai* disease case became finally clear. The cadmium as part of the effluents of a zinc-refining plant located at Kamioka on the upstream of the river Jintsū was the cause. Thus the source agent was also clearly established. The river happens to flow very rapidly northwards up to a certain point, and over a stretch of about 15 kilometres to that point the river bed is higher than rice fields on both sides through deposition of earth which has flowed with the rapid stream. Because of this alluvial fan formation, the river floods almost every year, and whenever it does, dirt and sand from the river, and with them cadmium also, overflows on to the adjoining fields. This explains the fact that the *itai-itai* patients were found mainly in the neighbourhood along this 15-kilometre stretch, that is the area of the town of Fuchū where Dr Hagino had his office.

In his testimony to the House of Councillors in 1967, Hagino revealed that there were 205 patients of the *itai-itai* disease he diagnosed, of whom 201 were females and 4 males and 117 had died. The incidence appeared to be especially heavy among fecund women. The technical chain from the intake of cadmium to the contraction of the *itai-itai* disease also has come to be established as firstly the impairment to urinary cell-tubes of the kidney by cadmium, followed by the re-absorption impediment causing discharge of phosphorus and calcium into the urine, with the consequence of softening of the bones.

The time was ripe by 1967 for bringing the *itai-itai* disease problem to court, and the initial action taken by the Anti-*Itai-Itai* Disease Council of the Toyama Prefecture was to make a visit to the Kamioka Mining Plant of the Mitsui Metal-Mining Company for the first time to request the payment of compensation for the victims who had died and of medical treatment allowances for those who were still alive. The Council representatives visited also the *kōgai*-contested spot in Niigata where the law-suit proposal just happened to have been decided. Hagino 's testimony in the Diet was a further inspiration; and the decision to sue the Mitsui Metal-Mining Company was taken on 9 March 1968 by 31 members of the disease victims and families, asking for the total damage payment of 62,000,000 yen (5 million yen for those who had died and 4 million yen for those who were still alive). This was the first law-suit of the case in the region, to be followed by six more, claiming for the total damage payment of 1,340,050,000 yen.

It happened that the Minister of Welfare at the time was Sunao Sonoda, who, though in the conservative cabinet of Eisaku Sato, was more sympathetic to *kōgai* victims than the bureaucracy itself and took an initiative in designating officially the *itai-itai* disease as '*kōgai* disease' on 8 May 1968. After making public a definitive statement on the causal relation between the *itai-itai* disease and the cadmium discharged by the Mitsui Metal-Mining plant, Sonoda commented, as if to forestall a dissenting argument:

> For the purpose of confirming a *kōgai* phenomenon it is not necessary to elucidate the causal chain thoroughly between the disease and its cause. When relevant experts and scholars have found the link to be unmistakable, we can be satisfied with the affirmative answer.

The Mitsui Metal-Mining Company, defendant in the law-suit, was not to be easily humbled. After all, Mitsui ranked at the top of the *zaibatsu* structures of prewar Japan and resuscitated itself again in the post-occupation period as an undisputed financial and industrial combine. The Kamioka Mine started as a silver mine as early as in the sixteenth century, and after some vicissitudes it came to be at first financially controlled by Mitsui after the Meiji restoration and by 1889 was bought up entirely as a mining branch of the Mitsui *zaibatsu*. However, when Japan went on to the gold standard in 1897, the price of silver plummeted, occasioning the shift in the priority production at Kamioka first from silver to lead and then to zinc from 1905 onwards. Thus it was that the first report of the *itai-itai* disease appeared in 1912. The outbreak of the First World War in 1914 brought a windfall boon to the Kamioka mine which was enjoying a near monopoly position in the production of zinc in Japan. It was rather characteristic of the Kamioka mine to enjoy a prosperous period whenever a wartime demand for its products was strengthened as in the 'Fifteen-year War' (1930–45) and the war in Korea (1950–3). By the occupation order for dissolution of *zaibatsu* the erstwhile Mitsui Mine Company was divided in 1950 into the coal division and the metal one, the latter becoming the Kamioka Mine Company. Although the merit of the earlier integration was lost through this dissolution, the Kamioka Mine Company could still take pride in its near monopoly position in the production of lead and zinc in Japan. Its sale of galvanized iron grew sharply due to the special procurements at the time of the Korean war and the company changed its name to Mitsui Metal-Mining in 1952.

The defendant in the civil law-suit on the *itai-itai* disease which began in 1968 was this Mitsui Company with robust pride in its history and inveterate confidence in its settled judgements. The central point in the dispute in the court was the cause-and-effect relation. Against the plaintiff's claim that 'the source material which has caused the *itai-itai* disease is the cadmium contained in the drainage and smelting waste of the Kamioka Mine Factory of the Mitsui Metal-Mining Company,' the defendant made an objection to the effect that (1) there is no relation between the *itai-itai* disease and the cadmium; (2) the Ministry of Welfare statement of May 1968 lacks scientific basis; and (3) no record can be found in the world of any case of chronic cadmium poisoning caused by the oral intake of cadmium. It took three years until March 1971 for the trial to come to its conclusion, during which time Mitsui kept on demanding an expert opinion in the court for a satisfactory scientific proof of the medical mechanism for the contraction of the *itai-itai* disease from cadmium. At the end, the court turned down this request and President Okamoto of the Toyama District Court pronounced judgement on 30 June 1971, favouring practically all the claims of the plaintiff side, ordering Mitsui at the same time to pay a total amount of 5,700,000 yen for damages. The characteristic aspect of the judgement was the affirmation of the principle that the causal relation illuminated through epidemiological research was sufficient for legal purposes. The impact which the affirmation of this principle had for other *kōgai* law-suits at the time and later was pregnant, indeed.

Mitsui decided to appeal immediately, still claiming that the disputed causal relation had not been proved. But the verdict of the Nagoya High Court on 9 August 1972 was the same as the one of the lower court, and Mr Shimpei Omoto, president of the Mitsui Metal-Mining Company, grudgingly[29] conceded that they would no longer appeal the case to a higher court and would be willing to settle the other pending law-suits without any further ado. Thus the day after the decision by the court, Mitsui signed with the plaintiff side two covenants and one agreement. 'The Covenant on Reparations for the Itai-Itai Disease' affirmed the responsibility of the Kamioka plant for the occurrence of the *itai-itai* disease and promised to pay the compensation as requested to all the plaintiff patients and also the cost of the litigation. 'The Covenant on Soil Pollution Problem' spelled out the responsibility of the Kamioka plant for polluting topsoil and causing damage to agriculture in the region where the *itai-itai* disease has occurred and promised to compensate for the damage caused to the rice-producing farmers and also to contribute to the task of restoring the productivity of the farm land. And finally, 'The Agreement for the Prevention of *Kōgai* in the Future,' signed between Mitsui and four organizations of victim-residents in the region, authorized the latter organizations to commission their own experts to enter the relevant places of the plant for inspection for the purpose of preventing any further occurrence of *kōgai* in the region.

With these documents duly signed and made public, one would have thought that the *itai-itai* disease problem came more or less to an end. But the history was less plain-sailing than expected. There were four outstanding problems after the court decision in June 1971, namely: (1) the certifying of the *itai-itai* disease patients and the medical assistance for them, (2) compensation for the damage to agriculture, (3) restoration work on the contaminated soil, and (4) the prevention of any further *kōgai* which may occur.

As for the first of these problems, under the new legislation called 'The Compensation for *Kōgai* Health Impairment Act' of 1974, the *itai-itai* disease patients had to be officially certified by an expert committee appointed by the Toyama Prefectural Office. But somehow a rollback trend began to prevail around the middle of 1970s, and for one thing, the chairman of the certifying committee was changed to a person (Kin-ichiro Kajikawa, head of the Medical Faculty of Kanagawa University) who was critical of the hypothesis that cadmium was the cause of the *itai-itai* disease. Thus, from about 1975 on even those who were diagnosed as *itai-itai* disease patients by their own doctors could not be certified. The criteria for certifying were made more strict by the committee and its 'closed door policy,' so to speak, continued until April 1993 when the Ministry of Welfare intervened to alleviate the criteria, resulting finally in the certification of 13 female patients towards the end of 1993.

As for the compensation for the damage to agriculture, negotiations continued between Mitsui and the victim-farmers until April 1974, when an agreement was reached for the reparation payment of 750 million yen. More difficult was the problem of soil restoration. Here inevitably arose two problems at issue: one was the exact acreage space to be restored, and the other was the proportion of the cost to be borne by Mitsui. The initial designation of the land space by the Toyama Prefecture in 1974 was the limited-size area (about 650 hectares) on the left bank of the river Jintsū. But through negotiations with the victim-farmers, the prefectural office agreed by 1977 to expand the area to 1,500 hectares to include the region on the right bank of the river also. Actual restoration work, however, was slow in making progress, accomplishing only about one-third of the plan by 1992, that is 20 years after the court decision. As for the matter of sharing of the cost, the covenant signed in 1972 stipulated that Mitsui was to bear the total amount. But here again, the Toyama Prefectural Office, in its mediating capacity, proposed to reduce the proportional burden of the Mitsui to 35.1 per cent (about 600 million yen) for the first stage of the restoration work and to 39.4 per cent (about 440 million yen) for the second stage. (The balance in both cases was to be borne by the state and the local autonomous bodies.) The reasons for the reductions were firstly that the 'natural pollution' had existed over the stretch of many past centuries and secondly that there were some mining activities before Mitsui started its operation at Kamioka. Both of these reasons were disputed by expert research people.[30] In any case, of the remaining two-thirds of the designated area, about one-half has been diverted to non-agricultural uses and the soil-restoration of the remainder was promised to be completed by 2004.

The fourth of the post-trial problems was the implementation of the practical task in pursuance of the 'The Agreement for the Prevention of *Kōgai* in the Future' of August 1972. This was undertaken energetically enough by the experts commissioned for the task by the organizations of the victim-residents. On-the-spot inspection inside the Kamioka plant was carried out twice in 1972 for the purpose of ascertaining the concrete nature of the research problems required to bring about a radical reform in the Kamioka's anti-*kōgai* measures. This subsequently led an organization of five research teams (on river water discharge, smoke emission, the cadmium balance, river Jintsū inspection, and waste pile problem), each of which to be assigned to a different university team. A comprehensive report combining the research outcome of the five teams was submitted in August 1978 to the liaison council of the cadmium-victims' organizations, and on the basis of this report an agreement with the Kamioka plant was confirmed that it would take a set of those concrete steps autonomously which were needed to neutralize the *kōgai* source entirely. It was also agreed then to set up a system of regular monitoring by the residents in the region. At least in this respect, the post-trial cooperation by Mitsui was more creditable than a number of other business firms which were defendants in the *kōgai* law-suits.'[31]

NOISE POLLUTION OF THE OSAKA INTERNATIONAL AIRPORT

One other major *kōgai* litigation in the postwar period was the case of the noise pollution of the Osaka International Airport which was unique in the sense that the Supreme Court reversed the decision of a lower court that was favourable to the anti-*kōgai* plaintiff side.[32] The origin of this law-suit dates back to December 1969 when some residents in the vicinity of the airport brought a suit to the Osaka District Court for the banning of the night-time flights and for the claiming of compensation.

The story of the Osaka international Airport is somewhat unique in the sense that it 'evolved' from a small local airport to an inter-national one for jet planes, and this under the strong pressure of the business community of the Osaka area. The airport lies inland some 17 kilometres north-west of the central part of the city of Osaka. Original construction began there in July 1936 with an area of 53 hectares, intended mainly for single-engined planes of six-person capacity. Its operation started in September 1938, and already in the following year the Osaka business community organized a special committee to promote the upgrading of the airport into an international one, with a plan of tripling the space area and of com-pleting the construction by 1942. But the Pacific War intervened, necessitating first the conversion of the airport into a military one and then, after Japan's defeat in the War, into an American base.

During the occupation period, the US military carried out uni-laterally an expansion of the airport to 221-hectare size, renaming it as the 'Itami Airport' and making use of it routinely during the Korean War. Through the coming into effect of the Peace Treaty in April 1952, Japan regained air autonomy in the formal sense. But the Security Pact between Japan and the USA, which was signed simultaneously with the Peace Treaty, enabled the USA to keep on controlling a number of bases including the Itami Airport. It was only in March 1959 that the US military agreed to the complete reversion of the Itami Airport to Japan, whereupon the Ministry of Transportation changed the name of the airport from 'Itami' to 'Osaka' and took steps to notify the municipalities in the region (cities of Itami, Toyonaka and Ikeda) 'a rebuilding plan of the airport' which had been drafted in advance. This plan envisaged an expansion of the airport by 82.5 hectares so that it could adequately serve as an international airport accommodating jet-planes' landing and take-off. For this purpose, not only a vast area of land had to be purchased anew, but also there was an inevitable problem of somehow appeasing the residents in the region on the question of aircraft noise. The business communities in Osaka and Kobe areas were so intent on expediting the expansion plan, allegedly in the hope of countering what they themselves called 'the business ground subsidence,' that they had organized a promotional organization called the 'Itami Airport Council' immediately after the reversion by the US military in 1959 and soon afterwards (in July 1960) began their public campaign by distributing a report called 'Jet-plane noise is little different from that of propeller planes.' The expansion plan had to be approved by the municipal assemblies in the region. And in the case of Toyonaka City the assembly's approval was obtained in December 1961 by a margin of just one vote; as for the case of Itami City, voting in the assembly took place on 5 April 1962 while 900 policemen guarded the building against the thronging citizens, and in the temporary absence of the Speaker (a member of the Socialist Party), who was conferring in the Speaker's room on the question of allotment of observers' tickets, the vice-speaker (a member of the conservative wing) opened the proceedings and forced the vote on the question to obtain the approval. Thus began the land-purchase programme for the expansion of the airport in November 1962, which was barely completed as planned by July 1964. Even before this, however, that is in June of that year, the government allowed the use of the airport for jet-planes although the initial plan was to wait for such operation until the 'B'-runway, 3,000 metres long, would have been constructed. The reason for this haste was apparently the eagerness of the 'airplane clan' to beat the inauguration of the bullet train service between Tokyo and Osaka in October 1964. The completion of the 'B'-runaway was in February 1970.

Such was the background to the law-suit on the noise pollution of the Osaka International Airport which was filed in December 1969 to the Osaka District Court. Before we discuss the details of this law-suit, we must evaluate the adequacy of this airport of 317-hectare size in the light of basic common-sense on airports in the jet age.

Since major items of airplane *kōgai* are noise and vibration, countermeasures against them consist mainly in (1) the provision of a sufficiently wide space for airports, (2) the improvement in the technology for abating noise and vibration, and (3) the limitation of flights and/or the time restriction in the use of runways. As for the first point above, a standard requirement for space area in the case of an inland airport would be: a 4,000-metre runway with spare room of 2000-metre length each on both sides plus a similar land-space facility which falls at right angles with the above providing for any changes in wind direction. This would mean an area size of $[4,000 \text{ m} + 2 \times 2,000 \text{ m}]^2$ or 6,400 hectares. In the United States, they have, for example, the Dallas–Fort Worth International Airport which is as big as 7,000 hectares. In view of such consideration, the area size of the Osaka International Airport, which is only 317 hectares in size, has to be branded as woefully inadequate, even having one runway of 3,000 metres for jet planes. It was inevitable that the households living within the threshold value of noise (WECPNL 85)* numbered as many as 42,000, and in such circumstance we can easily understand that especially the third counter-measure cited above was of imperative urgency.

One is tempted to ask how it was that such a defective airport came into existence. Clearly, it was due to the elementary negligence of *ex ante* assessment. With the coming of the jet age, it became a matter of common-sense practice in almost every country to make a careful assessment in advance when a new airport is planned. Typical was the example of the planning of the third London airport in 1968. On that occasion, the Roskill Committee started its assessment work, first selecting some 80 sites as possibilities, and then choosing four out of them as candidate sites after applying a number of relevant criteria such as the access convenience, its proximity to industrial centres, the prospective contour line of noise, etc. The next step was a series of public discussions with the residents of the relevant regions, after which concrete blue-prints were drafted and an intense discussion began within the Committee. The decision reached by the majority was to recommend Cabrington site to the government.

---

*WECPNL = Weighted Equivalent Continuous Perceived Noise Level (as defined by the International Civil Aviation Organization in 1971).

Altogether nine volumes of the Committee's Report were printed and were submitted for public review, after which another series of discussions was held between the Committee and resident citizens, as a result of which Foulness site was the one finally chosen. Such was the degree of care with which the selection of the site for an inland airport was made. In the case of the Dallas–Fort Worth airport in the United States also, the authorities responsible for its establishment spent two years, in advance of their final decision, for public dialogues with residents and organizations in the region such as trade unions, PTA, chambers of commerce, etc. The procedure they took was to send a detailed prospectus to each of these citizens' groups, suggesting to them that the planning experts would come to them for explanation and discussion at the time and place of the latter's convenience.

In abysmal contrast with such Western experiences was the case of the Osaka International Airport, where the authorities in charge, i.e. the Ministry of Transportation, was intent in accommodating the wishes mainly of the business community, to make haste in operating jet planes even before the 3000-metre-long 'B'-runaway was completed. Complaints by nearby residents against the noise pollution could be heard soon after the first flight of a jet passenger plane on 1 June 1964, and they came to be organized in a number of forms as such flights increased markedly in the following years.[33] Finally, it was in May 1968 that a mass gathering of citizens from the Takashiba district of Kasai adopted a resolution to bring the matter to court, joined subsequently by a few other citizens' groups in the nearby districts. Sensing the widening magnitude of the protest movements, the government proposed in November 1969 'to prohibit in principle the landing and take-off by jet planes in the Osaka International Airport between 10:30 p.m. and 6:30 a.m.,' this to be effective, however, from February 1970. Such proposal could hardly assuage the protesting mood of the noise-pollution victims in the region, and a formal step by them to sue the state was taken on 15 December 1969.

Thus began, for the first time in Japan, a large-scale law-suit on noise pollution. The trial of the case was unique in a number of respects, namely: (1) that the state itself was to be the defendant; (2) that the principle of 'public interest' was to be judged in the courts; (3) that an injunction was urged; and (4) that the plaintiff's argument was structured in terms of environmental right.

The first trial decision by the Osaka District Court (February 1974) went only as far as approving compensation for the past damage to a limited group of residents, which decision of course did not satisfy the plaintiff side, and an appeal was filed to the Osaka High Court. A decision by this court was given in November 1975, recognizing almost all the claims made by the plaintiff side. Details of the decision included: (1) the injunction on flights ordered from 9:00 p.m. to 7:00 a.m., (2) until this injunction is actually observed, the payment of 10,000 yen per month to each of the plaintiffs, and (3) as for the compensation for the past damage, amounts ranging from 146,600 yen to 1,128,000 yen are to be paid to each victim depending on the degree of the damage suffered.

The significance of this decision was in a sense epochal because it opened the gate for the direct regulation of the *kōgai* source through the policy instruments of the injunction and the polluters pay principle. In addition, the fact that the government *public works* were subjected to the court trial and also the fact that the compensation for the possible *future* damage was recognized – these were the epoch-making events in the history of *kōgai* in Japan. One other episodic event remembered in connection with the trial was that the judges of the High Court spent 15 hours in two visits to the scene of the airport noise and wrote in their judgement that 'such an inspection tour for checking of evidence should be an important starting point for any judgement on the alleged damages.'

From the standpoint of the pollution victims in the region, the one hour between 9:00 p.m. and 10:00 p.m. was what they called 'the crucial hour' and the High Court decision approving the injunction from 9:00 p.m. was appreciated most by them. In the subsequent negotiations between the plaintiff side and the government, which lasted nine more years until the final 'amicable settlement,' this 'crucial hour' issue came up repeatedly as a major bone of contention. The immediate problem for the plaintiff side after the High Court decision was to ensure that the defendant state would not appeal the case to the Supreme Court and also to have the injunction implemented without delay. The Ministry of Transportation did make some administrative effort to put pressures on the airlines to observe the nine o'clock time limit for domestic flight planes. However, the state decided to make an appeal finally in February 1976, submitting to the Supreme Court a 280-page long appeal statement with critical comments on the High Court judgement on most of the disputed points. Contested in particular was the question of 'public interest' served by airplane flights.

What is called for in the deliberation by the Supreme Court is not the re-examining of evidence but rather an inquiry into the legal propriety of the decision handed down by a lower court. In view of this, one is somewhat mystified by the fact that it took almost six years to come to its decision (from February 1976 to December 1981). This procrastination is explained firstly by the change of the tribunal in charge, when the conclusion was almost reached after the two and a half year deliberation, from a minor one of four judges to a major one of all the members of the court. Apparently the state managers were alarmed by the direction in which the minor tribunal's judgement was taking and put pressure on the chief justice of the Supreme Court (Hisao Okahara), claiming that the points at issue were of grave importance with possible repercussions on other trials of a similar character. Then, the chief justice Okahara's retirement age came six months after this change, and in addition, four other members of the Court had to be replaced within another year. Thus the inquiry by the Supreme Court had to be started afresh in 1980 with newly appointed judges included, and the conclusion was reached for the third time in the Court in December 1980. It was unprecedented that the Supreme Court reached its conclusion three times on one and the same issue. The final decision was given on 16 December 1981, reversing a number of important judgements of the Osaka High Court, such for example as on night-time flights and on the proposal of the compensation payments for future noise damages. The court ruled the injunction over the flight schedule itself as unlawful, thus negating even the decision of the earlier District Court which had recognized the restriction of flights after 10:00 p.m.

Thus the litigation which lasted for 12 years ended in labour in vain for the pollution victims. This was the occasion when public opinion cited the case as a glaring example of submission of the judiciary to the administration. In any case, however, practical negotiations were needed between the pollution victims and the administration on a number of concrete problems which were in dispute. Above all, the question of restricting flights after 9:00 p.m. was 'crucial' in the mind of the residents in the region, but in a series of 'amicable settlement' negotiations which were conducted after the Supreme Court decision of December 1981, the administration side persisted in their refusal to include the flight limitation clause in the 'settlement' agreement. A compromise was finally reached through the intervention of 'The Eleven-City Mayors Council' of the region which obtained a verbal commitment by the Airflight Bureau chief of the Ministry of Transportation to the effect that 'the Ministry shall maintain the policy of not setting up any flight which falls after 9:00 p.m.' Another problem in dispute was the amount of compensation to be paid by the state for the 'amicable settlement.' The pollution-victims' side demanded 5.5 billion yen against the state proposal of 700 million yen. Here too, the final compromise reached was for 1.3 billion yen. And thus on 17 March 1984 the 'amicable settlement' was concluded.

There were two somewhat theoretical problems on which the Supreme Court decision reasoned differently from the opinions expressed by the plaintiff side, namely: (1) the legal validity of the concept of 'personality right' (*jinkaku-ken*) and also of environmental right, and (2) the practical meaning of 'public interest' as applied to the civil air-flight activities. As for the first point, the plaintiff side argued from the very outset of the trial that the 'personality right' and the environmental right were backed up by Article XIII (the pursuit of happiness clause) and Article XXV (the right to live clause) of the Constitution, thus entailing the important right to protect citizens from *kōgai* and also to prevent *kōgai* in advance.

The argument of the state against this was that Article XXV was a programme provision of abstract and doctrinal character and that both the 'personality right' and the environmental right, not being stipulated in any positive law, could not be used as a ground for an injunction measure. The Supreme Court echoed the assertion of the state without any qualification. However, the Osaka High Court discussed the question in detail, and although it reserved its opinion on the efficacy of the environmental right in support of an injunction, it admitted that the 'personality right' of pollution victims was being clearly infringed and could be cited as valid ground for an injunction. The judgement of the Osaka High Court, though negated subsequently by the Supreme Court, has actually come to be accepted by many constitutional scholars, so that a standard commentary on the Constitution of Japan has been wont to quote the above interpretation of the 'personality right' as a positive implication of Article XIII.[34]

As for the second point above, namely, the practical meaning of 'public interest' as applied to civil air-flight activities, the disagreement in the courts (the High Court and the Supreme Court) centred on the comparative weights given to the benefit (the revealed social and economic demand) on the one hand and the cost (the pollution damages claimed by residents in the region) on the other. The Osaka High Court judged the cost in the above sense to be sufficiently high to call for the limitation of the benefit in the above sense to some extent. However, the Supreme Court ruled that the 'public interest' revealed in the benefit was much higher than the alleged damage in the case. On the other hand, the plaintiff's argument was that the 'public interest' in protecting the environmental right of residents in the region should be higher than satisfying the demand of air-flight passengers, 90 per cent of whom were one kind or another of tourists.

Here was a certain kind of cost–benefit analysis which in a general sense is commonly used in the assessment of public works. The Roskill Committee, referred to earlier, also relied rather heavily on a particular type of cost–benefit analysis in its comparative evaluation of alternative sites for the third London Airport. Estimation of the benefit by the Committee was in terms of 'time-saved' for passengers having different time values, and estimation of the cost was mainly in terms of the cost of removal for those who had to be evacuated. Such analysis required concrete supposition of object-persons in each case and was bound to cause a great deal of controversy. The difficulty stems from the normative character of what is called 'social and economic demand.' For those economists like Milton Friedman who considers the free-market decision to be the optimum solution, the answer is simple and clear cut. But we know that there are such things as market failures and also that the revealed market demand is sometimes not in harmony with the normative dictates of society. It is quite often the case that the 'public interest' demands a priority consideration for the weak and the indigent who are unable to register their basic requirements in the form of monetary demand in the market.

A pedestrian example of this kind in Japan was the fate of public bath-houses in cities, which some two generations ago used to be a necessary facility in urban life, but which gradually came to be substituted for by installing of bathrooms in private houses with the general rise in the standard of living. Thus by the late 1960s the number of customers in public bath-houses started declining rapidly with the natural consequence of an increase of bath rates to make both ends meet. But the citizens who still had to depend on such public facility were in the category of relatively poor stratum. As one after another of the bath-houses began to go bankrupt, a question was naturally raised as to the desirability of subsidizing them in view of the 'public interest' entailed in the need to satisfy the basic demand for hot-bath taking by the poorer people. It is clear enough that the magnitude of revealed effective demand in the market as such for a particular commodity or service does not warrant it to be judged as a matter of 'public interest.' Think of the thriving business of *pachinko* (pinball games) shops in Japan at present. Probably only a few people will infer their maintenance as a matter of 'public interest.'

There is another aspect on the question of 'public interest' in the civil air-flight activities. That is related to the character of airports – the necessary complement to air travel which presumably is a matter of 'public interest.' There are some who would impart a 'public interest' character to any establishment of a structure or a facility so long as it has been carried out as 'public works' on the assumption that 'public works' would not be affirmed unless they partake of 'public interest.' In the case of the Osaka International Airport, however, the Supreme Court, in particular, reasoned more concretely to derive the 'public interest' character of the disputed airport from the 'public interest' character of air travels for which the airport was essential. Such derivational interpretation does have some ground to the extent that the 'public interest' in the sense of enabling the trans-national air-flight requires the provision of an adequate international airport which *ipso facto* becomes a matter of 'public interest.' But far more important is the consideration that an airport is closely wedded with 'common property resources'[35] the management of which calls for collective or public action, thus becoming a matter of 'public interest.' For example, such *kōgai* phenomena as noise and vibration pollution are unavoidable in the vicinity of an airport for jet planes, and these *kōgai* attributes constitute none other than the befoulment of common property resources. The question of environmental amenity is actually much broader in the case of the Osaka International Airport, including the congestion on access roads and even the negligence of renovation of the areas that were previously residential. These considerations, however, were quite foreign to the position taken by the administration from the initial stage of the trial in 1970 to their last pleading in the Supreme Court in 1980, simply parroting the words of 'the public interest character of the airport' without elucidating its meaning any further.

CHAPTER FIVE

From Stockholm (1972) to Rio (1992)

The 1972 Stockholm Conference on the Human Environment marked a turning point in two senses; firstly, as its rallying signal of 'Only One Earth' bespoke eloquently enough, it heightened the general concern over the environment on a global scale, and secondly, in its attempt to enlist developing countries in the Conference, it sought to frame development issues as environment ones, thus expanding the topics to be dealt with quite widely to cover, for example, the relief of poverty.

At around the same time when the Stockholm Conference was marking such turning points, Japan's economy was also experiencing a turn of the tide from the period of exceptionally high growth to that of less than remarkable performance. Some economists suggested at the time that the two decades of high growth were nothing but an inevitable process of 'catching-up' with Japan's own potentiality which had been held in check during the war-time and immediate postwar conditions. In other words, there could be a transcendental explanation for Japan's growth performance, which, on the assumption of a country's innate capability of maintaining a certain long-run trend line, would state that Japan was simply coming back to her innate trend line after a lapse caused by the dissipation and isolation incidental to the war. Such an explanation appeared to be plausible enough up until around 1970 if we could assume that Japan's long-run growth rate of real GNP was more or less what she demonstrated to have been capable of in the course of her development from the early Meiji Era, or from the 1870s, i.e., between 3.5 and 4 per cent per annum. If the trend line were drawn with a 4 per cent growth rate starting from the 1934–6 average as 100, the hypothetical index would stand at 267 in 1960 and 324 in 1965, against which actual figures stood at 162 in 1960 and 248 in 1965. But by 1970, whereas the former comes up to 395, the latter goes slightly above it to 407, the implication being that growth up to 1970 was more or less within the range of the assumed long-run trend line. If we go, however, a few more years to 1973, the gap widens to 444 on the trend line against 499 as actual attainment. It is plain that we require a more substantive explanation than this trend-line hypothesis.

A brief summary may be given here on the factors which could be cited in explaining the eventual deceleration of the growth rate at that time. In the first place, most of the growth stimulating effects of postwar temporary factors had been more or less taken advantage of by the end of the 1960s, such as the favourable effect of the exchange rate determined with an allowance similar to 'a convalescent golfer'[1] along with the catch-up process in latest technologies, the hothouse effect enjoyed during the period while liberalization measures were temporized, and the once-for-all effect of the subsidized provision of factory sites through reclamation of convenient shore-lines. Furthermore, the structural shift of industries toward high value-added sectors, which contributed to the high rate of growth, had gone almost as far as it could by the first half of the 1970s, and such factors as special tax-relief measures for industries and the so-called 'the low interest-rate policy' had increasingly come to be frowned upon by the general public and it is doubtful if they could be relied upon with similar assurance as in earlier years. Such unique features of Japan as the general practice of 'administrative guidance' and the high propensity to save by households were still in place; but these factors alone could hardly have sustained the inordinately high rate of private investment as was observed in the decades of 1950s and 1960s. As the saying goes, you can pull with a string, but you cannot push with it.

In other words, it was inevitable that the 10 per cent growth-rate period would come to an end sooner or later, although the Japanese capitalist class was reluctant to recognize the trend as the decade of 1970s opened, as exemplified by the Kakuei Tanaka Plan for remodelling of the Japanese archipelago, about which a reference was made earlier in Chapter Three.[2] The immediate effect of Tanaka's coming to power in July 1972 with this Plan publicly announced in advance was a boom in land prices especially in those regions which the Plan had named specifically as newly to-be-developed industrial centres. All the more was it a shock for the Tanaka regime and its supporters

when in October 1973 the dikes that had been erected around petroleum prices were removed and within four months the crude oil
price (Arabian light crude) rose from $3 per barrel to $11.65.[3] The
so-called 'first oil shock' thus visited Japan with convulsive effect.
Japan is peculiarly vulnerable to price rises in raw materials and fuels
on the world market, and the effect on its economy of the four-fold
increase in the price of oil between October 1973 and January 1974
was almost instantaneous, as can be seen in the marked drop of
several components of effective demand in *real* terms from the latter
half of 1973 to the first half of 1974, as shown in Table 5.1. It is
especially to be noted that 'private consumer expenditures' and 'private investment in plant and equipment,' between them, accounted
for practically all the decline in the sources of effective demand, and
thus was ushered in, in Japan also, a period of 'stagflation' where a
recessionary trend coexisted with inflation.

Although, characteristically in Japan, the new situation was
immediately grasped more vividly than in other countries, as

	Percentage change from July–December 1973 to January–June 1974	Relative shares of each component in the total decline (%)
Private consumer expenditures	−8.5	40.5
Current expenditures of government	3.7	−2.3
Government capital formation	−6.6	5.4
Private investment in plant and equipment	−19.8	58.3
Investment in inventories	−0.6	0.2
Exports and income from abroad	−1.6	−2.2
Gross national demand	−9.2	100.0

Table 5.1 *Changes in effective demand components from 1973 to 1974*

Source: Economic Planning Agency: The Institute of Economic Research. Calcula-
tions are based on the real-term figures expressed in 1965 prices.

marking a historical transition basically conditioned by a new 'price revolution,'[4] this time involving an irreversible shift upward in the cost of raw materials and industrial fuels, it was realized at the same time by the business community as well that here was a turning point in the economic growth rate and also that the preceding high-growth period was accompanied by some flagrant cases of environmental disruption on which one after another of court decisions were coming out in favour of pollution victims. On top of this, the impact of the Stockholm Conference of 1972 struck the fidgety complacency of the Japanese government to become awakened to the international implication of environmental problems and also to their broader scope than it was accustomed to wrestle with. Thus the key word in Japan shifted from *kōgai* to '*kankyō*' (the environment), expanding the coverage of concern to such matters as 'the conservation of nature,' 'the protection of wild life,' 'urban housing' and amenity in general.

STOCKHOLM, BEFORE AND AFTER

The Stockholm Conference on Human Environment had an impact on a world scale both before and after it was held in June 1972. Preceding it, there was a heated discussion, as we referred to the matter earlier, in connection with the need to invite developing countries to the Conference, for which purpose the scope of agenda items had to be expanded. Then, it happened that there were two outstanding themes that were of global interest just about the same time. One was the warning on the so-called 'population explosion' and the other was the general view expressed by the Club of Rome in 1972 in its report, *The Limits to Growth*.

An early warning on the population problem was that of Thomas Malthus (1766–1834) whose *Essay on the Principle of Population*, published in 1798, postulated 'universal tendency for population – unless checked by limited food supply – to grow exponentially, or by a geometric progression.' Malthus based his observation partly on that of Benjamin Franklin who had written that in the American colonies where resources were abundant population tended to double every 25 years or so. Malthus knew that this certainly was exceptional. But with an annual growth rate of 2 per cent, population would double in 35 years, and such possibility was not too far from what was happening in many parts of the world in the twentieth century. The population of the world in 1800, that is about the time Malthus sounded his alarm, is estimated to have been 919 million, and the latest figure is 5,720 million for 1995, or more than six times as great in roughly 200 years. It is significant, however, that the number of years required for doubling from two billion to four billion was 45 years (1928–73) and that, in particular, low income countries have shown annual growth rates of more than 2 per cent in the postwar decades.[5] The United Nations estimated at the time of the Stockholm Conference that the population of developing countries would occupy about 77 per cent of the world total by the year 2000 and pointed to a number of serious implications of this in terms of resource uses and the environment. Thus it was that the UN Secretary General proposed on 20 September 1972 to call the year 1974 as the 'World Population Year' and took an initiative in organizing a number of expert commission meetings in preparation for the world congress on population to be held in Bucharest, Romania, in August 1974.

One of the serious concerns generated by the population problem is the well-nigh certainty of the shrinking resource base as the world population keeps on increasing at the present rate with the most likely rise in the standard of living in general. An attempt to deal with this problem produced a timely publication just before the holding of the Stockholm Conference, namely *The Limits to Growth* written by the so-called MIT group (Donnella Meadows, Dennis L. Meadows, Jørgen Randers and William W. Behrens III) for the Club of Rome. This publication coincided with another technical report endorsed by a group of noted natural scientists in the United Kingdom: 'A Blueprint for Survival' (*The Ecologist*, January 1972), whose message was quite similar to that of *The Limits to Growth*, and both together happened to underline dramatically the following year by the OPEC oil price hike. Essentially, however, what the Meadows' group did was to use mathematical equations and a huge computer to prove the basic dilemma between a finite system and exponential growth. Quite often, simple extrapolation was naively applied to important parameter values to derive a specific conclusion. For example, predicted magnitudes of per capita real income (at 1968 prices) for the year 2000 were shown to diverge markedly among various countries to the extent of Japan topping the list ($23,200), followed by the USA ($11,000), and with India ($140) and

China ($100) near the bottom. A number of economists[6] commented on the social scientific naiveté of the nonchalant modelling employed by the authors of *The Limits to Growth*, but the book's impact on public opinion through the decade of 1970s was hardly negligible, as was suggested by the authors of *The Resourceful Earth* that *Global 2000 Report to the President* (1980) was 'a direct lineal descent' of the Club of Rome report.[7]

Apparently, President Carter of the USA noticed the emerging picture of a new population/resource balance as the world population was moving towards four billion and he could not deny the inability of US Government agencies to provide a coherent set of projections in important areas such as energy, water and food. This lack of global foresight capability led him to launch the 'Global 2000' study in 1977. Thus a study was undertaken by the US Council on Environmental Quality and the Department of State in cooperation with 17 specialized government departments and agencies and produced the Report to the President in 1980. Two paragraphs, which are often quoted, summarize the 'Major Findings and Conclusions' of *Global 2000* on its page one:

> If present trends continue, the world in 2000 will be more crowded, more polluted, less stable ecologically, and more vulnerable to disruption than the world we live in now. Serious stresses involving population, resources, and environment are clearly visible ahead. Despite greater material output, the world's people will be poorer in many ways than they are today.
>
> For hundreds of millions of the desperately poor, the outlook for food and other necessities of life will be no better. For many it will be worse. Barring revolutionary advances in technology, life for most people on earth will be more precarious than it is now – unless the nations of the world act decisively to alter current trends.

A radical enough statement, this! we must say, and it is most likely that such thoughts as these must have been in the minds of many a participant at the Stockholm Conference. But an overriding orientation of the Conference turned out to be, as mentioned earlier, the need to frame development issues as environmental ones in order to enlist developing countries actively in the Conference.

Although on the one hand a voice of idealism was sounded as for example by Margaret Mead who eulogized the conception of the Stockholm Conference as a new Copernican revolution in the sense of reconverting man's position on this earth[8] and also by Prime

Minister Gandhi of India who proposed to change the catch phrase of the Conference (Only One Earth) to 'Life is One and the World is One' giving precedence to the unity and life of the human race over the physical oneness of the earth; on the other hand, the actual discordant pros and cons on the official table of the Conference apparently left the impression on Stanley Johnson, a correspondent of the *New Statesman*, that 'the environment was none other than a scene of politics.'[9] His impression was especially apt in connection with the drafting of the Declaration on the Human Environment, which was finally adopted on 16 June 1972 after repeated wrangling mainly to settle differences between the advocates of the 'North' and the 'South.' The bone of contention was whether or not to assign priority to the thesis asserted by Mrs Gandhi on the Conference floor that 'poverty above all is *the* cause of environmental pollution.' That this was going to be a controversial issue in the Conference where the participation by developing countries was considered essential had been realized beforehand by Secretary General Maurice Strong, and that was the reason the Founex meeting was convened in June 1971. A kind of compromise formulation at Founex on the issue of 'development and environment' was held on through the successive meetings concerned with human environment with a clever keyword 'eco-development' coined by Ignacy Sachs and later renamed as 'sustainable development.' In this process of conceptual evolution, the role played by the Cocoyoc symposium, held in Mexico in October 1974 under the auspices of UNEP and UNCTAD, was of special significance.

Although the final product of this symposium (The Cocoyoc Declaration) did not receive much public attention, its impact on the experts' opinion in the special field of 'development and environment' was considerable. For one thing, both UNCTAD and UNEP took the matter of preparation seriously and jointly held two expert-committee meetings in advance, one on 'the impact of the problems and policies of resource management by developed countries upon the world trade and development strategies' and another one on 'alternative patterns of development.' And out of this preparatory canvassing of views was produced a discussion paper for the Cocoyoc meeting with the title of 'Patterns of Resource Use, Environment and Development Strategies,' which served a good purpose of 'traffic control,' so to speak, for the symposium.[10] The concluding remarks in the Cocoyoc Declaration may be quoted here:

We recognize the threats to both the 'inner limits' of basic human needs and the 'outer limits' of the planet's physical resources. But we also believe that a new sense of respect for fundamental human rights and for the preservation of our planet is growing up behind the angry divisions and confrontations of our day. We have faith in the future of mankind on the planet. We believe that ways of life and social systems can be evolved that are more just, less arrogant in their material demands, more respectful of the whole planetary environment. The road forward does not lie through the despair of doom-watching or through the easy optimism of successive technological fixes. It lies through a careful and dispassionate assessment of the 'outer limits', through co-operative search for ways to achieve the 'inner limits' of fundamental human rights, through the building of social structures to express those rights, and through all the patient work of devising techniques and styles of development which enhance and preserve our planetary inheritance.

It can be acknowledged that here was a message of hope about the need and the possibility of designing and implementing environmentally sound strategies to promote equitable socio-economic development for countries both of the 'North' and of the 'South.'

Along the line of conception thus formulated was a further development in subsequent years of a concept of 'sustainability,' which was defined by Lester Brown in 1984 as 'the yardstick by which we measure progress, [or] the extent to which our economic and social systems are successfully adjusting to changes in the underlying natural resource base.'[11] Thus a further definition: 'A sustainable society is one that shapes its economic and social systems so that natural resources and life-support systems are maintained.'[12] As we have referred to this conceptual evolution in Chapter One, the idea was subsequently popularized in 1987 by the Brundtland Committee in its report, *Our Common Future*, and continued to serve as a useful keyword at the Rio de Janeiro Conference and after – the subject we shall discuss in greater detail later.

While this Founex-to-Stockholm-to-Cocoyoc line was becoming more or less dominant on the international stage where the environmental problems were discussed in the decades of 1970s and 1980s, there emerged another school of thought which attracted a great deal of attention especially in the United States. It grew primarily as a response to *Global 2000*, about which we mentioned earlier, and was most eloquently defended by the publication, *The Resourceful Earth*, 1984, edited by Julian Simon and Herman Kahn. In contrast to the summary paragraphs we quoted earlier from *Global 2000*, Simon and Kahn stated their conclusion in the same sentence structure as that of *Global 2000* but substituting their differing judgements in italics as follows:[13]

> If present trends continue, the world 2000 will be *less crowded* (though more populated), *less polluted, more stable ecologically, and less vulnerable to resource–supply disruption* than the world we live in now. Stresses involving population, resources, and environment *will be less in the future than now*. . . . The world's people *will be richer* in most ways than they are today. . . . The outlook for food and other necessities of life will be *better* . . . life for most people on earth will be *less precarious* economically than it is now.

This is no less a radical statement in the opposite direction than the one quoted earlier from *Global 2000*. But the editors give supporting empirical data abundantly, much of which, however, rely in the end on the availability of cheap abundant energy. The following statement by Bernard L. Cohen, one-time chairman of the American Nuclear Society Division of Environmental Sciences (1980–1) and one of the contributors to the volume, appears to justify the optimism of Simon and Kahn:[14]

> As a scientist I see no barriers to a bright future for America and for mankind. Irrespective of present trends, many minerals will eventually become more scarce and expensive, but we can develop substitutes for them. Food supply and environmental difficulties may well develop, but they can be solved. *The only thing we need to handle these problems is an abundant and everlasting supply of cheap energy, and it is readily available in nuclear reactors, including the breeder*. Given a rational and supportive public policy, science and technology can provide not only for the twenty-first century, but *for ever*. (Italics added.)

Thus the debate was shifted to another plane though general agreement is, as yet, far from assured.

THE KEYWORD CHANGES FROM 'KŌGAI' TO 'KANKYŌ'

THE OECD REVIEW

The decade of the 1970s after the Stockholm conference in 1972 ushered in a new stage of engagement with environmental problems in Japan, with the keyword changing from *kōgai* to *kankyō* (environment). And it was quite timely that in the middle of this decade the OECD Environment Committee decided to conduct a Review of Environmental Policies in Japan as a second one of its kind after the one for Sweden in 1973.

The Review was based on an extensive survey conducted in Japan in 1976–7 by the OECD Secretariat in cooperation with government officials as well as a number of experts in academia in Japan, and the final product was prepared by Professor Remy Prud'homme, formerly Deputy Director for the Environment in the OECD. The Report itself [15] runs to less than 100 pages, but is a model for this type of document in the sense that the exposition is lucidly concise and yet with a full explanation of important themes buttressed by comparative data for other industrialized countries. The main themes dealt with were:

(1) setting of standards, both quality standards and emission standards;
(2) compensation schemes of three kinds, namely: non-governmental, judiciary and administrative;
(3) the question of siting development projects, with residents' control or administrative control;
(4) achievements as revealed in the efficiency of policies and their economic implications.

It was quite natural that from the OECD point of view an aspect of comparative appraisal among its member countries was important. And we could cite a number of observations in the Report which struck many of us Japanese as uniquely edifying, for example, as follows:[16]

(1) Japan has won many pollution abatement battles, but has not yet won the war in environinental quality. (p 83) Environmental quality, or as it is often called 'amenities,' refers to quietness, beauty, privacy, social relations and other non-measured elements of the 'quality of life.' (p 87) This is indeed a new and difficult task. It will require new types of instruments and mechanisms. It is more difficult than pollution abatement, because the problems at hand are mainly of a social, not just technical nature. . . . What is required is careful global planning . . . this kind of planning has to take into account both the nature and the location of developments; it

has to find out what to do, and where to do it. This is why land use planning has an important role to play. In this new type of environmental policies to be developed the key element is probably the organization of public participation. (p 88)

(2) [The] Japanese approach appears to have had strong moral overtones. It did not attempt to nicely balance costs and benefits, along the lines advocated by environmental economists. . . . It is interesting to note that this approach worked rather well. Many apparent decisions proved to be particularly wise decisions. Automobile emission standards are a case in point. The standards for NO_x exhausts set in Japan were so stringent that they were generally considered 'unmeetable'; yet, in a matter of years, several automobile manufacturers developed the necessary techniques. The standards had actually been set without a detailed examination of whether they could be met; had such an examination been conducted, the standards would probably have been less strict, and low-pollution cars would never have been developed. (p 85)

(3) Economists are usually very fond of compensations. . . . Policy-makers, by contrast, do not like compensations. They tend to take compensations to be both immoral and impracticable, and they have, in most countries, been reluctant to pass bills granting money to victims of pollution. This is why there are not, in OECD Member countries, many examples of compensation. Japan is an interesting exception. It offers three different types of compensation:

  (i) Private compensation, which consists of pre-damage and after-damage compensation negotiated between polluters and polluted;
  (ii) judiciary compensation, which is after-damage compensation decided by the courts; and
  (iii) administrative compensation, which is after-damage compensation provided by a Law initiated by the Government. (p 37)

The payment of compensation for damage is an important element of environmental policies in Japan. What is particularly striking is the limited scope of judiciary compensation – which is in most other countries the main or the only form of compensation. In Japan, by contrast, most compensation is arrived at in the framework of a negotiation system which is 'before' the court system, or of an administrative system which is 'beyond' the court system. One could argue that this makes good economic sense because the legal system, in Japan and elsewhere, is slow, costly, and to some extent, haphazardous. But a deeper explanation is probably to be found in the notion of conflict-avoidance. . . . In a country where the desire for mutual respect and trust is so great, trials are socially disruptive, and it is not surprising that other ways have been devised to settle conflicts, or rather to suppress them. (pp 48–9)

[Thus, the OECD Review devotes a great deal of space to the Pollution-related Health Damage Compensation Law which was passed in October 1973 and came into effect in September 1974. We shall discuss this law later.]

The very first sentence quoted above, i.e., 'Japan has won many pollution abatement battles, but has not yet won the war in environmental quality,' was quite timely since the keyword in Japan was in the process of changing from '*kōgai*' (pollution) to '*kankyō*' (environment). Although the judgement expressed in the latter half of the above sentence was accepted generally in Japan, the first half in the sentence was felt debatable. The government, on the other hand, was gratified by the evident endorsement of Japan's achievements in the field of 'pollution abatement battles'; but the general public, on the other, was much more sceptical, especially as regards the assessment policy on which the administration kept on backsliding throughout the decade of 1970s, as we shall give an account of it later. It is history's irony that the visit to Japan by the OECD Review team happened to coincide with a period of reaction on the *kōgai* problem in general and yet the visitors failed to appraise the trend in a balanced manner.

THE ENVIRONMENT AGENCY ESTABLISHED

The decade of 1970s opened with the establishment of the Environment Agency as a wing of environmental control for the first time in Japan. Until then, the responsibility for controlling environmental pollution was mainly lodged in the Ministry of Welfare, and environment-related administrative activities of various kinds were dispersed among a number of other Ministries. The decision to set up an independent agency for the environment was made at a time of heightened awareness on *kōgai* problems which erupted at the end of 1970 in the so-called '*Kōgai* Diet.' But the transition itself was not plain sailing. For one thing, the authority of the Environmental Agency was limited to the seven 'typical *kōgai*' items specified in the Basic Law for Environmental Pollution Control (air pollution, water contamination, soil pollution, noise, vibration, offensive odour and ground subsidence) and in addition the subject matters under government control as specified in the Law for Natural Parks and the Law for Conservation of Nature. Thus some of the important areas closely related to the environment, such as sewage and water treatment plant construction and food and drug administration, remained in their original Ministries. Probably a more serious handicap for the Agency was the fact most of its members had to be recruited from other Ministries and retained close ties to their 'home offices.' Some were only temporarily assigned to the Environment Agency and would be returned to their former Ministries after two or three years of 'lease term.' An inevitable consequence of such leasing system was the divulging of inside information on specific projects by leased members to their former ministries which often leaked the information to the business community concerned. One of such examples was the case of a councillor, leased from the Ministry of International Trade and Industry earlier, who returned to his original ministry to become head of the Locational *Kōgai* Bureau and played a leading role in causing the introduction of the Assessment Bill to the Diet abortive.

The limitation of competence of the Environment Agency also had a type of consequence which was rather retrogressive from the environmental point of view. An example was in relation to the sewage control which had been reserved for the Ministry of Construction as its exclusive jurisdiction. Article II of the Sewage Control Act defines 'the sewage' as 'waste water pertaining to household and enterprise activities and rain water.' The question was the control value, for example, of BOD (biochemical oxygen demand) of the factory drains to be accepted in the sewage system. It ranged from 300 to 600 ppm, as contrasted to a far severer value of 20 ppm in Tokyo as prescribed by the Law for Prevention of Water Contamination. It was only natural that enterprises felt it more advantageous to connect their drain pipes to the sewage facilities, avoiding the scrutiny of water pollution by the Environment Agency. The sewage administration after all was a *service* activity by local autonomous bodies, and having no systematic punishing rule, it was not staffed adequately with personnel for violation check-up. The Environment Agency, on the other hand, was responsible for checking waste-water drains of enterprises into public outlets like streams and sea shores with powers to indict violation as judged in terms of its regulatory criteria specified by the Law for Prevention of Water Contamination. Jurisdictional disjunction in this regard was clearly an anachronism, and it was commented at the time that if Japan succeeded in covering entire islands with sewage facilities there would be no need for an Environmental Agency to deal with any industrial waste water problem.

In addition, the weight of the Environmental Agency in the hierarchical structure of the cabinet was regarded to be quite low, and probably for that reason, the minister in charge was changed a dozen times during the 1970s. A few of them[17] performed their function quite conscientiously, but most others were occupying the ministerial seat as a matter of political prize. A flagrant example of the latter was Shintaro Ishihara, a novelist–politician, who held his office from December 1976 to November 1977 and criticized the move for deleting the so-called 'harmony clause'[18] as a case of witch-hunting.

CONSERVATION OF NATURE

The gradual shift of the keyword from '*kōgai*' to '*kankyō*' in the 1970s reawakened the nation's awareness of the value of national parks and the need for conservation of nature.

At the time of Japan's defeat in the Pacific War, there were only 12 national parks in Japan and jurisdiction over them was in the hands of the Ministry of Welfare. But in the turmoil of immediate postwar bureaucratic reshuffling the officials who had been in charge of national-park management had to be transferred to a section of war-damage rehabilitation and for a time there was none to look after the problem of national parks. The occupation authorities, which were almost exclusively American, took a paternalistic attitude on the national-park problem and let Captain Walter Popham, who happened to be a landscape architect with some experience of working in the US National Park Agency, to take leadership in guiding Japan's resuscitation as regards national park ideas. A specialist, Charles A. Richey, was sent over from the US Bureau of National

Parks and he stayed for five months, from April 1948 to August of that year, to map out a comprehensive plan for the administration of the national parks in Japan.[19] The administrative guidance by the occupation authorities continued until Japan regained her independence in 1952.

A new turn was marked by the promulgation of the National Parks Law on 1 June 1957, which finally systematized Japan's park administration by establishing the classification of (A) national parks, (B) quasi-national parks, and (C) prefectural parks. By the time the Environment Agency came to take over the jurisdiction of non-urban park problems, there were, for the three categories above, 23 of (A), 44 of (B) and 279 of (C). But 21 per cent of the (A) category area and 44 per cent of the (B) category area were privately owned land, which meant that full public control of the utilization could not be ensured on all occasions. One of the problems on which experts' opinion was divided was about the major emphasis to be placed on the *raison d'être* of national parks; namely, whether they should be recreational facilities for the public or valuable nature reserves to be protected. The debate on such an issue pointed to the need for separate legislation for the conservation of nature as such, and even before the establishment of the Environment Agency, the Ministry of Welfare was exploring, as early as in 1970, the possibility of submitting a Law for the Conservation of Nature's Environment. This scheme was taken over by the Environment Agency, which drafted a concrete plan for legislation in January 1972. Its outline in a nutshell was as follows:

(1) The object of conservation shall include not only nature's endowment of beauty but also such superior natural environments as primeval forest, tideland, grass field and coppice.
(2) The importance of 'greens', in urban and suburban areas shall be stressed and they shall be maintained at the least as they are.
(3) Designation shall be in terms of five classes: primeval conservation areas, superior natural environment areas for conservation – with three ranks of Class One, Class Two and Class Three, and green areas for conservation (cities and their peripheral areas). The last category shall be under the jurisdiction of prefectural governors while the remainder shall be managed by the Environment Agency.

We can easily see that this outline was more ambitious for a new-born government agency than the ingrained bureaucratic division of power could tolerate. The immediate reactions from the Forest Agency and the Ministry of Construction (which was in charge of city planning and the conservation of urban and suburban greens) were negative, and the intense discussion for compromise lasted for about three months, ending with a number of concessions by the Environment Agency such as the conceding of permit power on lumbering of reserve forest to the Forest Agency. Even after the cabinet decision was reached on 6 June 1972 and the Bill was submitted to the Diet, arguments for amendments blocked the early passage and it was in danger of being tabled in the Diet because of the terminal date of the session. Furthermore, Mr Buichi Oishi, the head of the Environment Agency and thus the sponsoring minister of the Bill, had to rush to the Stockholm Conference in June – the circumstance which made the administrative officers in charge despair of any chance for the passage of the Bill. What saved the situation in the last minute was, according to Mr Oishi himself,[20] none other than the pressure of public opinion. Apparently mindful of reprobation by public for 'the responsibility of tabling the said Act,' Diet members scuttled along, while many other government-proposed Bills were being tabled, to pass the Nature Conservation Act in the committee (the chairperson being Mrs Shizue Kato) of the House of Councillors on the last day of the session and then pushed through the plenary session that night (16 June 1972). 'It was miraculous, indeed' was Oishi's comment at the time.

Article XII of the Law for the Conservation of Nature's Environment provided that the state should lay down basic policy as regards the conservation of nature's environment; and the necessary preparation for this task began in the spring of 1973, with the original draft worked out by administrative officials in the Environment Agency and then submitted for inter-ministerial coordination as well as for the experts' commission in charge of nature's environment. In this process of preparation, the major point of disagreement among the participating officials and experts centred on the question of implementing the environmental assessment. In fact, the final version of the Basic Policy left out reference to the assessment problem, and this was the first occasion when the negative attitude on assessment by industry oriented ministries was clearly indicated, to be repeated time and again as we shall deal with the question later on. In any case, the Basic Policy for the Conservation of Nature's

Environment was approved by the cabinet on 26 October 1973 and served as a kind of keystone to guide the administration in conservation matters. The preamble of this document, written in lofty style, came to be quoted often in subsequent years. Its opening words were as follows:

> Nature, forming an environment in a broad sense for human life, is none other than the mother's womb which fosters life itself and provides boundless benefaction to humans.
>
> In other words, not only does it perform the role as resources for economic activities, but in itself it constitutes a formative element of human life.
>
> Especially in our country, its unique cultural tradition has been that of man, nature and formative arts of man united as an organic unity.
>
> When we reflect upon the role of nature in our social life, we realize that the first step for all the policies shall be that we appreciate the value of nature highly and make the spirit of its conservation as a matter of habit in our daily life.

Parallel with this Basic Policy, which was a governmental guideline, there evolved a move among citizens' groups to set forth a declaration upholding the conservation of nature. The move actually started around 1964 when the executive members of the Japan Association of Conservation of Nature discussed among themselves about the advisability of proclaiming a charter setting great store by the conservation of nature. It took, however, 10 years before the final decision was reached on the textual details of the charter, and a ceremony was held on 5 June 1974 for the inauguration of the Nature Conservation Charter in the presence of the Crown Prince and Princess. The text of the Charter, essentially similar in content to that of the Basic Policy for the Conservation of Nature's Environment prepared by the government, was much briefer but was quite incisive. Its opening sentences went as follows:

> Nature, being a mother's womb for whatever is ordained with life including man, maintains its harmony in possessing solemn and delicate laws of its own.
>
> Man, being a part of nature along with the sun-light, the atmosphere, the water, the ground and flora and fauna, receives benefits as well as tribulations from nature, and by making most of them, has erected what is known as civilization.
>
> And yet, since we know not when, we have, in our eagerness to pursue the progress of civilization, forgotten the preciousness of nature, made

light of the delicateness of mechanism of nature, squandered its endowment under an illusion that nature was inexhaustible, and thus have impaired the harmony of nature.

This trend has been especially notable in recent decades, with such phenomena as the pollution of air, the contamination of water, the disappearance of greens, etc. causing disruption of equilibrium everywhere as regards the necessary conditions for the continuing life of living things in the world of nature; and thus nature's environment has deteriolated in high gear, so to speak.

Unless this circumstance is not expeditiously amended, man's life force is likely to be undermined at its depth, even the continuation of life itself might be endangered, and there is a danger of man's future facing a serious crisis. Moreover, once nature is disrupted, it is bound to take a long time for it to be restored and there may even arise cases where restoring to its original state is out of question.

Now is the high time that we are awakened to the solemn reality of nature; and discarding such conceited ideas as nature is to be conquered or nature is subservient to man, we should treasure nature and bring the concentrated efforts of the entire nation for the conservation of nature's environment, while endeavoring for its prudent use and not impairing its harmony.

Therefore, we proclaim herewith the Nature Conservation Charter.

Then in the latter half of the text, the Charter specified a number of concrete policies which were more or less similar to the ones described in greater detail in the Basic Policy which was drafted by the government.

On the occasion of the inauguration of the Charter, Mr Takeo Miki, then the Minister in charge of the Environment Agency, spoke quite frankly of 'the Charter's message to be the drastic conversion of value concepts held by administrative officials both in the central and local governments from that of economic efficiency to such standards as human health, happiness and yearning for beauty.' This was a welcome statement from a political leader. But unfortunately, felicitous words alone cannot have an effect on the practical stage of administration unless they are accompanied by tools of enforcement, as was proved time and again.

A notable exception in this regard, however, was the case of work stoppage on the construction of a skyline road for tourists intended as an access to the Ozé national park, a treasured swamp area at the height of 2,000 metres above sea level with numerous alpine flora. The construction plan for this access road had been approved bureaucratically before the Environment Agency came into existence in 1971 with prospective completion of a large parking area right near the Ozé swamp. But Mr Buichi Oishi, about whom we mentioned earlier as head of the Environment Agency, was a man of strong conviction as regards the conservation of nature and went on working to overcome all the bureaucratic barriers against his determination to stop the construction of the road in question. The tenacious opposition in the cabinet meeting against his ideas, especially by the Minster of Construction, was also finally overcome and the cabinet approval was obtained in favour of Oishi at the end of September 1971. Subsequently, the Commission on Natural Parks made a decision in December of that year to cancel the earlier plan of constructing the skyline road in question. It was a rare victory for the environmentalists in the field of conservation of nature – rare in the sense that the regular bureaucratic rail that had been laid was passed over.

As the keyword gradually shifted from '*kōgai*' to '*kankyō*' in the decade of 1970s, concern for nature's environment found its focus in a number of directions, one of which was a citizens' claim for access to the seashore as a matter of right. A new term was coined for this right in Japanese, namely 'Irihamaken'(the right to enter the beach), analogously to a historically antecedent term 'Iriaiken' (the right of common). And the citizens' group which initiated the movement using the keyword of 'Irihamaken' in 1973 was what was then called 'The Association of the Members of the City of Takasago.' The city faces the Seto Inland Sea, with the seashore lined with rows of pine trees, and was given the name of 'Takasago' – the title of a traditional Noh song played on auspicious occasions. The environmental conditions of the area began to deteriorate after a chemical factory was built on the reclaimed land and started contaminating the bay water with the drainage containing PCBs. As Keikichi Kihara in the book he edited with the title of *Irihamaken* wrote: 'The present-day environmental disruption, I believe, has to be conceived as a multi-faceted phenomenon consisting of three elements: *kōgai*, the destruction of nature, and the ruining of the historical milieu; and the city of Takasago is experiencing all these three simultaneously.'[21] The bay area was further assaulted by an oil-spill accident of the Mizushima *kombinat* in December 1974, which aroused the grass-root citizens to make an appeal at the national level and even came to

Tokyo to hold a protest meeting where 'the Irihamaken Declaration', was proclaimed. Its text, though brief, was as follows:

> From time immemorial, the sea has belonged to all people. Without any discrimination it has long been the common right of the residents of the region, to take a walk along the beach, to enjoy the scenic beauty, to go out fishing or swimming, or to draw sea water at ease, to gather drift-wood, to go picking shell-fish or sea weed, and otherwise to obtain some sustenance of life. And in the windbreak grove along the seashore there used to exist the right of common. To these things combined, we propose to give the designation of *Irihamaken*, which we believe belongs to the residents as a part of their rights guaranteed by the Constitution as an aspect of life in a healthy environment.
>
> And yet, in recent years, one after another of *kombinat* came to be constructed all over the country under the dictate of growthmanship; and especially through the reclamation of the seashore, not only has nature been subjected to serious destruction but also the *Irihamaken* of the citizens has come to be infringed almost completely as the enterprises occupied the reclaimed land up to the edge of the sea. Several of *kōgai* phenomena also are generated here.
>
> We declare herewith that we are possessed of the *Irihamaken* as an instrument of our movement for eradicating *kōgai*, protecting nature's environment from destruction and restoring nature's integrity.

Repercussions of this Declaration spread immediately to different parts of Japan where similar problems were in dispute. In particular, the citizens' protest movement in the city of Buzen in Kyūshū against the seashore reclamation for the siting of the Kyūshū Electric Generating Corporation was greatly encouraged by the Declaration which strengthened their earlier argument on the basis of environmental right. Combining this with the *Irihamaken* reasoning, the Buzen citizens' group decided to bring the matter to court in 1977 asking for an injunction against the siting of the corporation, which, however, was turned down as inadmissible for judicial deliberation. An appeal was made to the Fukuoka High Court. But again the court decision in 1981 was the same, except it was for the first time that a Japanese court gave a detailed explanation why the claim for injunction in a civil suit on the basis of the environmental right concept was inadmissible.

Another instance which is worth recording is the trial in the Ehimé prefecture in 1978 where the Matsuyama District Court turned down a law-suit in which residents of the town of Nagahama claimed the

free use of the seashore for swimming on the ground of *Irihamaken*.
The case is especially interesting because it elicited a court decision
in which it was stated that 'the seashore is a public entity in nature
under state control; and the possibility of sea-bathing by residents is
nothing but a reflex effect of the fact that the state might not prohibit
it.' It was commented in public at the time that by the same reasoning the possibility of breathing by the nation as a whole could be 'a
reflex effect of the fact that the state might not prohibit it.' Pompous
density of legal mind, this, indeed!

As we discuss the problem related to seashores, we inevitably recall
the matchless observation of Rachel Carson in her small, but classical work: *The Edge of the Sea*, which was published in 1955 before
she became famous through her serialized articles in the *New Yorker*
beginning 16 June 1962, later published in a book form: *Silent
Spring*. The geographic place of Carson's observation was the US
New England coast facing the Atlantic Ocean, but her description,
which we quote partly below, fits perfectly to many of the seashores
in Japan.

Like the sea itself, the shore fascinates us who return to it, the place of
our dim ancestral beginnings. In the recurrent rhythms of tides and surf
and in the varied life of the tide lines there is the obvious attraction of
movement and change and beauty. There is also, I am convinced, a deeper
fascination born of inner meaning and significance.

When we go down to the low-tide line, we enter a world that is as
old as the earth itself – primeval meeting place of the elements of
earth and water, a place of compromise and conflict and eternal
change. For us as living creatures it has special meaning as an area in
or near which some entity that could be distinguished as Life first
drifted in shallow waters – reproducing, evolving, yielding that end-
lessly varied stream of living things that has surged through time and
space to occupy the earth.

To understand the shore, it is not enough to catalogue its life. Understanding comes only when, standing on a beach, we can sense the long
rhythms of earth and sea that sculptured its land forms and produced the
rock and sand of which it is composed; when we can sense with the eye
and ear of the mind the surge of life beating always at its shores – blindly,
inexorably pressing for a foothold. To understand the life of the shore, it is
not enough to pick up an empty shell and say 'This is a murex,' or 'That is
an angel wing.' True understanding demands intuitive comprehension of
the whole life of the creature that once inhabited this empty shell; how it
survived amid surf and storms, what were its enemies, how it found food

and reproduced its kind, what were its relations to the particular sea world in which it lived.[22]

More appropriate, probably, to the *Irihamaken* claim in Japan today is the remark in Carson's personal letter to her longstanding friend Marie Rodell in 1957, to wit:

> The undisturbed shore is one of the best places to see Nature at work: in the geologic cycles by which the relation of sea and land is undergoing constant change, and in the flow of life by which species come and go, new forms are evolved, and only those that can adjust to a difficult environment can survive. Yet when man takes over all this is changed. Within the long cycles of the earth what we do probably makes little difference; yet within the restricted cycle that is completed within one person's life *the shore can never again be itself once man has 'developed' it.*[23] (Italics added.)

When Carson wrote this forty years ago, it is most likely that she could not have realized how pertinent the last sentence, quoted here, would become in the *Irihamaken* movement of the 1970s in Japan.

The *Irihamaken*, or the right to enter a beach, is clearly an aspect of 'amenity rights' (as defined by E.J. Mishan)[24] with reference to the non-market welfare significance of water-front on the seashore for human life. Similar claims to amenity rights have been made in Japan for inland water-front, such as those of rivers and lakes and are referred to by a coined expression: *Shinsuiken* (the water-savouring right or the right to enjoy the water-front). Rivers running through big cities, in particular, have frequently provided one sort or an another of *joie de vivre* in contact with water. The Thames in London, the Seine in Paris, and the Kamo in Kyoto are such examples. Especially in Japan where cities developed on alluvium plains created by the accumulation of earth and sand which rivers carried down, how to get on with rivers has been one of the most important political, as well as cultural, problems in her history. With steep mountains forming the backbone of the main island, rivers in Japan have the characteristic of flowing in a gush,[25] often causing serious enough floods. But three principles of coping with the water problem, namely, *chisui* (control), *risui* (utilization) and *hosui* (conservation), used to be practised more or less wisely in Japan with the long-term perspective in view until about the middle of the Meiji Era, or the end of the nineteenth century. However, technological development, itself, in the construction of river dikes triggered a legislative revision on the river control in 1896, introducing a system of what was known as 'the high-water construction work' which was intended to enable the river water to stream down to the sea quickly and 'safely.' Through the adoption of this system, rivers and river-side ground were detached distinctly in two and at the same time the river water-front areas became 'civilized' concrete walls – hardly suited for the exercise of *Shinsuiken*. There still remain, however, narrow limited sectors along the river-side in Tokyo. But such places have become the target of gentrification on account of the rise in the value of land.

As for the water-front of inland lakes and tide land, the *Shinsuiken* movement has won some battles mainly through energetic support of grass-root citizens. Memorable in particular was the fight for amenity rights, combining *Hosui* and *Shinsui*, or conservation and savouring, in the Lake Biwa area in 1979. The movement which aimed at reversing the eutrophication of the lake's water by stopping the use of synthetic detergents was fully supported, on the one hand, by Mr Masayoshi Takemura, then Governor of the Shiga Prefecture, but it was successful only through the cooperation of a host of housewives who gathered scrap cooking oil to manufacture amateurish soap to replace detergents. The end product was a local government ordinance for prevention of eutrophication of Lake Biwa (17 October 1979) – a unique example of grass-root initiative for environmental legislation.

Subsequently in 1984, Governor Takemura sponsored the World Environmental Conference on Lakes and Marshes, where a large number of citizens' groups participated to confirm the progress made in improving the water quality of Lake Biwa. Some of these citizens' groups suggested a need to hold a nation-wide assembly on 'lakeside districts and water-front cities' and succeeded in this endeavour on their own, with a meeting held in the city of Matsué in May 1985 gathering 700 persons from some 20 citizens' groups. It was on this occasion that the assertion of the *Shinsuiken* was publicly resolved by citizens' groups for the first time. The relevant passages in the 'Matsué Resolution 1985' may be quoted here:

> We, the residents of lakeside districts and water-front cities, have come to learn that we can enjoy the right to live in our home towns above all through savouring our water-fronts. In other words, we hereby confirm that we are possessed of the *Shinsuiken*, or the inherent right of savouring water-fronts. There are three principles that should be observed for the residents to be able to savour water-front in their daily lives. Firstly, the

water surfaced from the historical past should not be dissipated. Secondly, the water-front should be kept open to residents as a public resource. And thirdly, the quality of water should not be spoiled in any way through local development projects.

One of the reasons why the meeting was held in the city of Matsué was that in the background of the city is located Lake Shinji and Nakanoumi where a reclaiming project by drainage was in progress – a type of public works which has caused national controversy ever since then.[26]

CHAPTER SIX

Progress and setback in standards, compensation and assessment

With the establishment of the Environment Agency in July 1971, we could at least expect unification of environment-related policies within a single ministry along with a more positive approach in formulating and implementing them than before. The three issues we take up in this chapter, however, are typical in giving us a somewhat disappointing impression of the subservient position of the Environment Agency in the hierarchical structure of Japanese government.

STANDARDS FOR POLLUTION CONTROL

One of the reasons why the OECD review of 1977 complimented Japan for having 'won many pollution abatement battles' was, we surmise, that the quality standards for air pollution control, in particular, were far severer in Japan, as of 1975, than in most other OECD countries. Table 6.1, a comparative table for this purpose, is reproduced from the OECD Report for Japan.[1] Earlier, we quoted a comment in the Report that 'the standards for NO_x exhausts set in Japan were so stringent that they were generally considered "unmeetable"; yet, in a matter of years, several automobile manufacturers developed the necessary techniques.'

Only one year after this OECD Report was published, however, the Japanese government on 11 July 1978 issued a public notice to the effect that the quality standard for NO_2 as an average daily value was to be eased from 0.02 ppm to the range of 0.04 to 0.06 ppm. The earlier standard of 0.02 ppm had been in effect since May 1973 as a target to be attained within five years with special allowance of eight years for those areas where population and big industries were heavily concentrated. How such a policy retrogression came about is worth recording as a piece of drama fit for

	SO$_2$ (ppm)	Particulates (mg/m^3)	NO$_2$ (ppm)
Japan	0.04	0.10	0.02
Canada	0.06	0.12	0.10[b]
Finland	0.10	0.15	0.10
Italy	0.15	0.30	n.a.
USA	0.14	0.26	0.13[c]
Germany	0.06	n.a.	0.15[d]
France	0.38	0.35	n.a.
Sweden	0.25	n.a.	n.a.

Table 6.1 *Air quality objectives;* [a] *Japan and selected OECD countries, 1975*

Notes:
[a] All figures are average daily values.
[b] The figure is for Ontario: the figure for Saskatchewan is much lower: 0.01.
[c] For the USA, the NO$_2$ objective is set in terms of average yearly value (0.05 ppm); the figure given is therefore an equivalent open to criticism.
[d] The German standard is 0.05 ppm for 'long-term exposure' and 0.15 ppm for 'short-term exposure.'

text-book material in the history of environmental politics in the postwar Japan.

It may be recalled that Japan in the beginning of the decade of 1970s was still basking in palmy days of high growth rate on the one hand and also was undergoing a turning point, on the other, with respect to awareness of the importance of environment problems both on the part of government and the business community. Against this background, there occurred almost simultaneously two events: one in the United States – the passage of the Clean Air Act of 1970, or the so-called 'Muskie Law,' which prescribed some stringent targets for the reduction of major pollutants closely related to automobiles, and another in Japan – repeated occurrences of photochemical smog during 1970 to 1972 which caused much health damage to school children in Tokyo Bay side areas. These two events prompted the Japanese government, where the Environment Agency had just been set up, to map out a plan for setting adequate enough quality standards for pollution control. It was a necessary move if only for Japan's exports of cars to contend with the prospective hurdle of the Muskie Law. Thus began the first act of the drama in the form of a decision by the Environment Agency to submit the problem to the Central Anti-*Kōgai* Commission for concrete advice on control values for nitrogen oxides, hydrocarbons and carbon monoxide. The Experts' Committee of the Commission, headed by Dr Takeo Suzuki of the National Public Health Agency, came to a decision in April 1973, which was approved by the Minister in charge of the Environment Agency at the time, Takeo Miki, and became the official quality standards, as shown in Table 6.1 – clearly a far more stringent set of standards than in other industrialized countries.

The second act of the drama starts with the immediate reactions of the business community to the government announcement on the new standards. It was characteristic, however, that whereas the steel manufacturing group mobilized some academic circles in an attempt to prove that the prescribed standards had no scientific basis, the automobile manufacturing firms started to compete with each other in developing technological innovations to overcome, in particular, the barrier specified in the Muskie Law, obviously with an intention of obtaining preferential treatment for their products in the US market. It was in the middle of such domestic divergence of responses that the OECD Review team visited Japan, and their verdict praising the standards set for NO_x exhausts as enabling the development of necessary techniques. 'Necessity is a mother of invention' was an apt comment at the time. But the drama did not end with this.

The third act of the drama begins with a renewed offensive by the steel manufacturing group and others which became somehow more self-confident in the mid-1970s as the economic conditions in Japan after the first oil shock of 1973 were in the process of structural adjustment, and business in general was not in the mood for accepting additional cost for environmental control. While the automobile manufacturing industry was quietly busying itself in technological innovations, pressures from other sectors of the business community upon the officials of the Environment Agency became blatantly unrestrained. The opening salvo for this act was the official inquiry by Minister Ishihara on 28 March 1977 to the Central Anti-*Kōgai* Commission on the subject of 'the criteria and related matters in relation to the health impact of nitrogen oxide on humans.' It is to be noted that the inquiry this time was on 'the criteria' and not on 'the environmental standards.' The Commission set up a new experts' committee for this specific task and appointed Dr Takeo Suzuki again as chairman. But a star player at this stage of the drama was Dr Michio Hashimoto, head of the Bureau of Conservation of the Air in the Environment Agency, who occupied a key position in the bureaucratic line up on environmental matters. He had just congratulated himself for the praise from the OECD Review on the successful 'battles in the many pollution abatement.' But now he had to engage with contentions from both sides: the technical recommendation coming from Dr A Takeo Suzuki, chairman of the experts' committee on the one hand and the politically far stronger insistence that the earlier standard should be mitigated. Recommendation this time by the experts' committee was that 'the guideline level for NO_2 should be 0.04 to 0.06 ppm per day with the proviso that the safety coefficient of approximately 50 per cent should be applied to this in order to obtain an adequate enough quality standard. This would mean the repeating more or less of the 1973 recommendation of 0.02 ppm per day. The Ministry of International Trade and Industry, on the other hand, reflecting faithfully the opinion in particular of the iron and steel industry, was advocating at that time the environmental standard of 0.10 ppm per day, which was the level in force in the United States. Sandwiched between the two polar opinions in this manner, Dr Hashimoto found a bureaucratic solution by a convenient rationalization that the safety coefficient need not be applied to the guideline level. Thus the standards ranging from 0.04 to 0.06 ppm came to be officially established on 11 July 1978 to replace the earlier one of 0.02 ppm for NO_2. At the same time, the Environment Agency announced unilaterally that the coefficient of the 'Salzmann method of estimation' for the environment standard of NO_2 was to be changed by 17 per cent upward, thus automatically easing the standard, for example, to 0.047 ppm from 0.04. Upon fulfilling the thorny task of finding a compromise solution, Dr Hashimoto resigned in August 1978 from the position he had held for three years in the Environment Agency. Thus act three ended. But the drama continued further.

Act four of the drama opens with the immediate announcement by the heads of a number of local governments, such as Governor Minobe of Tokyo, Governor Nagasu of Kanagawa and Mayor Ito of Kawasaki, that they will continue to abide by the old standard of 0.02 ppm as the average daily value. This expression of noncompliance spread to many other regions, and finally in October 1978, the Liaison Association for *Kōgai*-patient Families sent delegates to meet Mr Yoshimasa Yamamoto, successor to Dr Hashimoto as bureau chief of air conservation, to question the scientific basis for the new 1978 standard. Yamamoto could not cope with the cross examination by the delegates on the occasion and was importuned to write a signed memorandum, saying that 'I have not studied the problem fully enough and therefore cannot explain to you patients on the scientific ground of the quality standard for NO_2.' This was a humiliating admission by a responsible high-level bureaucrat and not only elicited a harsh reprimand by the minister but also constituted an encouragement for the subsequent law-suit (October 1978) by a residents' group in Tokyo which included some certified *kōgai* patients demanding the revocation of the official notification on the new environmental standard for NO_2. This was a kind of administrative suit which was unprecedented. It touched on the question of the relation between the easing of the environmental standards and the total mass emission control, on which, however, the Environment Agency side kept on insisting that they were independent of each other. Although the plaintiff side, along with a supporting group of intellectuals, repeated the demand for a substantive trial on the question, the Tokyo District Court refused to go into a discussion of the practical effects of the easing of the standards and proclaimed the decision on 17 September 1980 stating that the plaintiff's instituting was unfit for judicatory consideration.

An appeal was made immediately to the Tokyo High Court, which turned out to be a stage where two key players of the drama were called to testify on the side of the plaintiffs, namely: Michio Hashimoto and Takeo Suzuki. Hashimoto appeared twice in the Court in 1985 and replied to questionings by defence lawyers on the plaintiff side, but he was rather eager to emphasize the point that the maintenance of the environmental standard in question was *not an obligatory* but *a desirable target* from an administrative point of view. He further confessed that at the time of the revision of the NO_2 standard in 1978 he was 'personally driven into a corner, so to speak.'[2] In effect, he remained non-committal on the issue contested in the Court. Suzuki, on the other hand, appearing in the Court in February 1987, testified, in particular, on the health-damage effect of multiple contamination of NO_2 with other air pollutants. But at the end of his testimony he stated decisively that at the time of the 1978 revision of the NO^2 standard the safety coefficient should have been applied to the guideline level.

Seven years passed for the Tokyo High Court to proclaim its decision on 24 December 1987, which turned down the plaintiff's appeal by saying that since the environmental standard is a policy target or a guideline for the administration in the process of promoting anti-*kōgai* tasks, it is outside the competence of the Court to pass a judicial judgement on pros and cons of the policy target or the guideline as such for the governmental policy.

However, the president of the Court, Mr Seichi Goto, added a special proposal at the end of his ruling to the effect that

> the prevention of *kōgai* is the earnest wish of the law and the nation; and as we think of the important role played by the environmental standard in promoting the anti-*kōgai* administration, it is highly desirable that its fixation, as well as its revision, should be conducted through procedures which reflect, as far as possible, the opinion and good judgement of the nation as a whole.

He also made a critical remark on the Environment Agency's failure to apply the safety coefficient at the time of their revision of the standard in July 1978. Thus, at least for the moment, the drama came to a close, aside from the details of coordinating the emission standard with the environmental quality standard.

COMPENSATIONS

As the OECD Review commented, most compensation claims in Japan are settled 'in the framework of a negotiation system which is "before" the court system or of an administrative system which is "beyond" the court system.' It is quite true that Japan had been much less dependent on the service of lawyers than, for example, the United States, for the settlement of civil disputes. Expressions like 'jidan' and 'wakai' (amicable settlement) were quite common for out-of-court settlements of one kind or another, the latter in particular having been in common use in those cases where settlement was agreed upon only after going through sharp disagreements on the points at issue.

In an earlier chapter we referred to a number of concrete instances of judiciary compensation, which took five years or more for the final settlement. One of such examples was the Yokkaichi pollution case, where the court decision was arrived at only in July 1972, more than 12 years after an air pollution victim was identified. This was the occasion which prompted anti-*kōgai* public opinion in general to propose an administrative compensation scheme in order to settle matters more expeditiously. Probably more significant, however, was the preference indicated by the business community for avoiding lawsuits which usually constituted an occasion of creating 'a dirty image' for the specifically identified polluting firms. If by some kind of a PPP (Polluters Pay Principle) system they could be exempted from any further involvement in *kōgai* disputes, they could carry on their business at ease. Thus it was more from the business community side that pressure was exerted on the government to develop an administrative compensation scheme. The state managers apparently felt in a similar direction, and as the Yokkaichi trial was approaching its conclusion in the spring of 1972, the government submitted an inquiry to the Central Anti-*Kōgai* Commission on the advisability of establishing an administrative compensation system. The Commission's subcommittee (Experts' Committee on the Charge System for Damage Compensation) published its interim report in December 1972, five months after the Yokkaichi trial decision, and the Central Commission sent the final report as of 5 April 1973. This became the basis for a law called 'Pollution-Related Health Damage Compensation Law' which came into being in October 1973, becoming effective in September 1974.[3] There was a certain ambiguity as to its major intent, that is, whether it was 'essentially structured as a damage compensation system in the nature of civil responsibility' (the wording in the Commission's final report) or a system in the nature of a kind of social security. At any rate, the law was intended at the same time to play the role of mitigating the pollution through the PPP.

Since this was a law for administrative compensation, all the key questions such as:

(i)   who is to be compensated and how
(ii) who is the one to compensate and how

had to be answered by administratively determined rules. And there arose a number of controversial points in the process, as we shall see.

For a pollution victim to be able to receive compensation under the system, there were three conditions: (1) he or she had to be a resident of one of the officially designated areas; (2) a certain number of years of residence in such area was required; and (3) he or she was suffering from one of the specified health impairments. As for the designated areas, there were to be two kinds: Class I areas, where marked air pollution was observed and where *non-specific* diseases due to the effects of such air pollution were prevalent, such diseases being chronic bronchitis, bronchial asthma, asthmatic bronchitis and pulmonary emphysema. Class II areas, where there were *specific* water-pollution related diseases, such as Minamata disease, *Itai-itai* disease and chronic arsenic poisoning. As of the end of April 1986, there were 41 areas throughout the country designated as Class I. And as for the number of years required as residence in the area, it was one year in the case of bronchial asthma and asthmatic bronchitis, two years in the case of chronic bronchitis and three years in the case of pulmonary emphysema. Thus the total number of pollution victims certified in the Class I areas was 95,000 by the end of April 1986.

What was being compensated is the next question. The law provides for several kinds of compensation benefits. First, medical care expenses are reimbursed. Second, a physical handicap compensation is paid monthly. The amount of the compensation paid to a pollution victim is a function of his age, his sex and his 'rank.' Victims are classified into four ranks, and to each rank corresponds a 'coverage rate.' Special rank victims and Rank I victims are people unable to work and badly hampered in daily life; the coverage rate for these ranks is 100 per cent. Rank II victims are people seriously restricted in work and impeded in daily life, the coverage rate for them being 50 per cent. Rank III victims are people hindered in work and slightly restricted in daily life, the coverage rate for them being 30 per cent. The general formula for the amount of compensation received by the victim is:

The average wage of the group he or she belongs to
times the coverage rate of his or her rank
times 80 per cent.

To give an example, a Rank II female aged 45 will receive about 38,000 yen monthly. The highest compensation, i.e. that paid to a special rank victim, male, aged 50–4, would be 174,000 yen monthly. There are less important types of compensation benefits, such as 'child compensation allowances,' paid to persons raising children under 15 years of age, designated as victims, and 'survivors' compensation payments,' paid to the surviving dependents of a person certified for a designated illness who dies as a result of that disease, to make up for the deceased person's lost earnings. Funeral expenses are also reimbursed.

Details of the compensation scheme give evidence to its somewhat eclectic character of mixing the administrative allowance element _with_ the burden to be borne by the polluters based on the principle of civil responsibility. This point was related to other ambiguities in the entire system.[4] But one controversial aspect of the compensation scheme was the gender discrimination inherent in the use of average wage as a basic parameter, giving rise to a consequence of extreme disparity between male and female in the old-age category. Also the method of selection of victims for receiving the compensation left much to be desired, since one had to propose on one's own initiative in order to be certified as a pollution victim by an official committee. Furthermore, the automatic exclusion of pollution victims outside the designated areas was a cause for much complaint as soon as the Compensation Law came into effect.

Even more questionable was the manner in which the 'who compensates' question was worked out. The flow of funds for compensation payment begins with the charges collected from polluting firms and agents on the basis of SO_2 emissions and syphoned into a juridical body having a special status (called the Pollution-Related Health Damage Compensation Association or PRHDCA) which distributes appropriate amount of money to the relevant local governments. This scheme, however, harboured three controversial issues: (1) The original recommendation by the Central Anti-*kōgai* Commission was to consider, as pollutants for the compensation purpose, not only SO_2 but also NO_2 and particulates. But the administration's decision was to limit to SO_2 only. This turned out to be a most serious issue subsequently. (2) Collecting of charges by PRHDCA was, in itself, a matter of convenience and constituted no ground for controversy. But in the process, the identification of the responsible polluters was kept secret. The PPP in this regard was only half effective. (3) While SO_2 emitting firms outside the designated areas were also called upon to pay *pro rata* charges,[5] pollution victims in such areas could not receive compensation under this system. This was a source of complaint from both sides.

The entire scheme was clearly designed for the eventual exculpation of the SO_2 polluting firms, since, partly thanks to the effective working of the PPP, SO_2 emissions gradually decreased to such an extent that the erstwhile polluting firms began to put pressure on the government towards the end of 1970s to rescind the designation of the Class I areas. Such pressure coincided with the easing of NO_2 quality standard; unless this was done it was feared by the business community that a possible revision of the Compensation Law to expand the scope to include NO_2 would reopen a new compensation headache for them.

It was in November 1983 that the Environment Agency officially asked the Central Anti-*Kōgai* Commission to reconsider the designation of the Class I areas. There were two steps in this procedure: firstly, again an experts' committee composed mainly of medical and public health specialists, and following this, another committee called 'working sub-committee' composed largely of legal specialists. The former's report did suggest the importance of NO_2 pollution anew, but gave enough ground for satisfaction for the business community on the improvement mentioned as regards SO_2 pollution compared with the 1955–65 period. The concluding words of the report were: 'It cannot be denied that there is a possibility that the present-day air pollution as a whole is having some effect on the natural history of chronic occlusive lung impairment.' The working sub-committee submitted its report on 6 October 1986 with a conclusion, referring to this dictum of the technical committee, that 'to say simply that "it cannot be denied that there is a possibility" is not strong enough to demand compensation for damages to the emission source-agents of air polluting materials as a matter of civil responsibility.' In effect, the working sub-committee denied the applicability of epidemiological judgement on the causal relation between the pollutants and specific victims. The sub-committee, with a conclusion of this nature, apparently did not realize that they were actually turning the clock back on the treatment of the question of causality in the environmental pollution case in postwar Japan. In any case, the Central Anti-*Kōgai* Commission accepted the recommendation of the working sub-committee which proposed:

(1) The designation of all the Class I areas are to he cancelled and no new certifying of pollution victims should be made.
(2) Payments to existing certified patients are to be continued.
(3) Policy should be reoriented from that of compensating individuals to that of improvement of regional environments.
(4) The establishment of a special 'fund' contributed by enterprises could be considered.

And these in turn became the final decision of the administration which received the approval from the Diet on 18 September 1987, and the steps for cancellation of the designated areas went into effect on 1 March 1988.

Reviewing the entire story on the Pollution-Related Health Damage Compensation Law, we cannot resist the impression that the scenario, from beginning to end, had been prepared by guileful men of the establishment. Immediate reaction, however, was generally critical of the evident machination by the Environment Agency which acted in collusion with leaders of the business community.[6] Admitting that the SO_2 pollution had decreased on the one hand, public opinion was particularly insistent that the nitrogen oxide pollution should have been, and still could be, included as a major category in the Pollution Compensation Law. Also it was pointed out that within the Class I designated areas newly certified patients just before the cancellation numbered as many as 9,000 within a year, with a net increase of 3,000 after deducting the number of those who were released from the system. The government decision of not allowing any more new certifications was most unrealistic. This was part of the reason, no doubt, why a great majority of 51 relevant heads of local autonomous bodies responded to the official inquiry negatively on the appropriateness of the 'revision' of the law.[7] The legal framework has been changed, but the substantive problems remain.

ENVIRONMENTAL IMPACT ASSESSMENT (EIA)

It is difficult to find a more laboured attempt for legislative realization than the case of environmental impact assessment in Japan which was once given up in 1984 after more than 10 years of striving and then had to wait a further 13 years before its final success in 1997. The chronicle of this process reveals in a way the characteristic interplay of politics and economics in postwar Japan.

The first flagrant occasion when elementary negligence of *ex ante* assessment brought about a subsequent law-suit was in connection with the Osaka International Airport in 1969. As we discussed this case earlier, the decision by the Osaka High Court was epochal in the sense that the anti-*kōgai* policy instruments of injunction and the polluters pay principle were applied to the state itself as the

defendant in the trial. It happened, however, that the United States –
considered by the conservative government of Japan as a senior
partner to be emulated in basic policy matters – passed new legislation in 1969, which was called 'The National Environment Policy
Act' (NEPA). At that time, Japan did not yet have an Environment
Agency, but a close study on NEPA began immediately among the
relevant official circles, who apparently were impressed by the
sophistication with which the American law was phrased and made
use of it as a model later when they were to draft the Japanese
equivalent.

The purpose of the US National Environmental Policy Act of
1969 read:

> To declare a national policy which will encourage productive and enjoy-
> able harmony between man and his environment; to promote efforts
> which will prevent or eliminate damage to the environment and biosphere
> and stimulate the health and welfare of man; to enrich the understanding
> of the ecological system and natural resources important to Nature; and
> to establish a Council on Environmental Quality.

And in Section 102 of the Act, it was stated:

> All agencies of the Federal Government shall –
> Include in every recommendation or report on proposals for legislation
> and other major Federal actions significantly affecting the quality the
> human environment, a detailed statement by the responsible officials on –

> (i) The environmental impact of the proposed action,
> (ii) any adverse environmental effects which cannot be avoided should
> the proposal be implemented,
> (iii) alternatives to the proposed action,
> (iv) the relationship between local short-term uses of man's environ-
> ment and the maintenance and enhancement of long-term prod-
> uctivity, and
> (v) any irreversible and irretrievable commitments of resources
> which would be involved in the proposed action should it be
> implemented.

The period from 1969 to 1972 was highly charged with environ-
mental awareness in Japan, what with the preparation for the
Stockholm Conference and the International Social Science Council
Symposium on the environment in Tokyo in 1970, what with the
revision of the Basic Anti-*Kōgai* Law to delete the so-called
'Harmony clause' and the drafting of 14 new laws related to the

environment, what with the consecutive court decisions in favour of
kōgai victims from the *Itai-Itai* disease case onwards, and what with
the establishment of the Environment Agency in July 1971. On top
of these events was now added the task of emulating the United
States in drafting an Environmental Impact Assessment Law.

The starting point for this action was a cabinet-level agreement of
6 June 1972 on 'the environment preservation measures in relation to
several kinds of public works,' which was intended to become the
basis for an impact assessment law. Confident that the government
would fulfil this promise, Buichi Oishi, then the minister in charge of
the Environment Agency, made a public statement soon afterwards
in Stockholm that 'it is my intention in Japan to adopt the approach
of environmental impact assessment whenever we propose a plan for
public works.' This intention was confirmed in a more concrete way
by Takeo Miki, who became the minister in charge of the Environment Agency in December 1972, both in his New Year address
of 1973 as well as in the Environment Committee of the Diet in
February of that year. It was in pursuance of such resolve by
Ministers in charge that the Central Anti-*Kōgai* Commission set up a
sub-committee on EIA, which worked out in June 1974 a guideline
for the operation of environmental impact assessment. Three basic
rules were proposed for the purpose as follows:

(1) It is proposed that *ex ante* estimation and assessment shall be made
on the degree and scope of the impact of developmental projects on the
air, the water, the ground, living things, etc., and also on the needed
countermeasures and possible alternatives. Environmental impact
assessment must be conducted in repetition at each stage of a developmental project, for example, at its conception, its basic policy formulation, and its practical execution. Thus in the cases of harbour planning,
the reclamation of public water-surface, and the siting of electric generating plants, environmental impact assessment should be repeated often
enough so as to improve the accuracy of the estimation.

(2) In order that the premises for environmental estimation and assessment can be made explicit, it is necessary to distinguish those matters on
which the estimation can be scientifically certain and those on which it is
uncertain. Inasmuch as science has its unavoidable limitations, it is necessary to secure, over and above experts' opinions, environment-related
information as fully as possible from the experiences and observations of
resident citizens in their daily lives and in the places of their work.

(3) The EIA should be re-examined continually on the basis of new
environmental information; and when any kind of trouble as regards

environmental preservation is observed, the ongoing developmental project itself should be reappraised immediately.

These guidelines became the basis for the subsequent proposals for EIA by the Environment Agency.

The Environment Agency was mindful enough of the expected opposition from other ministries on the EIA legislation and took time in working out the procedural aspect of the proposed assessment, which finally took the following itemized forms:

(1) The agency which is responsible for carrying out a developmental project shall conduct the initial assessment of the impact of that project and prepare a draft EIA document.
(2) The project operating office shall make that document public and make it known widely through holding meetings for explanation and otherwise.
(3) Steps shall be taken to ask for submission by residents in the region of their opinions on the draft EIA document and also to hold public hearings for the purpose.
(4) Steps shall be taken to elicit the opinions of the minister in charge of the Environment Agency and also those of heads of local autonomous bodies.
(5) The project operating office shall revise the initial assessment on the basis of the opinions expressed above and shall draw up the final EIA document and make it public, inclusive of details on the revising process.

Now the Environment Agency was ready to propose the EIA plan for legislative discussion and submitted a draft plan, first of all, to prefectural governors and mayors of ordinance-designated cities on 13 January 1976. Thus the whole matter became public and the first round of the bout, so to speak, began between the Environment Agency and opposition groups. There were altogether seven rounds in this bout which lasted until 1984, and in every one of them the Environment Agency was the loser in spite of the fact that in each successive round a fresh concession was made to the opposition side.

The immediate responses from the opposition side in the first round came from the Federation of Economic Organizations (*Keidanren*) and the Ministry of International Trade and Industry.

Keidanren, considered to be the most prestigious big-business group, opposed the EIA legislation on the following grounds:

(1) The items to be assessed, as well as the environmental quality levels to be attained, are, to say the least, unclear. If the law obliges enterprises in the procedural aspect only while the estimation method, etc., is technically undeveloped, there is a possibility of creating needless confusion as an inevitable consequence.

(2) An attempt to systematize reflections of opinions by local residents at the present stage is prone to promote social disorder inasmuch as the societal milieu in our country is not necessarily mature enough.

(3) The rights or wrongs of the carrying out of a developmental action should be judged comprehensively, that is to say, not solely on the basis of environmental considerations but also with reference to its impact on such socio-economic aspects as the effective utilization of land resources, the improvement in standards of living, and the promotion of social welfare. We should be especially careful not to cause miscarriage of a developmental project through unnecessary confusion by giving priority in the assessment to its environmental impact at the initial stage of the project planning.

The Ministry of International Trade and Industry was no less forceful in objecting to the EIA legislation by pointing out the following reasons:

(1) In the draft proposal by the Environment Agency as to the impact on the environment, the particular items to be assessed, the method of estimation, and the standard for assessment are extremely unclear. This may lead to a possibility of residents demanding unrestrained increase of burdens on the project operating agency and thus redound on the national economy as a sizable loss in time and additional cost.

(2) To prescribe the procedure of participation by residents in public works and factory-siting planning could mean that even a simple procedural oversight becomes a cause for litigation and thus generate the undesirable effect of causing a large number of meaningless law-suits. In the United States, we observe that due to the ambiguity of assessment standards, etc., there have occurred frequent cases of litigation and the solution had to depend on the judgement of the courts. If the Environment Agency's plan is legislated, there is a definite

probability that in a similar fashion as in the United States important projects of the state and enterprises will be delayed unnecessarily.

(3) Matters claiming prior settlement before the adoption of any EIA system are various other kinds of practices and experiences which are to be accumulated in the immediate future. The time is not quite ripe for a systematic application of EIA at the present stage to cover the whole of developmental projects in view. Practical policy should be the one of taking steps one at a time.

It might be noted that the Environment Agency did make a major concession to other economic ministries in the opening round of the bout by proposing that 'the agency which is responsible for carrying out a developmental project shall conduct the initial assessment of the impact of that project and prepare a draft EIA document.' But this concession was not enough, and the objections were so strong that the Environment Agency had to retreat and retracted the legislative proposal in May 1976.

The second round of the bout began under a new Fukuda cabinet with Mr Shintaro Ishihara as the minister in charge of the Environment Agency. This time, further concessions were made to the economic ministries by way of limiting the scope of residents' participation in expressing opinions to those who were locally concerned with the proposed project only and also by agreeing not to permit local autonomous bodies to prescribe such regulation as going beyond what the state has already stipulated. In addition, Minister Ishihara's guardless dictum on one occasion to the effect that 'there are some merits as well as demerits in developmental projects' was conveniently taken advantage of by the officials of economic ministries and emphasis on the economic fruits of developmental projects came to be highlighted in the public discussion. Again, the *Keidanren*, headed by Mr Toshio Dokō, made it clear that they were opposed to the EIA legislation, and with a new opposition coming from the Ministry of Construction citing a possible conflict with the City Planning Act, the Environment Agency lost its fighting spirit and decided for the second time in May 1977 to withdraw its legislative proposal of EIA.

From then on, successive rounds, from the third to the seventh, went on essentially with a pattern similar to the earlier ones; that is to say, a new eviscerating proposal made each time by one or another of economic ministries and the consequent concession by the Environment Agency without, however, success even in gaining a hearing on the legislative floor. One major concession on the part of the Environment Agency in the process was to agree to exclude the electricity generating plants from the list of developmental projects subject to impact assessment. By the time the bout reached the seventh round in 1984 the process of emasculation of the legislative plan became so pronounced that, paradoxically enough, the initial affirmative camp for the legislation turned to the negative side on the ground that the watered-down bill of the kind then proposed would do more harm than good. Thus, the Environment Agency finally gave up the legislative plan for EIA and agreed to compromise with a substitute idea of a cabinet-level agreement on 28 August 1984. Such denouement was unprecedented in Japanese parliamentary history in the sense that a public promise made by the administration for a legislative proposal had to be rescinded through seven rounds of striving because of the opposition by the very party in power itself.

During those nine years from 1975 when the Environment Agency took an initial move for the EIA legislation until 1984 when the proposal was finally given up, there ensued a number of episodic events illustrative of typical political dealings in Japan. Most flagrant among them probably was another paradoxical situation in the fifth round of the bout in 1980 when the negative side in the bout reversed itself to the affirmative ostensibly for the reason that a conservative Governor of Tokyo, Shun'ichi Suzuki, needed an umbrella EIA legislation of the state in order to override the then existing ordinance carried over from the progressive Minobé period. A responsible bureau chief of the Environment Agency was bold enough to reveal the significance of this policy reversal in a memorandum he drafted in favour of the legislative proposal. In addition, the memorandum contained a remark suggesting that in exchange for the agreement on the EIA legislation a revision of the Pollution-Related Health Damage Compensation Law could be considered to satisfy the demand of the business community. The memorandum was brought into the open in a Diet committee meeting, and the minister in charge of the Environment Agency had to disclaim the contents of the memorandum entirely and apologize for what his subordinate had done. At any rate, the fifth round ended in May 1980 with the decision by the Environment Agency to shelve the legislative proposal.

With the seventh round ending in August 1984, the central government became no longer inclined to pursue the policy of law-making for EIA, until the Basic Environmental Law of 1993 reopened the question about the need for EIA legislation. But as early as in the latter part of the 1970s, a number of local autonomous bodies, such as Kawasaki, Hokkaido, Kanagawa and Tokyo, had pioneered in passing ordinances for EIA, and public opinion was becoming quite receptive to the practice of impact assessment. It took 13 years of dormancy for the Environment Agency before legislation for EIA on the national level was finally enacted in 1997, about which we shall give some details in Chapter Eight.

CHAPTER SEVEN

Pharmacological and other pollutions

The dimensions of environmental problems broadened gradually, as the 'Earth Summit' of 1992 approached, both in time and space, that is, intergenerationally in time and globally in space. But before we pursue this evolution of our major subject matter, we must step aside briefly to review several cases of *kōgai* incidents of a rather special type in Japan at around the time of the Stockholm Conference – the incidents which illustrate the typical pattern of profit-oriented private enterprises supported by a pro-capitalist administration and condoned by a lack of vigilance on the part of consumers.

The following incidents are somewhat unique in this sense:

Pharmacopollution cases:
    (1) Arsenic milk poisoning
    (2) The Kanemi rice-oil disease
    (3) The SMON scandal[1]
Other *Kōgai* cases:
    (4) The Toroku mine *kōgai*
    (5) The hexavalent chromium *kōgai*

THE ARSENIC MILK POISONING[2]

This is a case of widespread baby-food poisoning, first turning up in June 1955 in the western area of the country, and by 1981 it was acknowledged that more than 10,000 patients were counted with 600 among them dying as a result. There were 6,093 persons still suffering from continuing health impairment 26 years after ingesting the milk in question, with 624 afflicted by severe mental retardation, developmental difficulties and brain-damage-related paralysis.

There were a number of causative factors which concurred to bring about such an incident. It happened that in the adding of sodium phosphate to the milk products as a stabilization agent in the spring months of 1955, the Morinaga Company, one of the top milk products manufacturers, used an industrial grade material which was one-third the regular cost of the pharmaceutical grade additive and *did* contain arsenic. This was clearly the basic cause. There was, however, a socio-economic factor occurring just around that time which was the beginning of the high growth period in postwar Japan when young female labour was in great demand and many of the working mothers with infants had to depend on the powdered milk for feeding. In fact, milk-producing companies as well as health professionals at the time championed the use of powdered baby milk, as a step in the direction of nutritional modernization, for non-working young mothers too. In addition, the recession of 1954–5 necessitated strenuous rationalization of all the major milk products companies, giving rise to an incident like the staphylococcus poisoning of skimmed powder milk produced by the Yukijirushi Company in March 1955. The use of industrial grade sodium phosphate containing arsenic by the Morinaga Company in 1955 was an aspect of economic rationalization at the time.

From June to August 1955, one after another infant patients were brought into hospitals in the Okayama Prefecture with common symptoms of diarrhoea or constipation, vomiting, a swollen abdomen and a darkening of skin colour. At first, there was no clue as to the cause of this commonly seen problem. But soon (that is, by 5 August) it was made clear that what the infants had in common was the intake of the Morinaga MF milk. And it was confirmed further that the strange sickness was related to products from the Tokushima plant of the Morinaga Milk Company, which subsequently (on 19 August) was advised by the Paediatric Department of Okayama University to re-examine its production process for possible imperfections. After that, the Company began using a purer form of sodium phosphate which was purchased through the regulated pharmaceutical channels. But by then arsenic was detected in the MF milk and the Public Health Department of Okayama Prefecture had to make a public announcement that poison had been found in the MF milk. Thereupon, the Ministry of Welfare of the central government issued an order for all MF milk to be withdrawn from the market and the Tokushima plant of the Morinaga Company to be closed. Thus began the contest between the Morinaga Milk Company on the one hand and the organization of the parents of the infant victims on the other.

The role played by the Ministry of Welfare in this dispute was not

up to the expectation of the victims' side in the light of the indisputable cause-and-effect relation of the poisoning that had occurred. In
fact, the Five-Men Committee[3] appointed by the Ministry ostensibly
for the purpose of 'fair and neutral settlement of the dispute' was
clearly biased in favour of the milk company in the recommendation
it proposed. Besides proposing a set of compensatory payments,
which fell far short of the demand by the victims' families, the
Committee's conclusion stated that 'it should be agreed that the poisoning has no lasting after-effects.' The recommendations were made
public in December 1955, less than five months after the first patient
of the milk poisoning visited the Okayama University Hospital, and
it was hardly possible to make any firm prediction about 'lasting
after-effects' without having a precedent of the kind somewhere else.

It turned out, however, that serious enough after-effects were
experienced by many of the patients of 1955; 14 years later, that is in
1969, painstaking research by Professor Hiroshi Maruyama of the
Osaka University, entitled 'Visits After 14 Years,' was made public
and immediately rekindled public concern over the arsenic in milk
problem. Before then, the Morinaga Company was apparently feeling unburdened because of the report of the Five-Men Committee
and further by the decision of the Tokushima District Court of 1963
which returned a verdict of 'not guilty' on the criminal charge of
poisoning. The victims' representatives, on the other hand, had come
together initially to organize an association, *Zenkyo* so-called, to
press for action by Morinaga on their compensation demands, but
this organization was disbanded as a condition for accepting
Morinaga's new proposal which was slightly better than that arrived
at through the deliberations of the Five-Men Committee. This was a
clear retreat by the *Zenkyo* leadership and a new organization was
immediately formed in the Okayama Prefecture for the express
purpose of providing protection for the Morinaga arsenic milk-
poisoned children, briefly called 'Mamoru-kai' (Association for
Protection).[4] In July 1957, this new organization entered into negotiations with Morinaga in which they demanded and received a memorandum from the company that acknowledged the company's
responsibility in paying the cost for periodic examinations for those
infants who had been poisoned. But not much concrete progress was
made until Professor Maruyama's report, 'Visits After 14 Years,' was
made public and aroused public opinion in 1969. It is significant to
realize that this was the year when public concern over environ-

mental problems started to grip Japan almost like an epidemic, and the renewed play-up of the arsenic milk poisoning incident in the mass media shifted the weight of argument in the direction in support of the poisoned victims. There were two contexts in which a turnabout could be observed.

One of them was in the criminal-case trial that had ended in the acquittal of the Morinaga men earlier, in which an appeal was made by the district prosecutor's office and the Takamatsu High Court dealt with the problem. The latter's decision in 1966 reversed the earlier one of the District Court, whereupon Morinaga appealed the case to the Supreme Court, which in 1969 supported the decision of the High Court. Thus the case had to be referred to the District Court again, where it took almost four years, from February 1970 to November 1973, to come to a final decision of sentencing three years' imprisonment to the factory head of Morinaga for negligence in ascertaining 'the foreseeable danger of poisoning.' All told this case took 18 years for the victims to win the day.

Another of the contexts in which Professor Maruyama's report made consequential impact was in the series of negotiations between Morinaga and the *Mamoru-kai*, now a united national organization for the victims. For some time, even after the public opinion critical of Morinaga spread nationwide after the publication of 'Visits After 14 Years,' Morinaga kept on oscillating in their concrete proposals of atonement, still continuing essentially to evade responsibility. But the *Mamoru-kai*, on the other hand, became more confident than before in the justness of their demand, and when confronted with the delaying tactics of Morinaga at the fifteenth negotiation meeting in December 1972, the *Mamoru-kai* converted the meeting into their national assembly on the spot and passed resolutions to spread the boycott movement against Morinaga products all over Japan and to take damage claims to the civil courts citing both Morinaga and the national administration as defendants. These tactics proved to be quite effective. For example, before the boycott movement had got under way, the Morinaga Company held 45 per cent of the market for powdered baby milk, but after the boycott started that share went down to 17–18 per cent. In the civil court trial, which began at the Osaka District Court in April 1973, the chief legal representative of the *Mamoru-kai* made a significant statement in the initial oral pleading to the effect that 'the demand for compensation included remuneration for all the victims who used the Morinaga milk in 1955, including even those patients who were not certified as suffering from any after-effects.' Such a demand, inclusive of that for uncertified victims, was epoch-making within the context of victim compensation negotiations related to environmental disruption.

In September 1973, two months before the decision of the Tokushima District Court on the criminal case – the decision which was expected to say 'guilty' for the Morinaga factory chief, the central government finally recognized its responsibility, at least in part, and proposed a three-party negotiation arrangement among the *Mamoru-kai*, the government administration and the Morinaga Company. This proposal was realized on 23 December 1973; and the signed agreement by the three parties contained the following five points;

(1) The Morinaga Company recognizes full responsibility for the MF milk-poisoning incident and will shoulder from now on all the obligations for the remedy and relief of the victims.

(2) As regards the measures to be taken for the victims, the Morinaga Company will respect the plans consistent with the permanent relief as proposed by the *Mamoru-kai* and will follow the judgement and decisions of the Relief Measures Committee to be established in accordance with the plans referred to above.

(3) The Morinaga Company will faithfully put in practice the instructions given by the Relief Measures Committee and will bear all the expenses required by the said Committee.

(4) The Ministry of Welfare will positively render assistance to the permanent relief programme and will cooperate with the Relief Measures Committee when this Committee requests administrative actions.

(5) The three-party negotiation meetings will be continued until all the problems could be completely solved.

Through signing of this agreement and the promise given by the Morinaga that they will advance three billion yen as a 'Relief Measure Fund' to the *Hikari* Foundation to be established as an organ designed to help relieve the Morinaga milk-poisoning victims, the 19-year-old contestation came to an end in April 1974.

As a post-mortem for the 'mystery' of the arsenic entering the production process of powdered milk at the Tokushima factory of Morinaga, it may be pointed out that the sodium phosphate purchased by the factory came originally from the Shimizu factory of the Nihon Light Metal Company as an industrial waste in the process of manufacturing alumina from bauxite. This waste material was purchased in September 1954 by the Shin-Nihon Metal Company presumably as an auxiliary material for the production of pigments. Before selling the said industrial waste, the Shimizu factory asked the Nagoya Industrial Laboratory for examination and was told that there were some foreign matters mixed in it. This analysis report was communicated to the Shin-Nihon Metal Company, which agreed to purchase nevertheless. However, the material was subsequently sold and resold to a few other agents, and after about a year and a half it was sold by the Kyōwa Sangyō Company to Morinaga as industrial grade sodium phosphate. It may be admitted that the factory chief of Morinaga had no way of fathoming this life story of the arsenic-containing sodium phosphate.

THE KANEMI RICE-OIL DISEASE[5]

This is another case of pharmacopollution illustrative of deficiency of the socio-economic system in coping with a modern product of science and technology. By 1973, that is, five years after the health impairment called 'Kanemi Rice-Oil Disease' was identified, over 1,000 persons had been designated as 'official victims,' although from 3,000 to 5,000 more were believed by medical authorities to have existed then. The 'culprit' of what was then called 'accidental food poisoning' was PCBs (polychlorinated biphenyls) and the offending firm was the Kanemi Corporation. The accounts of the incident here will be given in the following sequence:

(1) What is PCB?
(2) How it came about that PCBs seeped into the production process of rice-oil?
(3) How was the initial victim identified (in 1968)?
(4) What were the responses by the offending firm and by the government?
(5) How did the protest movement by victims develop, and also the court trials of the case?
(6) The final settlement in 1987.

The chemical substances known as PCBs, or polychlorinated

biphenyls, were first synthesized in Germany in 1881, and their uses were originally limited mainly to the electrical industry. After the Second World War, however, technological advances provided PCBs with more varied applications, and the first production in Japan by the Kanegabuchi Chemical Company with the trade name of 'kanekurōru' was in 1954 to the amount of 200 tons. Production increased to 11,100 tons by 1970, with the Mitsubishi Monsanto Company joining in this specific branch of industry.

> The chemical and physical properties of PCBs make them very adaptable. At room temperature, they form a colourless fluid (increasing in viscosity with the number of chlorine atoms) that does not conduct electricity or undergo chemical decomposition even at very high or low temperatures. PCBs are non-flammable and can theoretically be recycled. They have been used industrially as a heat-transfer medium, an insulator in condensers, transformers, and other electrical appliances, and as an additive in paints, insecticides, lubricating oils, plastics, and inks used in the manufacture of 'carbonless' copy paper. Thus, during the last 25 years, PCBs have on all counts become a technological success.
>
> It is just these technologically advantageous qualities, particularly their virtual indestructibility, that make PCBs a dangerous environmental contaminant. Once discharged into the environment, they are extremely difficult to destroy, retrieve, or render harmless. Furthermore, they concentrate as they move up food chains and are even harder than DDT for living systems to metabolize. High-chlorine PCBs accumulate in fatty tissues and are not readily excreted through urine or perspiration. The effects of PCBs on biological systems are thought to be similar to those of DDT: they interfere with sex hormone activities, exert a deleterious effect on liver enzymes, and are potentially carcinogenic.
>
> The first warning of PCBs' highly toxic effects came in 1936, when industrial health hazards, particularly a severe skin disease known as chloracne associated with the production and handling of the compounds, were reported in the United States. . . . For twenty years or more, however, these early warnings were ignored.[6]

It was such chemical compounds that were used by the Kanemi Corporation in the deodorizing stage of the rice-oil's manufacturing process, a stage in which the oil is brought to a very high temperature (210–30°C). To heat it to this degree, preheated PCBs were circulated through stainless-steel pipes running through giant vats.

Next comes the problem of how it was that PCBs seeped into the manufacturing stage of rice-oil itself. Needless to say, the Kanemi Corporation could not deny the fact they used PCBs for the deodor-

izing purpose, but when suspicion was raised on the seeped-in mixture of PCBs in the rice-oil about six months after the outbreak of
the disease, the factory chief of the company flatly denied such a
possibility. His explanation was that if by any chance PCBs were to
leak out, the vacuous condition of the deodorant vat would be
impaired and the temperature inside the vat would not rise as
expected and would be immediately detected by a watchman through
a measuring device which is installed. However, further examinations
by the research staff of Kyūshū University confirmed the fact of a
mixture of PCBs in the manufactured rice-oil, and the truth had to
come out on the details of the deodorizing process.

A number of corroborating facts was revealed soon afterwards.
For one thing, there was a sudden increase in the consumption of
PCBs between January and April 1968, actually a 10-fold increase
over the normal monthly volume of 20 to 30 kilograms. The company's management could have been aware of the leakage of PCBs
on this scale at the time. But apparently, Kanemi failed to make
periodic checks of the amount of PCBs passing through the pipes.
No safety equipment capable of detecting an accidental breach in
the metal was installed and the pipes were left exposed to the oil
without any protective sheathing. Furthermore, the heating mechanism was not a totally closed system. Water or vapour somehow
trickled in and mixed with the PCBs, forming hydrochloric acid,
which, at high temperatures, caused the pipes to corrode. Thus, several tiny openings of the size of pinholes developed in the steel pipes,
allowing PCBs to leak into the rice-oil. Eventually, Kanemi had to
accept this causal explanation.

When was the earliest occurrence of the PCB contamination for
which Kanemi was responsible? It could be conjectured from the
account given above that the contamination of the Kanemi products
might have begun coincidentally with the sudden increase in the consumption of PCBs in January 1968. Such conjecture was actually
confirmed in February of that year by the death of some 400,000
chickens in the western part of Japan and with an additional two
million of them falling sick with something similar to chick oedema
disease. At first, an epidemic of some kind was suspected, but
through an intensive investigation sponsored by the Ministry of
Agriculture and Forestry it was officially confirmed within about
three months that the causative agent was 'dark oil' which had been
mixed in the feed for chickens. This 'dark oil' was a product of the

Kanemi Corporation – a by-product of the process that transformed rice bran into the rice-oil intended for human consumption. Naturally as a result, the 'dark oil' was withdrawn from sale by Kanemi and the chicken disease no longer occurred. But while the suspicion was being investigated in the spring of 1968, a question was raised by an official research man to Sannosuke Kato, president of the Kanemi Warehouse Company, if the rice-oil for which 'dark oil' is a kind of raw material could be considered safe enough. Kato is said to have replied: 'Our rice-oil is perfectly safe. I myself am drinking it.'[7] This encounter was on 22 March 1968, and it was just about that time that the first patient with subjective symptoms of what came to be known as 'yushō' (oil disease) appeared.

However, it was not until 10 October 1968 when a reporter from the *Asahi* newspaper played up the case of 'Kanemi Yushō' in his reportage that human victims of the PCB-laced product became a national issue. It was commented that 'for the victims – and the public at large – it was seven months, 20 deaths and thousands of poisonings too late.'[8] How such procrastination occurred constitutes a story replete with socio-psychological implications.

Early complaints by the patients were that they lost their appetites and their bodies broke into a drenching sweat, or extreme fatigue set in and they could no longer work. But after a while, ugly boils exuding a strong-smelling pus appeared over every part of the body. Vision deteriorated, and from the eyes streamed a viscous discharge that quickly hardened into a paste. The following account was repeated with only slight variation by many of the victims interviewed after the *Asahi* reporter's disclosure:

> Before the October announcement, I made every effort to conceal my unsightly face and body from society. After the boils appeared on my daughter, she could no longer bear the sight of her own face and feared to look into the mirror. . . . On the train to the hospital, she hid behind a newspaper or a handkerchief, and my wife served as a screen. When she had to go out shopping, she always came back home in tears. What could we say when she cried, 'Strangers stare at me, and I can't stand the way their stares cling to my body'![9]

There is little doubt that such attempts by the victims to escape the 'cold-hearted eyes of others' contributed to delaying the recognition of the disease and clarification of its origin. Indeed, victims were so successful in isolating themselves from both society and each other that, until October, many families believed that they alone were stricken! Gradually, however, sufferers who chanced to meet in hospitals recognized their common plight. It was these rare contacts that eventually led to the discovery of the disease's origin – a discovery made not by medical or scientific authorities, but rather by one of the victims.

It was Tadashi Kunitaké, a young low-ranking employee of the Kyūshū Electric Power Company, himself suffering from symptoms of the *yushō* from the early summer of 1968, who persevered in searching for the cause of his own ailment by a positive attitude of contacting with other victims for exchange of information and of talking with doctors at the Kyūshū University Hospital and at the Omuta Health Center with a suggestion that the Kanemi rice-oil might be the 'culprit.' Failing to obtain any concrete response, Kunitaké revealed all the information he had collected to the *Asahi* reporter who followed up the lead, resulting in the nationwide publicity of 10 October 1968.

What were the repercussions of this newspaper revelation on each of the four major parties in the incident?

(1) As for the victims at large, they avidly welcomed the report, as if to say: 'The fear of a contagious disease is gone. We no longer have to put up with the cold stares of society. We now know that others like us exist, that we are not alone.'

(2) The doctors of Kyūshū University, on the other hand, did not take to the report so kindly. According to Ryuzo Kamino, later head of the National Federation of Kanemi Rice Oil Victims Associations, the scientific authorities were distressed because the announcement was not 'medically oriented' and because they had 'lost face' in not having been the first to identify publicly the disease and its cause. It is also known that in the case of Dr Masayasu Goto of Kyūshū University who had a fairly firm grasp of the entire problem, he preferred to wait to announce his findings at the annual meeting of the academic society to which he belonged (to be held several months later).

(3) Kanemi's immediate response to the Asahi's revelation was a straight denial of any responsibility of the company. When the Public Health Bureau of the City of Kitakyūshū advised the Kanemi Warehouse Company on the day after the newspaper's revelation that the company had better voluntarily

discontinue the sale of rice-oil until the causal relation could be cleared up, the company did not heed the advice, saying that 'there is no ground for thinking that our product was the cause.' It may be recalled that at about the same time the factory chief was denying the possibility of PCBs seeping into the rice-oil production process.

(4) Eight days after the *Asahi* scoop, the national media carried a report that revealed the role of government agencies in this tragic history of the Kanemi *yushō*. It was a report that suggested government ineptitude, if not malfeasance, in its handling of the early warning signs in the form of the death of over 400,000 chickens in February 1968. The Ministry of Agriculture and Forestry confirmed then within three months that 'dark oil' containing chlorinated hydrocarbons was responsible for it. But when the occurrence of human victims became a public issue in October of that year, the lack of communication between that ministry and the Ministry of Welfare became a bureaucratic barrier, and although a joint research committee was set up by the two ministries, it took more than a month to come out with an interim report which did not go beyond saying that the hypothesis of PCB poisoning in the case 'required further investigation.'

Faced with these responses, the victims now found themselves entering a new stage of the incident, namely, that of coping with three major problems – medical treatment, official clarification of responsibility, and compensation for damages. The question of medical treatment was most difficult. Up to then, no effective treatment for PCB poisoning had been discovered, in Japan or elsewhere. Although medicines did relieve minor symptoms, such as headaches and stomach pain, no basic treatment existed to remove or counteract PCBs accumulated in the human body. Like other chlorinated hydrocarbons, PCBs are fat soluble. Some (those containing relatively few chlorine atoms) are gradually discharged, but others remain lodged in fatty tissues in and around the heart and liver. Even in the case of Kanemi victims whose initial PCB concentrations have diminished, however, physical abnormalities persist. These include depression, fever, coughing, pains, irregular menstruation, depressed growth, teeth abnormalities and skin problems. PCBs leave their mark for life.[10]

While controversy continued over the problem of medical treatment and also over the issue of formal certification which was required for the purpose of negotiation with the Kanemi Company for a financial settlement, the victims split into factions over the best way to compel the company and government to accept legal responsibility for the disease and provide adequate compensation. But the problems of organizing Kanemi victims into a unified movement were much more complex than in most other pollution disease cases, largely because the victims were spread out over 23 prefectures.

In the end, different victim groups filed seven civil suits, and the Fukuoka prosecutor's office brought a criminal suit against the Kanemi Company. The first civil suit had already been filed in December 1968 against the Kanemi Warehouse and its president Kato for 'a charge of professional negligence resulting in injury and damage.' Then in February 1969, an action demanding compensation from Kanegabuchi Chemical Industry for the production of 'kanekurōru' (PCB) was added in the trial. This civil suit, usually referred to as 'the Fukuoka Kanemi Suit,' came to a judgement on 5 October 1977 with all-out endorsement of the plaintiff's claims. The criminal suit also resulted in a decision in March 1978, with a sentence of one year and a half imprisonment for the factory chief of the Kanemi Company. Such decisions, favourable for the victims, however, were not necessarily repeated in the other civil suits which followed.

There were two basic issues on which court judgements differed: the question of responsibility and that of the cause of contamination. On the question of responsibility of the state, the court judgements were made five times, of which three of them denied and the plaintiff side lost. As for the product liability as regards 'kanekurōru,' the responsibility of the Kanegabuchi Chemical Industry was affirmed six times, but was denied once in the High Court. On the question of the cause of PCB contamination, it was somewhat enigmatic that the courts could not be unanimous on the hypothesis of pinholes in the steel pipes. An alternative explanation was 'a mistake in construction.' At any rate, a generally most unfavourable judgement for the victims was that of the Fukuoka High Court on 15 May 1986. It was there that the Kanegabuchi was absolved of their product liability and the cause of PCB contamination was attributed to 'a mistake in construction.' Administrative responsibilities of the two ministries (that of Agriculture and

Forestry and also that of Welfare) were also denied in that judgement.

The immediate reaction of the victims' organizations to this High Court judgement was indignant disappointment over the reversal of practically all the gains won through the preceding trials, and they were resolved to appeal to the Supreme Court, while at the same time commencing varied kinds of protest movement including a sit-down protest for 108 days in front of the Kanegabuchi Chemical Industry. However, it happened that there was another one of the civil trials which had gone to the Supreme Court whose decision on 27 February 1987 recommended an amicable settlement among the disputing parties. This decision was suggestive of the likely response of the Supreme Court if and when an appeal were to be made on the High Court judgement of May 1986. And further, both Kanemi and Kanegabuchi were inclined to accept the Supreme Court suggestion of 'amicable settlement.' It was a difficult decision for the victims' organization to do the same inasmuch as the question of the state responsibility, which for them was of paramount importance, was still unsettled. But they too finally agreed to withdraw their litigious claims. Thus on 25 June 1987, the 19-year-old litigation on the Kanemi *yushō* came to an end with an 'amicable settlement.' Besides the compensation payment made by Kanemi, Kanegabuchi too, which was absolved of their product liability by the Supreme Court on 27 February 1987, agreed to shoulder the burden of 10.8 billion yen in total for the settlement. The end was as if no court trials were needed; it could not be denied that what remained in the minds of many victims was a sense of mortification only.

THE 'SMON SCANDAL'

'The SMON episode is a tragedy for the human race, a scandal from the standpoint of the medical profession, and a disgrace in the light of ethics and morals.' This was the summary comment by Olle Hansson, who made an intensive study of the SMON problem in Japan and was the author of the book, *Om SMON-scandalen*.[11] SMON stands for subacute myelo-opticoneuropathy (semi-acute spinal and optical nervous disorders) and was one of the two major pharmacopollution events in postwar Japan along with the episodic occurrence of the thalidomide incident. It took some time, however, for the causal agent of SMON to be confirmed as 'chinoform,' a medicine for intestinal disorders, being a trade name in Japan of 'oxyquinoline' marketed worldwide by the Ciba-Geigy Company of Basel, Switzerland. What is peculiar in the case of SMON was that its widespread occurrence in Japan was unique in spite of the fact that 'oxyquinoline' products with different trade names had been sold 'for 45 years in almost every country in the world.' (Ciba-Geigy's statement.) Thus, an explanation is required for the extremely disproportionate occurrences of the impairment of health in Japan from the essentially same product. We shall try to give an answer to this problem in the course of the following discussion.

The initial marketing by Ciba (which amalgamated with Geigy in 1970 to become known by the present name) of a product essentially similar to chinoform was in 1934. But it was only in the postwar period that Ciba's product came to Japan in joint operation with two pharmaceutical companies, Takeda and Tanabé. The earliest report that could be identified as a symptom of health impairment due to chinoform was in 1955 when unexplicable nervous disorders combined with constipation and/or diarrhoea were reported sporadically in the Wakayama and Miyé Prefectures. It was from 1959 onwards, however, that SMON patients turned up in large numbers in one community after another. Most of them had taken chinoform as prescribed by their doctors, but doctors themselves did not even suspect any causal connection between chinoform and SMON symptoms. For one thing, chinoform was at first advertised as effective for protection against dysentery and in fact was often distributed by town officials to citizens on the occasion of a visit by Imperial dignitaries for a precautionary reason. Besides, many doctors were so innocent as to prescribe a greater use of chinoform when patients showed the clearly recognizable SMON symptoms. Thus the record[12] shows that the number of SMON patients, which was 153 by the end of the 1950s, increased to 1,128 by 1965 and to 8,697 by 1970.

As late as in 1970, however, the causal agent of SMON symptoms was still indeterminate. At a professional meeting of the Public Health Association in October 1969 a technical report supporting the hypothesis of the infectious nature of SMON was made public, and in February 1970 Professor Yukishige Inoué of the Kyoto University advanced a theory, on the basis of his diagnosis of five SMON patients in the Okayama Prefecture, that SMON was caused by a special type of virus. This 'virus hypothesis' was reported as a top news story by *Asahi Shimbun* on 6 February 1970, saying that 'the Inoué hypothesis was borne out by a serum test, this being good news for medical care.'

The Ministry of Welfare became so concerned with an unusually large increase of SMON patients from 1968 to 1969 (an increase of 5,386 persons) that they decided to set up a SMON Research Council on 2 September 1969, which elected a virus specialist Dr Reisaku Kono as its chairman. During the deliberation of this Council, reports were made twice (by Dr Yasuo Toyokura and Dr Zengo Tamura, both of Tokyo University) that one common characteristic symptom of SMON patients was staining of their tongues, urine and faeces with a green colour. Actually, Tamura, who made his report on 29 and 30 June 1970, was successful in producing a yellowish crystal from the green-stained urine of SMON patients and identified that crystal as chinoform itself. This was a startling revelation for many members of the council. But Tadao Tsubaki, professor at the Niigata University who had played an important role in the Niigata Minamata case earlier and also a member of the council, had been himself suspecting the guilt possibility of chinoform in the SMON occurrence, and immediately began a full-scale epidemiological research in the Niigata and Nagano Prefectures. He checked 171 patients in the region and found that there was none among them who had *not* taken any dose of chinoform and that nearly every one of them had taken 1,200 milligrams or more per day for two to five weeks and had suffered from nervous disorders within two or three weeks after the use of chinoform. It was significant that in one of the hospitals in the Niigata Prefecture the additional use of chinoform for a recuperating patient actually aggravated the toxic effect and the decrease in recipe improved the patient's condition. Professor Tsubaki communicated the result of this research finding on 6 August 1970 to *Asahi Shimbun*, which reported it as a singular news item on the following day.

The research result of Professor Tsubaki gave occasion to the decision on 7 September 1970 by the Central Pharmaceutical Council to recommend the suspension of the sale and use of chinoform, followed immediately on the following day by an administration order of the Ministry of Welfare to the same effect. From then on the occurrence of new SMON patients declined drastically in Japan. The ministry's decision was at the stage when the confirmation of causal relation was still in the realm of conjecture. But the supporting facts followed one after another, first by Professor Hirotsugu Shiraki of the Tokyo University, a consultant of the Tanabé Pharmaceutical Company, who confirmed the chinoform hypothesis through experiments with animals in June 1971 but was restrained by the Tanabé executives from making his discovery public.[13] But other supporting reports followed from a number of hospitals in different regions, and finally on 13 March 1972 a general meeting of the SMON Research Council came out with the conclusion that 'from the epidemiological facts and a number of experiments that have been conducted, we have come to a judgement that an overwhelming majority of health impairments due to SMON has been caused by the ingestion of chinoform.'

Now that the causal relation of the SMON ailment had become determinate in Japan, there began a new chapter, so to speak, in the contestation between the victims on the one hand and the offending parties on the other. Soon after the SMON Research Council in Japan came out with a decisive statement on the causal relation between chinoform and the SMON disease, the Ciba-Geigy Company suspended in May 1972 the sale of entéro-vioforme, a product similar to chinoform, in the United States on the ground of 'marketing reasons.' But at the same time, the Ciba-Geigy Company drafted a statement, later made public in court, which was a counterargument against the decision of the SMON Research Council of Japan in March 1972. It stated in part:

A theory that nervous disorders associated with SMON are caused by chinoform is an opinion that cannot be accepted in any other part of the world but Japan, no matter how prevalent its influence in Japan might be. . . . The chinoform type of product has been widely used in the world for the past 70 years and the total number of SMON patients reported during that time in countries other than Japan has been only a little over thirty. This constitutes approximately one in 100 million persons. . . . If it is true that there have occurred 10,000 patients in Japan with a population of 100 million, it is clear enough that SMON is a peculiar ailment limited to Japan. . . . Those who accept a theory of chinoform's guilt for SMON are actually delaying the scientific inquiry of the SMON phenomena . . . and appear to be engaged instead in the modern practice of witch-hunting.[14]

On the other hand, the September 1970 decision of the Ministry of Welfare to suspend the sale and use of chinoform gave an activating impetus to the organized activities of SMON patients. The

earliest regional organization came into being in 1967 in the city of
Yonezawa where some SMON patients were reported as early as in
1959. From then on, other regional organizations began to crop up,
and finally in November 1969 an attempt was made to organize a
nationwide association of SMON victims, called the 'National
SMON Society.' This society, however, could not be wholly united
on particular litigational demands and had to be split within a few
years. But it was thanks to this organization that the first SMON
law-suit was filed to the Tokyo District Court in May 1971. This was
followed by one after another of regional law-suits, which eventually
totalled to 32 of them, with 5953 victims on the plaintiff's side . . .
truly a mammoth trial in court unprecedented in Japan's history. As
the regional trials were going on, on the one hand, the need for a
truly national organization of SMON victims came to be strongly
felt, with a result that in March 1974 the 'National Liaison Council
for SMON Associations' ('Suzenkyo') was successfully organized.

In the long history of the SMON Incident in Japan, the year 1976
marked a kind of turning point. For one thing, Olle Hansson,
requested by the plaintiff's side, agreed to come to Japan to testify in
the Tokyo District Court in March 1976. Cross examination by the
lawyers of Ciba-Geigy turned out to be so counter-productive that
Hansson wrote afterwards[15] that 'the persons who rendered greatest
service for me in the Japanese court were the legal advisers of Ciba-
Geigy Company.' It is most instructive to read the stenographic
record of the cross-examination on that occasion.[16] Then on 10 June
1976, soon after Hansson's testimony in the Tokyo District Court,
three defendant parties, that is, Ciba-Geigy and two Japanese
pharmaceutical companies, proposed suddenly to the court that they
would rather agree to an out-of-court settlement. In a statement
made by a Tanabé proxy, representing the three defendant companies, three points were made: namely, (1) that they affirm that
there was a causal relation between chinoform and SMON in Japan;
(2) that they will not shrink from the responsibility of shouldering
social implications in this regard in Japan; and (3) that they will
promise to pay appropriate compensations to the patients who had
submitted themselves to the use of chinoform. While *Suzenkyo* was
hesitant in accepting this offer of 'amicable settlement' so-called, the
presiding judge of the Tokyo District Court, Tsuneo Kabé, proposed
in September 1976 that he would advise on his own authority that
the two contesting parties in the trial had better agree to the out-of-

court settlement. This, indeed, constituted a crucial turning point for *Suzenkyo*, for there were a number of points on which a court decision was preferable in that: (1) by making the legal responsibility of the defendants explicit, legislative innovations in relation to pharmacopollution cases could be secured; (2) such semi-permanent countermeasures as pension plans and rehabilitation facilities could be won only through a victory in the court decision; and (3) out-of-court settlements may not be able to rescue those patients who have difficulty in obtaining diagnostic document. The Ministry of Welfare also made it clear that it would prefer to have the responsibility of the state determined in one way or another by a decision of the court. While these reactions were creating a mixed impression of uncertainty among the relevant quarters, Tanabé came out at the end of October 1976 with a reversion of their earlier commitment by resurrecting the virus theory and denying the causal relation between SMON and chinoform. They proposed to the Tokyo District Court to allow a special witness for presenting the case of the virus theory, and when rejected, Tanabé challenged the three judges of the court. But in the end, the Supreme Court dismissed this special complaint.

The presiding Judge Kabé of the Tokyo District Court kept up his efforts of persuading the relevant parties by presenting, on 17 January 1977, an official view in favour of an 'amicable settlement,' referring in particular to the responsibility of the state. This proposal was accepted by Prime Minister Takeo Fukuda on 28 June 1977 and subsequently by Takeda and Ciba-Geigy also, and these three defendants sat down with a portion of the plaintiff patients on 29 October 1977 for the first instance of amicable settlement. Tanabé, still persisting in the virus theory, refused to accept Kabé's proposal.

Meanwhile, trials went on in a number of other regions, and in one of them, that is, in the Kanazawa area, the decision by the court on 1 March 1978 marked the first occasion when the SMON trial resulted in a victory for the plaintiff patients, although in a number of respects the decision went only half way in meeting their claims. However, a momentum was gained in the direction of a satisfactory solution of the SMON problem, and the second victorious trial for the victims came on 3 August 1978 in the Tokyo District Court where the first SMON law-suit of May 1971, referred to earlier, had been still pending. The decision stated by the presiding Judge Kabé was so straightforward and decisive that Olle Hansson referred to it as 'a victory of justice and wisdom, bound to carry weight beyond the boundaries of Japan.'[17]

Kabé stated unequivocally that the cause of SMON was chinoform, that the toxic nature of chinoform could have been foreseen already in 1955, and that SMON was a disease with sociological implications. In explanation of this last point, Kabé made a critical comment on the medical system of Japan, referring especially to the common practice of administering medicines liberally for a long stretch of time. All the parties in this trial appealed. But successive decisions in Fukuoka (14 November 1978), Hiroshima (22 February 1979) and Sapporo (10 May 1979) all turned out favourably for the side of plaintiff patients, even to the extent of approving the general principle of compensating those patients without the documentary proof of having taken chinoform.

Such a trend in the court decisions finally induced Tanabé to accede to the procedure of an 'amicable settlement' on 16 May 1979, and thus a prospect of a grand finale for the SMON incident could be more or less assured. The next step was the signing of what was called a 'Confirmation Document' by *Suzenkyo* on the one hand and all the defendant parties in the trials on the other. The 'Document' specified details about compensations to be paid and other relief measures for SMON patients and was intended to serve as a concrete guideline for deliberations in those court trials which were then still pending. Its highlights were as follows:

Lump sum for settlement (the basic amount) *

Degrees of health impairment	Serious	25 million yen
	Medium	17 million yen
	Light	10 million yen

Life annuity for health care   30,000 yen per month

Condolence money   One million yen per head

> * There were additional amounts to be paid, calculated separately by age groups, and also with special consideration for mothers who had an immature child at the time of their contraction of SMON.

It was on 15 September 1979 that the signing of this 'Document' was finalized. With this ground-work done, the pending regional lawsuits throughout the country subsequently reached an agreement smoothly, and when the Hiroshima SMON Society won its law-suit in 1987, all the court proceedings related to the SMON incident came to an end – no less than 16 years since the first suit was filed in the Tokyo District Court.

It may be recalled that when the presiding judge of the Tokyo District Court, Tsuneo Kabé, proposed in September 1976 an out-of-court settlement by the two contesting parties, one of the reasons why the *Suzenkyo* took the position preferring a court decision was that by making explicit the legal responsibility of the defendants, legislative innovations in relation to pharmacopollution cases could perhaps be secured. This was a pending question that could not be passed over by the government. And here too, the *Suzenkyo*'s insistence bore fruit when the Diet on 7 September 1979 passed two laws, the Law to Establish a Relief Fund for the Side-effect Damage due to Pharmaceutical Products and the Law for the Partial Revision of the Drugs, Cosmetics and Medical Instruments Act. This latter was to enable the government to guarantee the financial debts of pharmaceutical companies when the latter have to borrow for the payment of compensation as in the case of the SMON incident.

The last question we have to tackle is an explanation of the prodigious disproportion of the occurrence in Japan of SMON damage from chinoform compared with the experiences in other countries where identical products were sold. A number of considerations are relevant to this question, but it is certain above all that the SMON incident made us realize how important the *public* nature of the medical and pharmaceutical industry is for a modern society, especially where a free enterprise system prevails.

One unique characteristic of the SMON incident was that the 'culprit' of the pollution was, unlike contaminants like arsenic and PCBs in other pharmacopollution cases, a product presumed to be a provider of 'safety' and 'health' itself. It was a case of negative external economy of a commodity with a positive use-value. Occurrence of this incident involved four parties, all of which have to acknowledge a share of responsibility in the widespread pharmacopollution which eventuated in Japan in the period roughly from 1955 to the end of the 1960s; the four parties being (1) the pharmaceutical companies which marketed the product, chinoform in this case, (2) the medical profession which allowed its widespread use, (3) consumer patients who lacked sufficient vigilance, and (4) the central government which was negligent in its administrative responsibility.

The roles played by these parties are actually interrelated as integral aspects of the country's medical system which requires a separate institutional inquiry.

(1) As for the role of pharmaceutical companies, like Ciba-Geigy, Takeda and Tanabé, the profit-oriented conduct of their operations as private enterprises in a market economy was inevitable, and the extravagant advertisement of their products and their reluctance in admitting their responsibility for product liability were characteristic enough.

(2) As for the role of the medical profession, the general delay in identifying the cause of SMON disease by it has to be mentioned, but at the same time, as Olle Hansson suggests in his book,[18] it has to be pointed out that so many of the doctors in Japan depend for their living upon the income they can obtain from the sale of medicine they prescribe, thus tending to carry the matter to excess in the case of chinoform also.

(3) As for the role of consumer patients, what Galbraith called the 'dependence effect' has been especially marked in the doctor–patient relations in Japan, in that patients blindly follow what they are told by their doctors and seldom bring matters to court when their doctors commit a fault. Also there is a tradition in Japan, probably cultivated through the historical reliance on Chinese medicine, to believe that more is always better.

(4) As for the role played by the government, it cannot be denied that pre-authorization tests for new medicines have often been inadequate and also that there were so many instances in which government complicity with private enterprises and professional groups for a particular prejudicial position could be discerned.

For the explanation of an uncommonly widespread sale of chinoform in Japan in the decades of the 1950s and 1960s, it may not be irrelevant to point to the social climate at the time when the exceptionally high growth rate of the economy created a condition of euphoria, weakening the sense of restraint in every direction. At least the firms which were enjoying 40 times increase of the sale of a particular product in 14 years must have been in the mood of forward stampede only.[19]

THE TOROKU MINE KŌGAI

Probably no better example of 'the law's delay and the insolence of office' in environmental disputes in Japan can be found than in the incident of the Toroku Mine *Kōgai* of arsenious acid pollution. The incident illustrates the structural discrimination which often characterizes particular *kōgai* phenomena – in this case the prejudicial stance toward underdogs in society by the people in the élite stratum.

Toroku is an isolated mining hamlet, remote from 'civilization' in the inland mountain area of Kyūshū, inhabited only by 48 households with 191 members in 1988. Mining there originally was for copper and lead, but from 1918 on, the production of arsenious acid (or arsenic trioxide) was started with a rather primitive technique. Already in 1922, the pollution damage on stockbreeding and agriculture became evident, and a painstaking report of the blight was drafted by a local veterinarian (Mr Bokuzen Ikeda, by name) in 1925. The production of arsenious acid at the Toroku mine reached a peak in 1925 (491.2 tons), continuing the operation until 1942 with less performance. After the war, the mine activity was reopened in 1955 until it was closed in 1962.

By this time, the pollution damage to local residents as well as paddy fields was so manifest that a professor in the Agriculture Department of the Miyazaki University (Bunji Saito) compiled a report and submitted it to the Nobeoka City Office, which, however, persuaded Professor Saito not to make it public, saying that 'publication could cause a social uproar.'[20] The mining right at Toroku mine was in the hands of a small company called Nakajima Mining until 1967, when it was transferred to the Sumitomo Metal Mining Company, a major corporate tentacle of the rejuvenated Sumitomo *zaibatsu*. The mine had already been closed five years earlier and the new proprietor Sumitomo decided to forfeit the Toroku mining right in 1973.

Such is the brief history of the Toroku mine. The fact that the mine was closed in 1962 and the mining right was forfeited by the proprietor in 1973 might suggest that the question of the mine *kōgai* was more or less a past history when the decade of the 1970s opened. But this was hardly the case. Besides, the process that led the Toroku Mine *Kōgai* into an instance of national notoriety is not unrelated to 'the law's delay and the insolence of office' referred to at the beginning of this section. We owe to the devoted efforts of two public-spirited citizens for bringing a closed-book incident to a burning current issue. They were Masatake Saito, a young school teacher just out of college and Kazuyuki Kawahara, an *Asahi* reporter stationed at its Miyazaki branch office.[21]

It happened that M. Saito married a local girl in 1968 and noticed a certain health impairment of hers which could be traced to her grade-school period when arsenious acid was still being produced in Toroku. Suspicion arose in his mind that the effluents of the Toroku mine, though a thing of the past, might have caused a more general pollution damage in the community, and he began his energetic investigation through interviews with the older-generation people in the area. The entire story he could gather was so startling and yet systematically coherent that he decided to mobilize for cooperation a number of his colleagues in the school to prepare a paper to be read at the Prefectural Research Convention of the Japan Teachers Union (JTU) in November 1971. Saito's report was repeated at the National Convention of the JTU in January 1972 and this was the occasion through which the Toroku Mine *Kōgai* became a widely known issue throughout the country.

The role played by K. Kawahara was, firstly, an unearthing of the 1925 veterinarian's report, mentioned earlier, from a storeroom of Takachiho Town Office in January 1972 and copying the whole thing. He was especially moved by a remark at the end of the said report, saying that 'how the capitalists in this incident oppressed the simple and honest farmers is plain to be seen.' With a strong sense of justice, Kawahara made up his mind to leave his career position in the *Asahi* and joined the organizational movement to aid the victims in 1974. His particular contribution at that stage was in the way of pamphleteering for which he made full use of the research he had personally undertaken.

Before Masatake Saito made his report public at the Prefectural Research Convention of the JTU in November 1971, there were a number of occasions during the Toroku mine's active days when the local government offices were called upon to make some comments on complaints from the Toroku area over the damage to humans and agricultural and livestock industries. But the official responses used to be either flat denial of damage or deliberate disregard. When the news of Saito's indictment in November 1971 was reported in the press, however, both the Miyazaki Prefectural Office and the Environment Agency reacted immediately. The former initiated a group check-up of Toroku-area residents at the end of November 1971, taking, however, only six hours for 224 of them. There were several among them who were sent to university hospitals for further examination. But on 28 January 1972 the Environment Public Health Bureau of the Miyazaki Prefecture made a public announcement to the effect that 'hardly any causal relation could be found between the health impairment of the residents and the arsenic poisoning and such possibility in the future is likely to be very small.' There were three technical staff from the Environment Agency present on that occasion, who concurred with this judgement, adding that 'the Toroku incident, if anything, is a case of workers' accident.' They even ventured a specific comment on the 'Kiémon family case'[22] as having been, if at all, the victims of tuberculosis.

With such official responses on the one hand and an aroused nationwide public opinion on the other there was created inevitably a social setting of confrontation. A number of medical specialists cooperated with the victims' society and the aid organization called 'Mamoru-kai' (Association for Protection) to confirm the nature of a complex ailment from which the poisoning victims were suffering. Thus, the Environment Agency finally had to eat their words and decided in February 1973 to designate 'the chronic arsenic poisoning' as a '*kōgai* disease.' In doing so, however, the symptoms officially specified for this designation purpose were limited to the characteristic skin colour abnormality and the perforated nasal septa. An objection against this limitation was voiced immediately by a number of medical specialists, who pointed out that the health impairment of the Toroku residents included nervous disorders, troubles with respiratory and digestive organs, eyes and bones, caused not only by arsenious acid but also by heavy metals and sulphur oxides. Thus the confrontation still continued.

Soon after the nationwide publicity was created through Masatake Saito's report at the National Convention of the JTU (January 1972) and seven of the victims, in the first instance, were certified as patients of chronic arsenic poisoning by an experts' committee set up by the Miyazaki Prefecture (July 1972), Governor Hiroshi Kuroki of the prefecture became apparently constrained to take an initiative in 'solving' the infamous problem in his prefecture through his mediating efforts. He went to Tokyo in August 1972 to meet the president of Sumitomo Metal Mining, Kenjiro Kawakami, for this purpose and obtained the latter's basic consent on the matter. Thus began the series of governor's mediation in the City of Miyazaki from December 1972 onwards, altogether on five occasions for 87 victims until October 1976. The typical manner in which the mediation was conducted was an interview for each victim in an isolated manner allowing no legal aid and with an average offer of 3,100,000 yen as 'consolation money.' Besides, in the confirmation paper which each victim was asked to sign after the meeting, there was added afterwards, without his or her knowledge, a sentence saying that 'I shall make no additional claim.' Out of the 87 victims who were qualified to be called to the mediation meeting through the official certification of their disease symptoms, 14 of them refused to sign, one of them making a bitter parting remark that 'the meeting was like a rape behind closed doors.'

The manner in which the prefectural office conducted the mediation meetings intensified the determination of the victims' organizations to fight it out in the court, and the first law-suit against Sumitomo was instituted in December 1975 by 11 victims including their inheritor members, demanding on average 30 million yen per person as damage compensation. The major points of contention in the trial were: (1) the responsibility of the proprietary enterprise, (2) the question of legal prescription, (3) the causal relation and disease symptoms, and (4) the effectiveness of the governor's mediation. On all these points, Sumitomo's assertions were one-sidedly clear; namely, that (1) in fact, Sumitomo was not operating the Toroku mine, thus had no legal responsibility; (2) the Mining Act stipulated the prescription of 20 years, thus all the claims regarding the Toroku mine had lapsed; (3) the causal relation between the disease and what was claimed to be the source-agent had not been proved; and (4) the confirmation document at the time of the governor's mediation stated clearly that no additional claim shall be made, thus disallowing any further negotiation about claims.

These points had to be thrashed out in court, and it took more than eight years until March 1984 for the decision of the court, by which time 12 out of 23 plaintiff patients had died in between time. The delay in the court proceedings is mainly accounted for by the obstinate manner in which Sumitomo defended its assertions. At any rate, however, the decision of the court was decisively in favour of the plaintiff side; namely, it affirmed the responsibility of Sumitomo under the Mining Act, denied the application of the prescription, took a broad enough interpretation of the causal relation and ordered the reparation payment by Sumitomo of 30 to 40 million yen per person to plaintiff patients. Since there were at the time about 6,000 non-working or abandoned mines in the country, the court decision of affirming the responsibility of Sumitomo for the Toroku mine which had been closed in 1962 and forfeited by the company in 1973 was considered to have far-reaching repercussions.

Understandably, Sumitomo appealed immediately. The Fukuoka High Court Miyazaki Branch started its proceedings in August 1984 and took four years to come to its decision. Sumitomo stuck to its earlier position of 'no responsibility,' reinforcing its original argument with a specially invited witness from the United States, Dr Charles H. Hein, a toxicologist and professor at the University of California. But again, the decision of the High Court on September 1988 was essentially the same as the one in the lower court, the main difference being an allowance for the payments already received by the patients under the Pollution-Related Health Damage Compensation Law. Because of this allowance Sumitomo's liability was reduced from 506,230,000 yen in the lower court decision to 308,500,000 yen in the High Court. Sumitomo appealed again immediately to the Supreme Court. Thirteen years had passed since the instituting of the trial by 23 Toroku victims, of whom only nine were alive then with an average age of 75 and five among them bedridden all the time.[23] In such circumstance, to keep on the litigational fight for another several years could mean an almost futile effort for the ailing victims whose number was further expected to decrease by death. 'Solution by all means while we are still alive!' was the heartrending voice of the few surviving victims. Legal aids as well as the long-standing supporters of the Toroku victims felt that an 'amicable settlement' (*wakai*) might be the only realistic solution and proposed this procedure in April 1990 to the secretariat of the Supreme Court. It took some time, however, for this to become a reality, mainly for the reason that the Sumitomo Metal Mining Company insisted that they could not agree to any settlement without an explicit statement on 'no responsibility of the company' and the victims' side, in turn, would not consent to a settlement with no mention of the company's responsibility. It was probably legalistic sagacity of the Supreme Court officials to have suggested a compromise wording that satisfied both sides on this rather basic question, and the initial step for the *wakai* was taken on 31 October 1990. The gist of the agreement suggested by the Supreme Court was as follows:

(1) It is confirmed that Sumitomo Metal Mining did not, either before or after the acquisition of the mining right, engage in any operation in conformity to the Mining Act, nor establish any facilities for operation.

(2) The total payments of 464,750,000 yen incurred on Sumitomo for provisional execution shall be returned by the recipient patients to the company, which in turn shall pay the same amount as 'solatium' to them.

(3) It is confirmed that this 'solution' does not make up for the damage as specified in the Pollution-Related Health Damage Compensation Law (Article 13 paragraph 1), nor is it premised on the reparation obligation under the Mining Act.

The victims, at that stage, had no other possible alternative than to accede to this obviously pro-Sumitomo *wakai* statement, and on 2 December 1991 the formal ceremony for 'amicable settlement' was held in the Miyazaki Summary Court. On that occasion, the agreement signed by both sides made explicit that there was no legal obligation on the part of Sumitomo to pay damage compensation. It took no less than 20 years since a local school teacher, Masatake Saito, made his public indictment of the incident to come to this denouement with the *de facto* reversal of the three lower court decisions in favour of the victims. There still remained the remedy and relief for the surviving patients through the benefits obtainable from the Pollution-Related Health Damage Compensation Law, and just as significantly, there also still remained sources of arsenic pollution in the Toroku area in the form of metal-waste mound and river water contamination.

The significance of the Toroku Mine *Kōgai* lay not only in revealing bureaucratic negligence and the élite capitalist's indifference to the suffering of the indigent, but also in presenting a typical case of '*kōgai* disease' comparable to the one in the case of Minamata.[24] What distinguishes '*kōgai* disease' from ordinary poisoning cases is, first of all, the mechanism of its occurrence. Victims are not confined to a particular workplace and to a particular group of workers as in the case of an accident at work. Patients are spread over an entire community or several communities and from the young to the old. Symptoms show up in a syndrome, forming a pyramidal shape, so to speak, with a slighter case of poisoning at the base. Such configuration defies a clear-cut certifying of the disease for the purpose of damage compensation. Further, the poisoning process may be indirect in the sense that the carriers of the toxic material could be either one or all of the three media, namely, water, atmosphere and food. Lastly, the pollution effect tends to last for a long time. The Toroku Mine *Kōgai* fits these characteristics perfectly; thus, it was appropriate enough for it to be designated as '*kōgai* disease,' along with the Minamata and *Itai-itai* diseases. And for that reason also, as Professor Masazumi Harada has warned, the so-called 'specialist' of conventional type often fails to comprehend the many-sided implications of the '*kōgai* disease.'[25] At least, the Toroku case gave us a good lesson in this regard.

THE HEXAVALENT CHROMIUM KŌGAI

Occupational diseases of various kinds used to be fairly common in the early stages of industrial development, a typical one being silicosis among coal miners. They were generally considered as a kind of social cost and were gradually remedied through the instituting of labour legislation. England gives us a classical example of such development in the nineteenth century, as illustrated by the publication of Friedrich Engels' *The Condition of the Working Class in England in 1844* and the subsequent reformist measures legislated by Parliament. Japanese capitalism too shares such historical experience, albeit in a less enlightened fashion. As was mentioned in an earlier chapter, labour conditions in many of the industrial plants in Japan were often so deplorable that external disamenities caused by these plants were a matter of lesser urgency for the workers inside.

Hexavalent chromium pollution is an occupational disease, known to have caused in most cases lung tumour or lung cancer. A record exists, reported in 1935 by a medical specialist (by the name of Pfeil) attached to a German chromium acid chloride factory, who first discovered two lung cancer patients among the workers in the factory during 1911 to 1912, confirming subsequently five fatal victims of lung cancer there. Soon after this occurrence, which was recognized as an instance of occupational disease, steps were taken by that factory to keep the work-place airtight and to instal dust-collecting facilities and in addition to strengthen the supervision of workers' health, thus succeeding in checking the re-occurrence of lung cancer patient completely. Japan's experience of the occupational disease associated with the production of chromium acid chloride came much later with the successful application of the so-called 'charge method' by the use of rotary kilns in 1933. Dr Pfeil's report appeared two years later, and it is difficult to believe that the precedent experience in Germany remained entirely unknown among the professional people in Japan until the hexavalent chromium *kōgai* was brought to public notice in 1975, when not only the occupational disease aspect was revealed to have been quite extensive but also a widespread *kōgai* arose through the dumping of mineral refuse on to a number of vacant spaces outside the factory. The belated revelation of the incident was again through the indictment by a few public-minded individuals, and the entire story fills another page of Japan's disgraceful record as regards environmental disruption.

It is significant that public knowledge of this incident came not from the fact of the occupational disease which had a long enough history in the enterprise concerned but from the alert reaction of a young man by the name of Hisakazu Fujiwara to a rumour in the spring of 1975 that strange yellowish dust with harmful effects was observed on a vacant land space in the Edogawa ward of Tokyo. Fujiwara, being an employee in the Kōgai Bureau of the Tokyo Metropolitan Government, became suspicious of the *kōgai* possibility in this rumour and decided to start investigations on his own. In the file of documents in the Kōgai Bureau he found a report, dated May 1973, which gave details of dumping of 80,000 tons of mineral refuse by the Nippon Chemical Industrial Company (NCI) on the land space in question. No further action was taken, however, by the Kōgai Bureau at the time, which apparently conceded to an appeal by the regional Land Adjustment Union that the revelation through an official investigation would induce the lowering of the land price there.

While Fujiwara was wondering what to do, he read an item in the newspaper reporting a protest demonstration by citizens against the NCI for its plan, suspected as an 'export of kōgai,' of setting up a chromium production plant in the Republic of Korea. He immediately got in contact with one of the active members of this citizens' group, Yuji Matsuoka, and discussed with him the organization of a group called 'the Association of Ward-Inhabitants Demanding Liquidation of Kōgai in the Bokuto Area.'[26] The association soon expanded itself to a group of 35 kindred spirits composed of a carpenter, a mailman, a taxi-driver, etc. They proceeded to examine the degree of chromium contamination of the soil with the cooperation of research staff of the faculty of Agricultural Chemistry of Tokyo University, and from the stagnant water in the centre of the land space where the mineral refuse had been dumped; for example, the measure of chromium contamination was found to be as high as 940 ppm, compared with the sewerage standard of 0.5 ppm as prescribed in the Water Contamination Prevention Act. Armed with such fruits of research, the Ward-Inhabitants Association decided to hold a press conference on 16 July 1975. Thus was the particular *kōgai* instance publicized. But this was only the beginning. To an inquiry about the specific places where mineral refuse had been dumped in the past, the NCI would only reply that all the dumping had been done by a subcontractor trucking company which must have found convenient places from their point of view. At least the information on approximate total quantity of disposed mineral refuse was coaxed out of the company, but the identifying work of altogether 100-odd specific places where the dumping had been done was almost entirely due to the work of one person, Muneaki Tajiri, then the head of the Kōgai Regulation Bureau of the Tokyo Metropolitan Government. His name was mentioned earlier in Chapter Four in the section on 'Pollutions Compounded in the City of Yokkaichi.' It happened that Ryokichi Minobe was elected as Governor of Tokyo in 1967 on a joint ticket of the Socialist and the Communist Parties, and on Minobe's suggestion Tajiri joined the Tokyo Metropolitan Government in 1974.

Told that the NCI had no list of places where the dumping was done, Tajiri decided to interview all the truck drivers who could be identified as having carried out the actual dumping job. Dumping had actually begun in 1933, and many of the truck drivers had retired by 1975 when Tajiri started his investigations. Were it not for his superhuman efforts in locating the retired drivers one by one and overcoming their often hostile reluctance in revealing the needed information, it would have been impossible to complete the final finding of 172 places (a total area of 82 acres) where 330,000 tons of the NCI mineral refuse had been dumped. Thus began the immediate countermeasures, the ordering of the NCI to carry out reduction treatment of the surface soil with sulphate of iron and paving the contaminated areas with asphalt.

It was during the negotiations on this matter between Tajiri and the NCI that information was revealed that there were some 80 NCI workers who were suffering from perforated nasal septa and that eight of them had died from lung cancer during the period between 1970 and 1974. Significantly enough, this *public revelation* of a flagrant case of an occupational disease came *after* the disamenities inflicted upon the public from the same cause became known, and this fact gives indication of an old-line character of the enterprise concerned.

The NCI was established in 1893 in Tokyo as a manufacturer of potassium iodide and developed into a representative maker in the realm of the inorganic chemicals industry through the period of WWI when imports from Germany were suspended. In particular, the demand for domestically produced potassium bichromate rose enormously, and at one time NCI's production of bichromates accounted for 80 per cent of the total supply in Japan. The company used to employ a large number of Korean immigrants and had a reputation of traditional indifference to the welfare of its workers. Such attitude was typically shown immediately after Tajiri's public disclosure of the contaminating effects of the mineral refuse dumped by NCI. Kan'ichi Tanahashi, president of NCI, had to submit himself to a press interview on 14 August 1975, on which occasion he made two points without equivocation: firstly, that the degree of polluting possibility of the mineral refuse dumped outside was infinitely less than that of the hexavalent chromium inside the plant, a fact borne out by the absence of any damage incurred on the residents living near the dumped location; secondly, 'dumping by the NCI' was not a correct statement since the mineral refuse was used for reclaiming purpose at the request of the respective landowners.

Such attitude on the part of the NCI president was clearly a challenge both to the victims of the pollution among the company employees who had kept tight-lipped about their plight in the past and to the local autonomous body which had taken special pains in tracking down the dumped places. It was only a few days later (17 August 1975) that the chromium victims' association was organized and within a few months decided to present a set of claims against the NCI. At the same time, an energetic research was started in two directions: one on the past record of actual health impairment caused within the NCI plant and another into the technical aspect of soil contamination by hexavalent chromium. For this last purpose, the Tokyo Metropolitan Government set up on 25 September 1975 a special committee called the 'Experts' Committee for Countermeasures against Soil Contamination due to Hexavalent Chromium' headed by Dr Takeo Suzuki. This Suzuki Committee's report, made public in October 1977, remains as a classical research document on the subject, probably the first of the kind in the world.[27]

For the investigation of past instances of the occupational disease inside the NCI plant, it was again Tajiri himself who went to see the factory chief of the Komatsugawa plant of NCI and sought out from him doggedly the information on the subject. It was revealed to him then that the cases of perforation in the nose began to occur at the beginning of the 1950s and that a file of individual medical cards as of 1967 showed 80 victims of occupational disease, 62 among them being the nose perforation cases. A more surprising revelation was the fact that the NCI labour union had published in their organ in 1964 a detailed warning article on the subject of chromium poisoning, provoking, as a consequence, the company officials to a high-handed step of interfering with the election of union officers so that pro-company members could subsequently sit at the top of the union. In effect, the occupational disease information compiled by the union could not be publicized outside the company, and even the normal step of applying on the grounds of 'worker's accident' was not allowed for the stated reason that the company's public image would be damaged. Novice workers in the plant were customarily told by the old-timers that 'you will become a full-fledged member here only when you will have perforations in your nose.'

The attempt of the victims' association to negotiate with NCI got nowhere, faced as it was with the callous attitude of company officials who would not even agree to sit at the table of negotiation. Thus a decision was taken finally to bring the matter to court, and the formal start of court battles by the victims' association against NCI began on 1 December 1975, with 208 plaintiffs all told including later participants in the trial. The points at issue in the court could be summarized as follows:

(1) What is the toxic character of chromium? The NCI had admitted to a few of consequential health impairments, such as skin tumour, rhinitis and perforated nasal septa. But how about the harmful effects on lungs, stomach, liver, kidney, etc., which NCI has not yet acknowledged?

(2) Given the hypothesis that health impairments caused by chromium extend to the whole body – a hypothesis which is affirmed by the plaintiff side – how far has NCI been aware of it?

(3) As to the cause of the disease and/or death of each of the victims, can NCI prove that it has nothing to do with chromium?

(4) What kind of counter-measures has NCI been taking for the purpose of forestalling occurrence of damages due to chromium?

(5) How does NCI propose to deal with the damage reparation demands of the plaintiff side?

Once the law-suit got started, NCI's strategy was two-sided: on the one hand, the company worked for the splitting of the victims' association by organizing 'the Retired Employees' Association' to which many of the victims were invited to join in the name of eight trade union organizations including the Federation of Trade Unions in the Synthetic Chemical Industries, headed by Kaoru Ota; at the same time, the company began their court argument by denying any causal relation between chromium and lung cancer. The first part of this strategy, embodying an offer of graduated compensation to the victims with 10 million yen as a limit, succeeded to the extent of finalizing the settlement with some 190 members of the Retired Employees' Association on 19 October 1977. As for the second part of the strategy, however, the opposition encountered by NCI was definitely formidable from their point of view. The central point in the dispute was:

(a) The causal relation between chromium and lung cancer.

(b) If NCI admits to a causal relation, when did it first become aware of it?

(c) Are there not other cancer possibilities caused by chromium?

On point (a) above, NCI retracted its initial denial of the relation in the course of the trial. On point (b) above, NCI continued to insist that it was only in 1975 that they became aware of it for the first time. One could extenuate the company's knowledge gap insofar as Dr Pfeil's report on the subject in the 1930s, referred to earlier, was concerned, but decisive evidence unfavourable to NCI's position emerged in 1980 through the discovery of the medical report on a former employee, who had worked for 20 years in the NCI plant and died in October 1935 from lung cancer. It was on the file of the Tokyo University Hospital and the discovery was rather fortuitous. In any case, NCI could no longer pretend that the first time they became aware of any relation between chromium and lung cancer was in 1975. Through this revelation the tide definitely turned in the court proceedings in a hapless direction for NCI.

At the final stage of the trial, that is early in 1981, NCI did admit the *epidemiological* relation between chromium and lung cancer, while still denying the *causal* connection, and further continued to deny other types of cancer possibilities caused by chromium (point (c) above). But by then, the plaintiff side had presented detailed technical research results, notably one by Dr Tatsuo Sano of the Research Institute of Labor Sciences, giving persuasive enough ground for believing that the health impairment due to chromium poisoning could be to the whole body. Thus the prospect of losing for NCI in the court was becoming almost indisputable.

On the other hand, while the court proceedings were going on over the problem of occupational disease, the external *kōgai* aspect of the mineral refuse dumping was developing with a momentum of its own. There the problem was the urgent need to neutralize the contaminating effects of the dumping in widely scattered areas in Tokyo. As was mentioned earlier, the Suzuki Committee set up by the Tokyo Metropolitan Government had made its report public in 1977, and this report became the basis for the Tokyo government office to call upon NCI to take immediate counter-pollution steps. For this purpose, an unusual type of united front was organized between the local autonomous government office and the citizens' groups concerned. It was in December 1977 that an organization called 'Conference with Residents Participating for Counter-measures against the NCI Chromium Kōgai' was set up, briefly referred to subsequently as 'Counter-measures Conference' (*Taisaku Kaigi*).

NCI, however, while issuing a statement with an intention of refuting the Suzuki Committee's report, refused to sit down for the negotiation on the question of decontaminating the dumped areas on the ground that *Taisaku Kaigi* included representatives of the victims' organization involved in the pending trial. The company was more belligerent here than in the court in contesting the pollution effect of chromium, calling it a 'phantom *kōgai* without any victims involved.'

The Suzuki Committee did not remain silent on such accusation and published a detailed rejoinder, and Tajiri sat down repeatedly from December 1978 onwards with the NCI representatives trying to obtain an agreement on the lasting treatment of the contaminated areas but without success. Finally, Tajiri thought of a tactic often used in Japan of putting pressure on the company through the parental bank, which in this case was the Industrial Bank of Japan. He sent for the bank executive in charge of the NCI account and warned him of the possible consequence of NCI's obstinate evasion of the social responsibilities. This last-resort tactic on Tajiri's part apparently worked, and NCI finally shifted its position in March 1979, indicating its willingness to take steps to restore the soil conditions of the dumped areas in conformity with the instructed specifications. The mass media in general agreed at the time that the application of the 'polluters pay principle' in this case owed its success to the harmonious cooperation achieved in the *Taisaku Kaigi* which was a united front between the local autonomous government office and the citizens' groups concerned.

As for the trial on the occupational disease issue, which was going on while the dispute on the *kōgai* aspect came more or less to a propitious settlement, the final decision was scheduled to be announced on 28 September 1981, that is five years and nine months since the litigation started, and 242 members of the plaintiff side (89 victim-employees and 153 family members of 38 former employees who had died from lung cancer) awaited expectantly in front of the Tokyo District Court on that day. The presiding judge Isamu Tsuchida's verdict was decisive and in a number of ways epoch-making. For one thing, it was the first time that a court trial had ever dealt with a case of occupational cancer disease, and further, in ordering NCI to pay compensation for the damages incurred on the victims amounting in total to 1,054,620,000 yen, the court made it quite explicit that the causal relation required was the epidemiological one only and also that there was a case of infringement of 'personality right' which meant that the required compensation was to be uniform regardless of age or gender. Also the question of prescription was disregarded to allow compensation for the victims who had left the company more than 20 years before the start of the trial. And Kan'ichi Tanahashi, president of NCI, finally appeared on 28 March 1982 at the memorial service for the NCI chromium victims to express his regret for the entire incident, thus closing one of the most shameful pages of postwar industrial pollution in Japan.

CHAPTER EIGHT

Implications of globalized environment problems: sustainable development

'THE EARTH SUMMIT' OF 1992

The span of 20 years which separated the 'Only One Earth' Conference in Stockholm and 'The Earth Summit' in Rio de Janeiro marked an evolution in the thinking on environmental problems in the world community. The shift in emphasis is best evidenced in the contrast we can observe between two declarations: one 'of Human Environment' adopted at the Stockholm Conference and another 'on Environment and Development' at the Rio meeting. Both began with lofty statements of principles:

> [Stockholm] 'Man has the fundamental right to freedom, equality and adequate conditions of life, in an environment of a quality which permits a life of dignity and well-being, and bears a solemn responsibility to protect and improve the environment for present and future generations.'

> [Rio] 'Human beings are at the centre of concerns for sustainable development. They are entitled to a healthy and productive life in harmony with nature. . . . The right to development must be fulfilled so as to equitably meet developmental and environmental needs of present and future generations.'

Further, both declarations ended with an appeal against the destructive weapons and warfare:

> [Stockholm] 'Man and his environment must be spared the effects of nuclear weapons and all other means of mass destruction. States must strive to reach prompt agreement, in the relevant international organs, on the elimination and complete destruction of such weapons.'

> [Rio] 'Warfare is inherently destructive of sustainable development. States shall therefore respect international law providing protection for the environment in times of armed conflict and cooperate in its further

development, as necessary. Peace, development and environmental protection are interdependent and indivisible.'

There is another respect in which the two declarations are essentially similar: that is the explicit exhortation given to priority consideration for developing countries. The Stockholm Declaration was more concrete in this regard, but it is summarized adequately enough in the Rio statement, i.e., 'The special situation and needs of developing countries, particularly the least developed and those most environmentally vulnerable, shall be given special priority.'

Other than the above three points of similarities, there are a number of significant differences between the two declarations of 20 years apart. A new orientation which we observe in the Rio Declaration is the recurrent use of the expression, 'sustainable development.' Actually, a detailed document called *Agenda 21* issued by the Rio meeting as a 'programme of action' has the subtitle: 'A blueprint for action for global sustainable development into the 21st century.' We did have an occasion earlier to refer briefly to the concept of 'sustainable development' but we have to grasp its meaning more fully in this section. Before we do so, however, an additional difference between the two declarations must be mentioned. That is a greater degree of globalized approach in the Rio document than in the Stockholm one in the sense that 'cooperation in a spirit of global partnership' among states was given a priority emphasis compared with the prerogative of sovereignty.

'Principle 16' of the Rio Declaration states, for example: National authorities should endeavour to promote the internationalization of environmental costs and the use of economic instruments, taking into account the approach that the polluter should, in principle, bear the cost of pollution, with due regard to the public interest and without distorting international trade and investment.

Another difference of import between the Stockholm and the Rio is the degree of concreteness with which 'a blueprint for action' was spelled out in the Rio Conference in the form of *Agenda 21*. This document has a structure of giving to each section the subdivisions consisting of:

> Programme areas
> (A) [the title of the area]
> Basis for action
> Objectives

Activities
Means of implementation
(B), (C), etc.

One can see that special care was taken in relating a specific objective to practical action that has to be taken.

Although the concept of 'sustainable development' is used as a central keyword in *Agenda 21*, its precise definition is not given anywhere in the document. It is most likely that the drafting committee for the occasion considered that the Brundtland Commission's detailed discussion (in 1987) of the concept was by then generally accepted in the world community. Therefore, we might reproduce here relevant paragraphs from the Brundtland report:

> Humanity has the ability to make development sustainable – to ensure that it meets the *needs of the present* without compromising the ability of future generations to meet *their own needs.* The concept of sustainable development does imply limits – not absolute limits but limitations imposed by the present state of technology and social organization on environmental resources and by the ability of the biosphere to absorb the effects of human activities.
>
> But technology and social organization can be both managed and improved to make way for a new era of economic growth. The Commission believes that widespread poverty is no longer inevitable. Poverty is not only an evil in itself, but sustainable development requires meeting *the basic needs of all* and extending to all the opportunity to fulfill *their aspirations for a better life.* A world in which poverty is endemic will always be prone to ecological and other catastrophes.
>
> Meeting *essential needs* requires not only a new era of economic growth for nations in which the majority are poor, but an assurance that the poor ones get their fair share of the resources required to sustain that growth. Such equity would be aided by political systems that secure effective citizen participation in decision making and by greater democracy in international decision making.
>
> Sustainable global development requires that those who are more affluent adopt life-styles within the planet's ecological means – in their use of energy, for example. Further, rapidly growing population can increase the pressure on resources and slow any rise in *living standards*; thus sustainable development can only be pursued if population size and growth are in harmony with the changing productive potential of the ecosystem.[1]
> (Italics by Tsuru.)

On a first reading of these paragraphs, one may not find any ambiguities on which one might stumble. But note the italicized words and try to pore over them as to what they exactly could mean. If we are speaking of a particular society with its historical traditions and the given socio-economic and cultural conditions, the words italicized in the above quotation might be understood without much ambiguity. But the Brundtland Commission was clearly thinking in terms of 'a global society,' where admittedly the diversity of cultures and belief systems exist. As the *2050 Project*,[2] which recorded the voices from the developing world, attested eloquently enough, the definition of 'sustainable development' by the Brundtland Commission did give 'a needed focus on the importance of long-term planning, but as a policy tool it was vague, providing no specifics about which needs and desires must be met and fulfilled and how.'[3] In Nagpal's summary words:

> Nowhere is the chasm between the developing and industrialized worlds more clear than in the discussion of the role of indigenous groups. Indigenous people and their spokespersons contend that Western societies place human beings in a position of dominance over nature, making the search for sustainability fruitless. In contrast, they feel that sustainability is not about prosperity but about living a life of dignity in harmony with nature.[4]
>
> In sharp contrast to this indigenous view of the primacy of the environment is the argument that sustainability is about 'a systematic shift in economic development patterns' and that there are no inherent inconsistencies between the object of the market system and the goals of sustainability so long as 'markets internalize environmental costs.' While many essayists would agree that 'getting prices right' is certainly a component of the transition to a sustainable future, they appear to be increasingly disenchanted with the exclusive focus on economic growth and market instruments. . . . If economic growth must come at the expense of the Earth's ecosystem, as many contend it does, such growth is nonsustainable. Equating development with growth and growth with increase in wealth are at the heart of the struggle between development and sustainability.[5]

It is clear enough that 'voices from the developing world' do place a greater emphasis on 'basic values' as an extension of 'basic needs,' thus to use the wisdom of indigenous groups, elders and tribal leaders to re-examine current structures of government and sources of knowledge. But we must point out for fairness' sake that 'Principle 22' of the Rio Declaration does state: 'Indigenous people and their communities and other local communities have a vital role in environmental management and development because of their knowledge and traditional practices.' On the question of 'equating development with growth,' however, *Agenda 21* of Rio is not quite safe from the criticism that it dodged the issue of 'development *without* growth.' It is true that 'economic growth' and 'sustainable development' are cited as two distinctly separate objectives in 'Principle 12' of the Rio Declaration, which reads: 'States should cooperate to promote a supportive and open international economic system that would lead to economic growth and sustainable development in all countries.' But in so many particular places in the pages of *Agenda 21* an impression of interchangeability between 'growth' and 'development' is not ruled out. This was probably unavoidable because, as Michael A. Toman wrote,

> for ecologists 'sustainability' connotes preservation of the status and function of ecological systems; for economists, the maintenance and improvement of human living standards. . . . Like many evocative terms, the word sustainability means many things to different people and can be used in reference to a number of important issues. The term inherently evokes a concept of preservation and nurturing over time. . . . Thus sustainability involves some notion of respect for the interests of our descendants. Beyond this point, however, uncertainty and disagreement are rife.[6]

At any rate, the general tone of criticism raised by the *2050 Report* was not entirely off the mark, for it cannot be denied that the Rio Conference in a number of ways fell short of fulfilling the mission it was charged with, due basically to concessions to commanding forces in the international politico-economic configuration. The most conspicuous in this regard was the basic stance taken by the conference of carrying the banner of free-market mechanisms. In this connection, we are reminded of the offensive for privatization launched by Mrs Thatcher's government of Great Britain after her election victory in May 1979, gradually gaining momentum throughout the world in the 1980s. The highlight of this worldwide trend was an international conference on privatization sponsored by the United States Agency for International Development (USAID), held in Washington, DC, in February 1986, where nearly 500 delegates from 45 countries assembled. They were addressed by Secretary of State George P. Shultz, who claimed that the conference symbolized a revolution in economic thinking. It has been an unusual revolution in that it is *a return to principles we once adhered to, but from which we had strayed.* They are principles of individual freedom and private enterprise that have changed the world more in 200 years than all the changes in the preceding 2,000 years.[7] (Italics by Tsuru.)

It may be agreed that George Shultz's pronouncement, quoted here, was more in the nature of a rallying call for a like-minded partisan group, and consensus among experts appears to be that the worldwide fashion of privatization has been more of a political than an economic action 'structuring [its] strategies to build political constituencies.'[8] Nevertheless, what John Naisbitt and Patricia Aburdene called 'a major megatrend for the twenty-first century'[9] must have prevailed in the minds of those in charge of finalizing the document *Agenda 21*, so that in the section on 'Promoting Sound Economic Policies' in the programme area entitled 'Encouraging Economic Policies Conducive to Sustainable Development,' for example, there appear statements like:

> All countries should . . . remove the barriers to progress caused by . . . the neglect of market conditions . . . [and] encourage the private sector and foster entrepreneurship by improving institutional facilities for enterprise creation and market entry . . . [and] provide scope for appropriate economic instruments, including market mechanisms, in harmony with the objectives of sustainable development and fulfilment of basic needs.

The social philosophy essentially identical with that of reliance on free-market mechanisms and privatization is reflected in the emphasis given in *Agenda 21* on its advocacy of free trade. The very first subsection in its Section 1 discussing 'Social and Economic Dimensions' has the title 'International cooperation to accelerate sustainable development in developing countries and related domestic policies' and leads off its exhortative paragraph with the statement:

> The international economy should provide a supportive international climate for achieving environment and development goals by:
> (a) Promoting sustainable development through trade liberalization;
> (b) Making trade and environment mutually supportive.

This advice is supplemented further towards the end of the same subsection with an admonition to 'all countries to remove biases against exports and in favour of inefficient import substitution and establish policies that allow them to benefit fully from the flow of foreign investment, within the framework of national, social, economic and development goals.' It strikes one somewhat odd that *Agenda 21*, while preoccupied with the role of foreign trade and investment in the current scene of international economic relations, fails to mention an important aspect of globalization today, that is the far-reaching activities of giant transnational corporations and their distorting influences. The omission was, most likely, deliberate, but it turned out to be a critical deficiency of *Agenda 21* as we shall discuss the problem of *kōgai* export later in this chapter.

As for the positive significance of free trade for worldwide welfare, conventional economic wisdom is known to have achieved general unanimity. Trade benefits all parties, as the conventional wisdom goes, by reaping the rewards of specialization, thereby fostering economic growth and contributing to the attainment of other economic objectives. As with the benefits of trade in general, however,

> this benign outcome depends on *several important conditions* that are not often met in practice. In today's harsh and increasingly competitive trading system, it is likely to be more difficult still because of the growing pressure to gain competitive advantage by externalizing environmental costs. . . . If the potential environmental benefits of free trade are to be realized, trading rules must recognize that environmental externalities amount to subsidies that are as economically distorting and unfair as any financial subsidy. The rules must not only discourage such 'eco-dumping' through these subsidies, they must also permit countries to protect themselves against eco-dumping by others. This, however, will require a sea change in the General Agreement on Tariffs and Trade.[10] (Italics by Tsuru.)

'Several important conditions' suggested in this quotation are:

A. No externalities
B. Stable prices, in particular of primary products specialized by developing countries
C. No dynamic differences, such as, for example, from banana production to higher added-value industries
D. No coercion in production or exchange, often observed in gross inequalities between trading partners
E. No international mobility of capital

When these conditions are not satisfied, the realm of free trade will bring about, in all probability, a situation where the strong will get stronger at the expense of the weak, as in the oft-quoted biblical affirmation to the effect that 'for those who have will be given more, till they have enough and to spare; and those who have not will forfeit even what they have.' (Matthew, 13:12) It seems clear enough that 'the era of free trade pure and simple is over. It has to be replaced by a "green" framework in which environmental issues are given due weight and non-governmental organizations play a much greater role.'[11]

At any rate, the aftermath of the Rio Conference saw the proliferation of organizations and committees newly created with assignments to implement one or the other concrete tasks specified in *Agenda 21*. Immediately, the United Nations Commission on Sustainable Development was organized to oversee that implementation; then the Global Environment Facility (GEF), which had come into existence already in 1991 as an international financing mechanism designed to provide developing countries with some additional financial incentive to tackle global environmental problems, was set to become, after the Rio Conference, the funding mechanism for the international conventions on ozone, biodiversity and climate change. The US government, for example, responded to *Agenda 21*'s challenge by the establishment of the President's Council on Sustainable Development (PCSD) in June 1993 with 25 members – leaders in industry, government, and environmental, Native American and civil rights organizations. Japan, too, responded by revising extensively the earlier Basic Law for Environmental Pollution Control in 1993, about which we shall discuss in the next section.

In spite of these and other myriad supportive organizations all over the world, the UN General Assembly had to make public in 1997, five years after the Rio Conference, 'a statement of commitment' in which an admission was made to the effect that 'we are deeply concerned that the overall trends with respect to sustainable development are worse today than they were in 1992.' The United Nations Environment Programme (UNEP), too, in its *Global Environment Outlook* of 1997 echoed this disappointment in the following manner:

> Despite [the] progress on several fronts, from a global perspective the environment has continued to degrade during the past decade, and significant environmental problems remain deeply embedded in the socio-

economic fabric of nations in all regions. . . . The reconciliation of environment and trade regimes in a fair and equitable manner still remains a major challenge. The continued preoccupation with immediate local and national issues and a general lack of sustained interest in global and long-term environmental issues remain major impediments to environmental progress internationally. Global governance structures and global environmental solidarity remain too weak to make progress a world-wide reality. As a result, the gap between what has been done thus far and what is realistically needed is widening.[12]

Why such a disappointing outcome? One basic reason that could have been foreseen was in the non-binding character of *Agenda 21* itself. It did not have the force of law, and no country is under legal obligation to implement its provisions. For example, on one of the most important issues raised in the Rio Conference, namely, what was known as the 'additionality' question, or the notion that the developed countries should either individually or collectively pay the costs of measures undertaken by developing countries to tackle global environmental problems and make the transition to sustainable development, chapter 33 of the *Agenda* affirms that 'implementation . . . will require the provision . . . of substantial new and additional resources'; but no specific transfer mechanism was actually set up. Furthermore,

Chapter 33 is an adroitly crafted diplomatic compromise that fails to bind anyone to anything. It notes that 'funding should be provided in a way which maximizes the availability of new and additional resources and which uses all funding resources and mechanisms. These include, among others: the multilateral development banks . . . the International Development Association (IDA) . . . GEF . . . private funding . . . debt relief.' No indication is given as to the likely or expected contribution of each.[13]

Such being the operative nature of the 'programme of action' for sustainable development, one cannot resist holding the impression that a topic like 'global environmental problems,' while admirably suited for high-toned oratory by political leaders,[14] has to be tackled with full awareness of the realistic obstacles which keep the implementation at bay. We encounter the same type of situation when we come to discuss the 1997 Kyoto meeting on the Framework Convention on Climate Change later in this chapter.

THE BASIC ENVIRONMENTAL LAW OF JAPAN (1993)

It did not take long for the Japanese government to respond to *Agenda 21*'s challenge by revising almost completely the 1967 Basic Law for Environmental Pollution Control. Soon after the end of the Rio Conference, the Environment Agency asked the Central Anti-*Kōgai* Commission and the Conservation of Nature's Environment Commission to draft a plan of the revision of the earlier Law, and the joint meeting of the two commissions submitted a report as early as on 20 October 1992. From that time to the cabinet decision on the draft new Basic Law on 12 March 1993 was the period when the time was consumed almost entirely by interministerial adjustment within the government while various non-governmental groups, such as the Japan Lawyers' Federation, the Citizens' Committee for Inquiry on the Environmental Legislation, etc., published their opinions with constructive criticism of the October draft report of the two commissions. There was practically no dialogue between the bureaucracy and public opinion on the subject.

Other than the motivating force coming from the international scene, there was a domestic reason for Japan to overhaul the legislative scaffolding of environmental control. During the quarter century from 1967 to 1992 there transpired a marked shift in the keyword from '*kōgai*' to '*kankyō*' (environment) in Japan, in addition to the many legislative failures in coping with *kōgai* problems themselves. It was inevitable that a radical revision of the Basic Law had to be proposed from the domestic bureaucratic point of view as well.

Pressed on by both international and domestic reasons, the Basic Environment Law was pushed through the Diet rather hastily, becoming effective on 19 November 1993. Probably on account of the haste with which the drafting was done, the text of the law has a typically bureaucratic style of guarded verbosity, as can be illustrated by Article 4, which has the title 'Creation of a Society Ensuring Sustainable Development with Reduced Environmental Load':

> Environmental conservation shall be promoted so that a society can be formulated where a healthy and productive environment is conserved and sustainable development is ensured by fostering sound economic development with environmental load, through practices on environmental conservation such as reducing as much as possible the environmental load generated by socio-economic and other activities, which are voluntarily and positively pursued by all the people sharing fair burden; and so that

interference with environmental conservation can be anticipatively prevented through enhancing scientific knowledge.[15]

There are two keywords in this article: 'sustainable development' and 'environmental load,' both of which are quite new in official documents of the Japanese government. As for the former, we have already discussed its implications, but the latter term is defined in Article 2 of the Law as 'any adverse effects on the environment generated by human activities which may cause interference with environmental conservation.' It may be noted that this definition of 'environmental load' corresponds to the second stage in the definition of *kōgai* as we discussed the problem in Chapter One; that is to say, it follows the first stage of 'sources' and is antecedent to the third stage of 'damages'; thus the term fails to pin down specifically upon the question of responsibility connecting 'damages' with 'sources.'

Still, this Article 4 along with Article 3 detailing the desideratum of 'enjoyment and future sources of environmental blessings' and Article 5 exhorting 'the active promotion of global environmental conservation through international cooperation' are referred to as the 'basic principles' in the Law; and the responsibilities of the State, of local governments, of corporations, and of citizens in conducting their activities in pursuance of such 'basic principles' are set forth. The responsibility of corporations, in particular, is spelled out (in Article 8) with exceptional detail, but the long-winded four paragraphs in that article amount to nothing more than to say that 'corporations are responsible for taking necessary measures in pursuance of the aforesaid basic principles.' However, there are two points in which the positive role of non-governmental bodies is understood: something which had never been officially acknowledged before in Japan. One is the recognition accorded to the importance of voluntary activities conducted by private bodies like NGO (Article 34 paragraph 2), and the other is the provision (Article 35 paragraph 2) which can be put to practical use in a critique when *kōgai* exports by Japanese corporations threaten to become a contentious issue.

Among the topics singled out under the general chapter heading of 'Basic Policies for Environmental Conservation,' the following three are of special importance:

A. Basic Environmental Plan
B. Environmental Impact Assessment

C. Economic Measures to Prevent Interference with Environmental Conservation

The 'Basic Environment Plan,' in particular, is considered to be of central importance, given its purpose of 'comprehensively and systematically promoting policies for environmental conservation.' (Article 15 paragraph 1) In view of such importance, a special committee was subsequently set up to draft a detailed programme for implementation, which was made public on 15 July 1994. We shall come back to this topic later.

As for the question of 'Economic Impact Assessment,' it may be recalled that there were actually seven occasions (up to 1993) when proposals were made by the Environment Agency itself and became abortive through the opposition by other ministries and the *Keidanren* (The Federations of Economic Organizations). It was, therefore, with a sense of renewed expectation for the EIA legislation finally to materialize that the provision for it in the Law was welcomed. However, the relevant Article 20 states:

> The State shall take necessary measures to ensure that, when corporations[16] are engaged in alteration of land shape, construction of new structures and other similar activities, they will conduct, in advance, surveys, forecasts or evaluations of the environmental impact of such activities and will give proper consideration to environmental conservation based on the results of them.

How inadequate such formulation is in meeting the requirements for the EIA legislation can be seen in the light of the discussions on the subject we had in the last section of Chapter Five. An especially deficient point was the failure to refer to the major project operating agency requiring *ex ante* assessment in Japan, namely: the government offices which plan and undertake public works. It may be recalled that the National Environment Policy Act (NEPA) of the United States, which did serve as a model for EIA legislation in Japan since 1969, stated explicitly that the coverage for the needed assessment included 'the proposed actions of all agencies of the Federal Government.' On this matter, too, we must come back later in view of the fact that a concrete step for new legislation began in 1997.

On the third topic mentioned above, or the 'Economic Measures to Prevent Interference with Environmental Conservation,' we may begin by quoting the text of the relevant Article 22 (paragraph 2), which, we must warn, is again circuitous and long-winded:

In consideration of the fact that the measures, which aim at encouraging persons who are conducting the load activities to undertake voluntarily to reduce the environmental load by means of imposing appropriate and equitable economic surcharges on them, are expected to be effective in preventing interference with environmental conservation, and that such measures are internationally recommended; the State shall appropriately conduct surveys and researches on the effectiveness of implementing such measures with regard to prevention of interference with environmental conservation and on the effects of such measures on Japanese economy; and should it be deemed necessary to implement such measures, the State shall make efforts to acquire the understanding and cooperation of the people with regard to utilization of such measures to prevent interference with environmental conservation. In this case, should such measures be implemented for global environmental conservation, the State shall take account of international considerations so as to appropriately ensure the effectiveness of such measures.

We can see that the tone of this paragraph is quite concessional to 'persons who are conducting the load activities to undertake voluntarily to reduce the environmental load'; and it was probably in the same purport that Article 22 begins in the first paragraph by stating the advisability of 'providing necessary and appropriate economic assistance' by the government to those persons referred to above. It is as if to say that the application of 'economic surcharges' is to be adopted on the assumption of prior governmental assistance. It is also to be noted that the last phrase in the above quotation has the implication that a policy measure like an 'environmental tax,' if unilaterally adopted by Japan, might redound to Japan's disadvantage in international competition, and that therefore we must consider 'international collaboration.' Such has been the opinion repeatedly insisted upon by the business world.

The Basic Environment Law consists of 46 Articles and was meant to cover the whole range of problems concerned with the environment, even including the provision (Article 10) on the designation of 'the Environment Day' which 'shall be June 6th.' Far more important for the Basic Law would have been to affirm the principle of 'Environmental Right' which was repeatedly contested in the environment-related law-suits in the 1970s and 1980s. It may be recalled, as was discussed in Chapter Three that this principle was proclaimed in the Tokyo Resolution of 1970 to the effect that above all, it is important that we urge the adoption in law of the principle that every person is entitled by right to the environment free of elements which infringe human health and well-being and the nature's endowment, including its beauty, which shall be the heritage of the present to the future generations.

The term *kankyōken* (environmental right) which came to be commonly used since 1970 is now broadened to cover *irihamaken* (beach access right) and *shinsuiken* (water-savouring right) as well as *jinkakuken* (personality right), and it was quite significant that the Osaka High Court, in its decision in 1975 on the Osaka International Airport case, admitted that the 'personality right' of noise-pollution victims was being clearly infringed and could be cited as a valid ground for injunction. It is true that courts in general have not been as enlightened as in this case. For example, when Matsuyama District Court pronounced a negative judgement on the 'beach access right' case in Ehimé Prefecture in 1978, it proclaimed that 'the seashore is a public entity in nature under state control; and the possibility of sea-bathing by residents is nothing but a reflex effect of the fact that the state might not prohibit it.' Still, the very whole issue related to the environmental right had been of such heated controversy both in the courts and in public that it was natural for the general public to expect that the Basic Environment Law would come out with some kind of statement on the subject. But it did not.

What is generally admitted is the point that legitimizing of the environmental right is needed when the property right has to be superseded in the interest of the conservation of environment, or for the situation where, by nature, the environment-related resources cannot be individually appropriated. The latter corresponds to what modern economists call 'inappropriable resources' exemplified by air quality and mountain views.[17] The Comprehensive Environment Law in Germany, though still in a draft stage, does provide a section on environmental right, calling it 'the right to demand intervention by the administration.'[18]

THE BASIC ENVIRONMENT PLAN

In pursuance of the stipulation (Article 15) in the Basic Environment Law, the Prime Minister submitted the problem concerning the Basic Environment Plan to the Central Environment Council for deliberation on 14 January 1994, which council in turn commissioned its policy-planning sub-committee to draft a concrete plan. Within six months 'An Interim Conclusion' was produced and made public, whereupon the council invited people to comment on it through public hearings and correspondence. Incorporating some of the comments made, the finalized report was submitted for the cabinet decision on 16 December 1994. The democratic procedure which was adopted in working out the details of the 'Basic Environment Plan' – a procedure which was commendably novel for the Environment Agency – elicited an expectation that at last a concrete plan more in accord with the dominant public opinion than in the past would emerge this time. But the end-product was disappointing mainly for the reason that major critical comments on 'An Interim Conclusion' communicated through hearings and correspondence were simply ignored. Between 'An Interim Conclusion' originally published and the finalized report on the 'Basic Environment Plan' approved in the cabinet decision, there was only a negligible difference.

The Basic Environment Plan suggests four keywords for long-run goals: 'circulation,' 'symbiosis,' 'participation' and 'international involvement', and it propounds five concrete policy measures around these goals, namely:

A. Actualization of a socio-economic system based on the circulation which minimizes environmental load
B. Symbiosis of man with nature
C. Realizing of the participation by all the subject-agents under the fair sharing of roles by them
D. Promotion of common basic policy measures related to the environment conservation
E. International involvement

Although the proposal, with literary embellishment, is itemized in a conveniently quotable manner, its sentences are presented in a typically bureaucratic style, lacking their sentence-subjects, thus leaving the question of responsibility ambiguous. The keyword 'circulation' is ambiguous enough, but when it is applied to the problem of an evolution of the socio-economic system as in the first policy measure above, we cannot but be puzzled as to its significance in the light of the dominant emphasis given to the free enterprise market system by the Japanese government. In this connection, more enigmatic is a statement given under the third heading of 'realizing of the participation by all the subject-agents, etc.' There, the proposed 'participation' is meant not for ordinary citizens, who are often the victims of pollutions, but above all for manufacturing firms, and the proposal is couched in the following phrases:

> Manufacturing industries shall cooperate in (1) the utilization of raw materials with minimum environmental load of reproductive resources, (2) a reduction of environmental load in the production stage through the adoption of the method of production of low-load type, (3) curbing of the generation of waste materials, (4) the effective treatment in general, (5) lengthening of the life span of products, (6) the promotion of development and production of the products which have the minimum of environmental load in the stages of consumption and waste disposal, and (7) using appropriate methods of disposal after the products, etc., are disused.

One gets the impression that this is a type of instruction that might be issued to manufacturing enterprises in a centrally planned society, and that it is highly questionable for the Environment Agency of Japan to be able to ask the country's major corporations to abide by them.

ENVIRONMENTAL IMPACT ASSESSMENT (EIA)

The absence of an umbrella assessment law did not mean that Japan lacked the experience of EIA before the legislative efforts succeeded in 1997. A number of prefectures and municipalities had their own assessment ordinances or what was called 'assessment guidelines' on the basis of which 'individual assessments' had been conducted. And also, when the legislative attempts failed for the seventh time in August 1984, the cabinet-level agreement became the substitute authorization for carrying out official assessments of specific projects. There were actually 370 cases of this kind between July 1986 and March 1997.[19] These instances, both the local government ones and the 'cabinet-decision' ones, covered a wide range of projects beyond the restricted application visualized in Article 20 of the Basic Environment Law which referred only to 'corporations' as project operating agencies. Thus when the Comprehensive Research Group on the EIA System was set up by the Environment Agency in July 1994, the coverage of the types of projects it had to deal with was

extended to public works of various kinds, such for example as reclamation projects, road construction, city planning, etc. The group
published its report in June 1996, which became the basis for further
deliberation by the Central Environment Commission, which submitted its report to the Prime Minister in February 1997. Thus,
finally the government draft plan for EIA could be voted in the Diet
to become a law on 13 June 1997.

The salient points of the law may be enumerated here:

(1) Innovations compared with the earlier assessment practised
without legislative authorization:

    A. The coverage was broadened, to the extent of including elec-
       tricity generating plants, large-scale forest roads, etc.
    B. The procedure of so-called 'screening' is to be conducted prior
       to the decision to carry out EIA.
    C. The procedure of so-called 'scoping' is to be conducted for the
       purpose of sifting the really needed specific items for assess-
       ment, thus saving time.
    D. A 'monitoring' procedure is proposed for the re-examination
       after projects went into practice.
    E. The earlier regional limitation of allowing only local residents'
       opinions to be expressed on projects is cancelled, thus giving a
       much wider participation of public opinion.

(2) The features which remained the same as before:

    A. Essentially, assessment is to be 'self-assessment' in the sense
       that it is to be done by the project operating agency itself,
       although the Environment Agency can express its opinion on
       the content.
    B. Assessment is still limited to the stage of execution of a project
       and not for the planning stage as in the so-called 'strategic
       environment assessment' practised in Europe today, in spite of
       the fact that the Basic Environment Law proclaimed in Article
       19 that 'the State shall consider environmental conservation
       when *formulating* and implementing policies which are deemed
       to influence the environment.' (Italics by Tsuru.)

At least, however, an improvement in the sphere of environmental control was committed in a law, although its enforcement date was allowed a two-year delay after its enactment, which means 13 June 1999. It remains to be seen what may happen before then.

The classical definition of external diseconomy, as in A.C. Pigou, was related to disamenities inflicted externally upon the public by an enterprise or a unit of activity *within* a country, either in the very neighbourhood or in the latter's vicinity; but in the context of global environmental concern today, similar events have come to be observed especially in the countries of the 'South' where external diseconomy is caused by an enterprise owned and operated by the countries of the 'North.' Such is the concomitant of direct investment by developed countries in developing ones in the form of transnational corporations and is referred to as the export of hazard[20] or the *'kōgai* export' in Japanese. A most glaring instance of such a phenomenon occurred in Bhopal, India, in 1984, and this was so typical of the global unfolding of environmental problems that it is worth giving a full account of the event, which follows:[21]

> At about 12:40 A.M. on December 3, 1984, Suman Dey looked at the gauges on the control panel in total disbelief. Dey was the control-room operator at the Union Carbide pesticide plant in Bhopal, India, and what he saw was so far out of the ordinary that it terrified him. Inside a storage tank containing the dangerous chemical methyl isocyanate gas (MIC), which was supposed to be refrigerated, the temperature had risen to 77°F. Pressure in the tank, which ordinarily ranged between 2 and 25 pounds per square inch (psi), had risen to 55 psi.
>
> Bewildered by the readings, Dey ran to the storage tank area to investigate the problem. He heard a loud rumbling sound and saw a plume of gas gushing out of the stack in front of him. Dey, along with the MIC supervisor on duty, Shakil Qureshi, and several operators, attempted to control the gas leak by turning on safety devices. Together they tried switching on the refrigeration system to cool the storage tank. They started the scrubber through which the gases were passing and sprayed water on escaping gases, hoping to neutralize them. When all these efforts failed, they fled the plant in panic.
>
> The Bhopal district collector, Moti Singh, and the superintendent of police, Swaraj Puri, were awakened in the middle of the night by the insistent ringing of their telephones. Singh and Puri were in charge of

district administration, the local police department, and civil defense efforts. They rushed at once to the police control room to coordinate emergency relief efforts. But they, along with hundreds of other governmental officials and Union Carbide plant managers, were caught sleeping in more ways than one. Nobody seemed to know what gas had leaked, how toxic it was, or how to deal with the ensuing emergency. The police and the army tried to evacuate affected neighborhoods. They were too slow, and instead of being told to lie on the ground with their faces covered with wet cloths, people were urged to run. 200,000 residents fled in panic into the night.

Morning found death strewn over a stunned city. Bodies and animal carcasses lay on sidewalks, streets, and railway platforms, and in slum huts, bus stands and waiting halls. Thousands of injured victims streamed into the city's hospitals. Doctors and other medical personnel struggled to cope with the chaotic rush, knowing neither the cause of the disaster nor how to treat the victims. Groping for anything that might help, they treated immediate symptoms. They washed the eyes of their patients with water and then soothed the burning with eye drops. They gave the victims aspirin, inhalers, muscle relaxants, and stomach remedies to relieve their symptoms.

Before the week was over, nearly 3,000 people had died. More than 300,000 others had been affected by exposure to the deadly poison. About 2,000 animals had died, and 7,000 more were severely injured. The worst industrial accident in history was over. . . .

In one sense, the Bhopal crisis was simply an industrial accident – a failure of technology. But the real story behind the accident goes much deeper than mere technology. It extends to the organizational and sociopolitical environment in which the accident occurred.

Organizational pressures within Union Carbide contributed to both the accident and the ensuing crisis. The Bhopal plant was an unprofitable operation, for the most part ignored by top Union Carbide officials. With several of Union Carbide's traditionally profitable divisions in the United States faltering, the Bhopal plant was a prime candidate for divestiture. . . .

But it was more than Union Carbide's financial difficulties that set the stage for the crisis. The economic, political, and social environment of Bhopal also played a contributing role. At the time of the accident, Bhopal was a peculiar combination of new technology and accident tradition sitting in somewhat uncomfortable relation to each other.

Though the city is nearly 1,000 years old, its industrial capacity, until recently, was primitive. In the last thirty years industrial growth was encouraged in Bhopal, but the necessary infrastructure needed to support industry was lacking. There were severe shortcomings in the physical infrastructure, such as supplies of water and energy and housing, transportation and communications facilities, as well as in the social infrastructure, including public health services, civil defense systems, community awareness of technological hazards, and an effective regulatory system. . . .

Not all industrial accidents become crisis. They trigger crises only when technological problems occur in economic, social, and political environments that cannot cope with them. The Bhopal accident became a crisis not because of technological problems alone but also because of environmental conditions outside the plant. The plant was operated by a company under pressure to make profits and/or cut losses; it was sanctioned by a government under pressure to industrialize, even though the appropriate industrial infrastructure and support systems were missing; and it was located in a city completely unprepared to cope with any major accident. It was these factors, combined with the technological failures that actually caused the accident, that expanded the initial event into a crisis.

One common characteristic of the *kōgai* export is the double standards in safety practised by multinational corporations. And the Bhopal disaster case is typical in this respect. The Union Carbide was operating a sister plant in Institute, West Virginia, and compared with this, the Bhopal plant was deficient in a number of respects from the standpoint of safety. For example:[22]

- In *plant design*, there was a lack of automatically operated emergency systems, and also a lack of instrumentation for detecting MIC leaks. (At Bhopal, this was done by the workers themselves sensing eye irritation and tearing, then trying to locate leak sources.)
- In *plant operation*, there was a lack of fixed water-spray protection from fire and vapour releases in the MIC operating and storage areas; also, personnel turnover was high resulting in untrained people doing hazardous tasks, besides the training of workers was done by rote memorization only.
- In *executive management*, Carbide USA is alleged to have approved turning off the MIC coolant system ('chiller'), a measure which effected significant savings in energy operating costs. It is unthinkable that such a vital safeguard would be sacrificed at a US plant with large-scale storage of MIC.
- In *community relations*, the community was not informed about the very dangerous materials used at the factory. Thus, there was

no emergency planning with local medical, police or other officials; even as the victims were arriving at the hospitals, Union Carbide failed to provide vital information about the toxic effects and the treatment to use.

- As regards *civil liberty matters*, compensation for wrongful death and personal injury in India is not only minimal, but moreover, virtually inaccessible to Bhopal victims in Indian courts as they normally function.

Although the Bhopal instance was of disaster-scale as a *kōgai* export, it can hardly be regarded as an exception in the practice of double standards, as we shall see presently, citing the cases of Japanese experience. Therefore, it is of special significance to refer in this connection to remarks in a memorandum written by Lawrence Summers in 1991 when he was vice-president of the World Bank, suggesting that the Bank should 'encourage more migration of the dirty industries to the third world' with a somewhat unconditional statement that 'the economic logic of dumping a load of toxic waste in the lowest-wage country is impeccable.' He cited three grounds for this statement, to wit:

First, the costs of pollution depend on earnings forgone through death or injury; these costs are lowest in the poorest countries. Second, costs rise disproportionately as pollution increases; so shifting pollution from dirty places to clean ones reduces costs. Third, people value a clean environment more as their incomes rise; if other things are equal, costs fall if pollution moves from rich places to poor ones.[23]

Essentially this is 'a philosophy of discrimination' that could perhaps be applied to a situation within a single country, e.g. in the United States. It is indeed amazing that a responsible officer of the World Bank could be so completely at ease with this logic of cost-benefit analysis. But the truth of the matter may well be, as Mr Bruce Rich, an attorney and specialist on World Bank affairs, commented that '[Mr. Summers] finally put in writing the full implications of the current neo-classical economic model that reigns at the World Bank and elsewhere.'[24] Be that as it may, instances of double standards in industrial hazards in the world today are legion, especially in connection with the production of pesticides as enumerated in the full four-page list in Jane Ives' volume.[25]

Japan, of course, is no exception in this regard, her major field of activities being in Asia. Some prominent instances of the kind in recent years are the following:

- It was in 1977 that Kawasaki Ironworks, harassed by *kōgai*-protesting citizens in the neighbourhood of its Chiba plant, decided to move its sintering process section to the Mindanao Island of the Philippines. (The sintering process generates a great deal of sulphur oxides and nitrogen oxides, which are sources of pollution.) For this purpose, a local subsidiary called the Philippines Sintering Corporation (PSC) was set up with the financial assistance of JICA (Japan International Cooperation Agency) to the amount of 730.7 million yen.

- Another instance of *kōgai* export to the Philippines was the establishment of the Basar Copper Smelting Plant in the Isabela region of Leyte Island in 1977. This case was a joint venture with three Japanese companies participating (Marubeni, Sumitomo Shōji and Itochu) and was again supported by generous semi-official funds of the JICA and OECF (Overseas Economic Cooperation Fund). Once the operation started by the plant in 1983, complaints by residents around Isabela Bay began to be heard repeatedly in connection with the fish they were eating.

- Probably the most typical and significant instance of Japan's *kōgai* export to an Asian country was the establishment in 1982 of the Asia Rare-Earth Company (ARE) in a suburb of Ipoh City in Malaysia, a joint venture of the Mitsubishi Kasei Corporation of Japan with the Bay-Mineral Company, the biggest rare-earth ore-dressing company in Malaysia. The principal activity of this ARE was the extraction of rare earth (such as ittoleum) indispensable for high-technology industry out of raw materials like monazite ore. In this process, a radioactive substance called thorium having a half-life of 14 billion years comes out as a by-product which tended to be casually dealt with as a waste material thus causing health impairment to the workers of the plant and some residents in the neighbourhood. The protest movement by the residents has often taken a violent form as at the time (May 1987) when the ARE reopened its operation ignoring the provisional injunction order by the local court. The historical background of this case was somewhat complex since the Japanese army during the last war discriminated severely against residents of Chinese origin, committing various persecutions against them, and it happened that the victims of the ARE *kōgai* were mostly of Chinese origin many of whom retained their historical enmity against Japanese. Here was another unfortunate by-product, for suppression by the Malaysian police against the protesting residents had the effect of widening the racial gulf between the two major ethnic groups in Malaysia.

- It has been stated time and again that the careless and uninformed use of pesticides accounts for an enormous toll of preventable death and disease in developing countries. And yet, according to a report by the US Audit Board for 1976, for example, approximately 30 per cent out of the 247,500 tons of agricultural chemicals exported by the US were of the kinds either banned or severely restricted in the US itself. In Japan, too, similar double standards have been practised by keeping effective still Article 16 of the Agricultural Regulation Act which states that 'this law does not apply to those cases of production and sale of agricultural chemicals for the export to other countries.' Thus, when chlordan, a chemical product used for the extermination of termites, was banned its production, imports and use in September 1986, its inventories in a semi-processed state in the hands of producers were exported to East-Asian countries. A similar step was taken, when the use of HCH, another type of agricultural chemical, was banned in Japan, by exporting the stockpile remaining in Japan to Thailand and Malaysia.[26]

The *kōgai* export is an aspect of globalization of the strained relations between economics and ecology, with the economics of the 'North' prevailing over the ecology of the 'South.' As a compensatory action by the 'North' for the benefit of the 'South' a reference is often made to the unilateral grant in the form of ODA (official development assistance), which initially had the contribution target of 0.7 per cent of GNP by 1985 for each of the developed countries. The average figure attained by 1992, the year of the Rio Conference, however, was only 0.34 per cent, and again the 0.7 per cent goal was agreed upon in Rio. In spite of this, as Mostafa Tolba, chairman of the UN Commission on Sustainable Development, revealed in his interview in June 1997,[27] 'Today, five years later, the figure is 0.27 per cent. . . . This is really something that the international community should be ashamed of.' Such a trend in *quantity*, in itself, is deplorable. But what is more important in the case of Japan, in particular, is the *quality* of the ODA activities.[28] When the International NGO Forum was held in September 1989 in Washington, DC, simultaneously with the annual assembly meeting of the World Bank and IMF, a special resolution entitled 'An Appeal to the Japanese Government' was adopted by the forum, in which an admonitory opinion was expressed to the effect:

> In view of the fact that Japan's ODA is causing, in fact worsening, the social and environmental problems in developing countries, we propose that Japan shall:
>
> A. Introduce an environment impact assessment system for the projects of development assistance.
> B. Listen especially to the voices of local residents who are likely to be affected by the projects.
> C. Make public all the relevant information related to the assistance items.
> D. Abstain from financing environment-disruptive projects, such as giant-dam-cum irrigation projects and felling of tropical forests.
> E. Give priority to small-scale projects that can be practised with the initiative of local residents.
> F. Provide funds for the restoration of the environment damaged by past project operations.[29]

If we are to describe in detail concrete cases of Japan's ODA projects during the two decades prior to this forum meeting, we can easily be persuaded that the particular points made in this 'Appeal' had good enough grounds to be made to the responsible government offices in Japan.

KŌGAI OF US MILITARY BASES IN JAPAN

Japan has been an exporter of *kōgai*, but has also been a victim of its importation. This, in the form of various pollution events caused by the US military bases provided under the US–Japan Security Treaty dating back to 1951 and revised in 1960. Okinawa, where the last ditch battle was fought before Japan's surrender, was reverted to Japan only on 15 May 1972 and thus has remained for more than half a century as America's military bastion occupying 20 per cent of the main prefectural island where 75 per cent of the US exclusive facilities area in all of Japan are concentrated.

Kichi-kōgai, a brief expression in Japanese to connote 'pollution and damage occasioned by the existence of military bases,' has sprung up in a number of forms, as listed below, most frequently in the Okinawa district. They are in the nature of '*kōgai* imports' for Japan.

A. Sexual assaults by US military personnel, which became the focus of international attention after the rape of a 12-year-old Japanese girl on 4 September 1995:

> More Marines and sailors were tried for rapes, child molestations and other sexual assaults at bases in Japan than at any other US military site in the world. Computer records of Navy and Marine Corps cases since 1988 show that bases in Japan, which have a total of 41,008 personnel, held 169 courts martial for sexual assaults. That's 66% more cases than the number 2 location, San Diego, which, with 93,792 personnel, had 102 cases.[30]

B. Noise pollution caused by military planes all hours of the day and night:

> In particular, such damage is serious in the vicinity of Futenma Airport in Okinawa where the noise measures at 75 per cent of the measuring points habitually exceed the environmental standard. Also, the use of Atsuki Airport in a suburb of Tokyo for training of carrier-borne aircraft has been creating long-standing protests by citizens in the region.

C. Accidents occasioned by low-level training flights, including incidence of shock waves and broken windows:

> On 3 February 1998 a US military plane on a low-level training flight cut a cable car line at an Italian resort, killing 20 people inside the gondola. At that time, US President Clinton immediately expressed his regret and announced that US forces would suspend low-level training flights until the cause of the accident became clear. In Japan, however, such training flights have been routine over four routes, which have never been officially disclosed, but were identified thanks to the research effort of a private group which obtained the details through the US Freedom of Information Act. Training to slip through radar screens of enemies to destroy ground bases and facilities could lead to serious accidents on the ground. In 1991, for example, a training plane along what was called 'the red route' sliced through a forest wire across a ravine in the Nara Prefecture, and the route was changed in January 1992 to

218   *The Political Economy of the Environment*

'the orange route' running from the Wakayama to the Ehimé Prefecture. Based on the Japan–US States-of-Forces Agreement, the altitude limit set by the Civil Aeronautics Law of Japan does not apply to the flight training of US military aircraft in Japan.

D. Damage and pollution occasioned by target practice firing with full charge, which was conducted across and over the No. 104 prefectural highway in Okinawa, starting on 30 March 1973 and repeated 163 times by the end of November 1995. The highway was closed each time the practice was taking place, habitually going on for three days, firing upward of 600 rounds of 155-millimetre howitzer.

Protest against this firing practice having been so strong from the neighbourhood made up of residential houses, schools and hospitals that SACO (Special Action Committee on Facilities and Areas in Okinawa) voted in April 1996 to transfer the firing site to five other places on Japan's mainland. The autonomous bodies nominated for this transfer suggested, instead, suspension of such firing practice all together and would not agree to accepting the new assignment. Nevertheless, the transfer step was confirmed between Japan and the United States.

E. Contamination of water and soil, especially in Okinawa:

The contamination of water caused by sewerage disposal at American bases was confirmed 65 times by the Okinawa Prefectural Office since the reversion of 1972. Especially serious has been the leakage of oils and fats from the Kadena air-base into the river Hisha which is a source of drinking water for citizens. As for the soil contamination, an accidental emission of PCBs occurred in the Kadena air-base at least twice (in 1986 and 1988) but was kept secret until it was brought to light by the media in January 1994. A similar contamination was reported in connection with the Clark and Supick bases in the Philippines, where, contrary to a US government report, the post-reversion research by environmental groups verified a serious degree of contamination of the soil by various chemicals, thus delaying the diversion of end use for public purposes due to unexpectedly large expenditures for decontamination.

As can be seen in these instances of *kichi-kōgai*, one common characteristic which stands out is again the use of double standards which the '*kōgai* exporter,' that is the United States, does not seem to hesitate in applying. In this case, however, it is significant that the '*kōgai*-importer,' that is the Japanese government, too, has fallen in with the adoption of double standards by itself, as is illustrated by its suspension of the Civil Aeronautics Law for low-level training flights by US military aircraft. Such accommodation appears to be motivated by the basic predilection of the Japanese government to be faithful to the United States as a partner in the US–Japan Security Treaty. The implications of this treaty are far and wide in the current politico-economic controversy in Japan, but this is not the place to sidetrack ourselves for it.

WARMING OF THE EARTH

As I write this section on 'warming of the earth,' the Kyoto conference on climate change has just ended. It is just about 30 years since Ambassador Aström of Sweden spoke in the General Assembly of the United Nations (3 December 1968) explaining the resolution his government proposed on the matter of holding a world conference on the human environment and gave as a concrete example of environmental disruption: the possible danger of the so-called 'greenhouse effect' through 'the rise in the concentration of atmospheric carbon dioxide produced by the intensive combustion of fossil fuels during the past few decades.' Serious consideration of this question at the international level began after the June 1992 United Nations Conference on Environment and Development (UNCED), on which occasion the Framework Convention on Climate Change (FCCC) was completed for signature. Thus began a series of gatherings under numerous acronyms such as COP (the Conference of the Parties), AGBM (the Ad-hoc Group on the Berlin Mandate), IPCC (the Intergovernmental Panel on Climate Change), etc. The Kyoto conference was to be COP3.

The complexity of the problem was recognized by everyone concerned in the international negotiating process, as was expressed in the introductory chapter of the volume on 'Economic and Social Dimensions' of the IPCC's Second Assessment Report as follows:

> Climate change presents the analyst with a set of formidable complications: large uncertainties, the potential for irreversible damages or costs, a very long planning horizon, long time lags between emissions and effects, a global scope, wide regional variations, and multiple greenhouse gases of concern.[31]

It was only natural, as *The Economist* wrote immediately after the Kyoto meeting, that:

> Put diplomats from 159 countries, plus lobbyists with at least as many agenda – hidden or open – into one place, and the result is bound to be hypocrisy, gamesmanship and sheer nonsense. Such was the case during the negotiations in Kyoto to reduce greenhouse-gas emissions, which ended this week. It was not until well past the formal deadline, amid gestures and language that were scarcely diplomatic, that delegates were able to cut a deal. Too bad it will never fly.[32]

If we are to summarize what finally transpired in the Kyoto meeting, the following three propositions are probably sufficient, namely:

(A) The industrialized nations are to reduce their average national emissions over the period 2008–12 to about 5 per cent below 1990 levels.

(B) None of the developing countries is required to set any limits. But between their refusal to accept any arrangement for specific emissions reduction and the US insistence that any new commitments on its part should be linked to the developing countries accepting new obligations as well, a compromise was reached in the form spelled out under (A) above, which was interpreted to imply that the developed countries, because of their past historical record, are obligated to take the lead in reducing emissions now by a significant enough measure.

(C) If a more or less uniform reduction target of the level specified under (A) is to be observed among the developed countries, it is only reasonable that a realistic approach should be worked out in the form of adjustment devices for mitigating of impact depending on particular conditions in each country. Proposals such as international trading of emissions rights,[33] joint implementation[34] and 'netting'[35] are in this category of adjustment devices.

It is quite evident that these three propositions are mutually dependent on each other, giving priority consideration to the position of the developed countries.

How Japan comes out when the above conclusion is applied to her case may be cited here as a concrete example. Although the overall average ratio of reduction for the industrialized nations was to be 5.2 per cent, the US pledge was 7 per cent, the European Union's average 8 per cent and Japan's pledge 6 per cent. The explanations which the Japanese government gave on this matter after the Kyoto conference were:

(1) The initial plan of reduction was 2.5 per cent.
(2) Adding of three gases in the plan (HFCs or hydrofluorocarbons, PFCs or perfluorocarbons, and sulphurhex [sulphur-6]) will have a minus effect in reduction of 2.0 percentage points.
(3) Through the absorption of gases by forests, a 3.7 per cent reduction becomes possible.
(4) In order to reach the target of 6 per cent, a 1.8 per cent reduction can be made by trading in emission rights and joint implementation with other countries.

Concerned citizens in Japan, upon hearing this official convoluted explanation, were tempted to ask if the government was really serious on the feasibility of attaining the 6 per cent target in the reduction of greenhouse gases. Emissions of CO_2 in Japan in 1995 had already exceeded the 1990 level by 8 per cent. The initial plan of 2.5 per cent reduction itself was admittedly a window-dressing figure without material grounds. And in particular, given the strict conditions set down in the provisions of the Kyoto protocol, the government's estimate of the absorption capacity of the forests was decidedly excessive. In preparing legislation implementing this target programme of saving CO_2-emitting energy use, the Japanese government had to count on 20 additional nuclear power plants to be constructed anew within the next decade. There are 53 nuclear power plants currently operating in Japan, generating about 30 per cent of the country's total electric power, and even a single additional new construction is encountering strong objection by grass-root public opinion, as was exemplified by a referendum in Maki, Niigata Prefecture, which turned down the project proposed by the Tōhoku Electric Power Company in 1996. The idea of constructing 20 new nuclear power plants within the next decade was most unrealistic, indeed!

Compliance by the United States to attain the 7 per cent reduction target is probably more problematical than the case of Japan. With only 4 per cent of the world's population, the United States produces more than a fifth of the greenhouse gases and yet came to the Kyoto convention hall in December 1997 with an uncompromising insistence on 'a zero reduction.' Ten days later, it agreed to the 7 per cent reduction – a most surprising volte-face. On the surface it was surprising, but behind this move was its belief that it could ostensibly attain the target by exploiting a number of loopholes which were allowed for in the protocol in return for the US concessions to the EU, one such loophole being the scope for trading emission reduction units. As *The Economist* has written, however, that

> in fact, the deal is almost certain to crash and burn in the American Senate, which strongly opposes deep cuts in American emissions, and has said unanimously that it will not accept any arrangement under which the developing countries fail to do their bit in some way. It is virtually unimaginable that the necessary 66 out of 100 American senators will now ratify the treaty. And if America fails to ratify it, many of the other 34 countries required to make cuts – Russia, Eastern Europe and most of the OECD rich countries – will have an excuse to drop out too.[36]

On the other hand, President Clinton has wisely indicated that he would not send the protocol to the US Senate for ratification until more progress was made on a number of issues, such as the rules and institutions that will govern international trading of greenhouse gas emissions, etc.[37] This US case exemplifies fairly well the purport of the observation, made in *Environment*,[38] to the effect that 'as with negotiations in trade, arms control, and human rights, matters of international environmental negotiation are closely and dynamically coupled to domestic politics.'

The problem of climate change, however, does have a characteristic significantly different from such topics as arms control and trade in that the objects of negotiation are global phenomena often transcending the unitary control of single sovereign states. The best example is the damage caused by emissions from transnational air transport. Members of several non-governmental green groups, including ASEED, Japan Save the Ozone Network and Climate Train, urged the official negotiators to include air transport emissions in the Kyoto talks during a news conference on 5 December 1997; the negotiators' response was that 'they are not discussing the effects of jet fuel because it is too difficult to decide which country should be held responsible for emissions during international flights.'[39] According to Dietrich Brockhagen, a German scientist who advises the European Commission on the greenhouse effects of air transport emissions, CO_2 emissions from planes constitute now about 2.5 per cent of man-made CO_2 in the world today, but this is expected to grow to one-third of the total greenhouse gases by 2050.[40] The relative weight of this scale cannot be ignored in the long-range discussion on warming of the earth. It may be recalled that when Ambassador Aström of Sweden proposed holding an international conference on the environment in 1968, one of the points he emphasized in his warning was the greenhouse effect giving an illustration of 'a four-engined jet passenger aircraft in normal flight emitting about two and two-third tons of carbon dioxide and one and a third tons of water vapour every ten minutes.'

Similarly, CO_2 emissions by transnational automobile trips on the European continent constitute a factor that is not negligible. We can actually widen the scope of such type of transnational interdependence further to point to Japan's purchase of a large quantity of pulp wood from some Asian countries causing excessive deforestation there. In 1985, for example, out of the total world-traded volume of 14 million cubic metres of pulp wood, Japan imported 11.8 million. And the pace of deforestation has been especially serious in the Philippines, Thailand and Malaysia. If the CO_2-absorbing capacity of forests is to be counted, we cannot make light of the transnational sale of forest products which is causing deforestation in the exporting countries.

CHAPTER NINE

A new life-style sought

> If the earth must lose that great portion of the pleasantness which it owes to things that the unlimited increase of wealth and population would extirpate from it, for the mere purpose of enabling it to support a larger, but not a better or a happier population, I sincerely hope, for the sake of posterity, that they will be content to be stationary, long before necessity compels them to it.
>
> It is scarcely necessary to remark that a stationary condition of capital and population implies no stationary state of human improvement. There would be as much scope as ever for all kinds of mental culture, and moral and social progress; as much room for improving the Art of Living, and much more likelihood of its being improved, when minds ceased to be engrossed by the art of getting on.
>
> J.S. Mill, *Principle of Political Economy*, 1848, pp 750–1

Global concern over resource sustainability and a healthy environment calls for serious rethinking of life-style especially on the part of developed countries like Japan. It is generally agreed, as the Brundtland Report stated, that 'sustainable global development requires that those who are more affluent adopt life-styles within the planet's ecological means – in their use of energy, in particular.'[1] *Agenda 21, The United Nations Programme of Action from Rio*, also included in its 'Programme Areas' the topic of 'focusing on unsustainable patterns of production and consumption,' emphasizing that 'developed countries should take the lead in achieving sustainable consumption patterns.' It is clear enough that the era of mass production and mass consumption, which characterized, for example, the high growth period of Japan, should now be a thing of the past. But we ask now: what type of life-style is it that is now required? A general statement, which is often quoted from the Brundtland Report, is: 'Humanity has the ability to make development sustainable – to ensure that it meets the needs of the present without compromising the ability of future generations to meet their own needs.'[2] This requirement sounds straightforward enough. But the keyword in this sentence is the 'needs' which, it should be realized, is quite complex once we try to visualize its implication in a concrete situation. The reason for its complexity is that 'needs' in a specific situation of a particular country have to be grasped by applying an equation with at least four variables: (a) the relevant population structure, (b) the availability of physical resources, (c) technological possibilities, and (d) the structure of demand ranging from the material to the spiritual. Although global conditions of the spaceship earth are directly relevant in the formulation of such an equation, one can of course discuss the 'needs' problem with reference to a specific country. Thus, I shall do so with a major focus on Japan.

As for the relevant *population structure* of Japan, we have fairly accurate demographic estimates for the future. The total population as of 1998 was approximately 126 million, of which the 0–14 age cohort and the 65-or-over cohort were just about equal. But the forecast for the year 2025 is 120.9 million, of which the 0–14 age cohort will be 15.8 million while the 65-or-over cohort will be 33.1 million, occupying 27.4 per cent of the total. The implications of such demographic structure for social security problem, for example, will be of major concern in the near future. For one thing, many of the members of the 'old age' cohort (65 years old or over) are, even now, not only capable but also willing to continue to belong in the country's labour force and yet are at present 'kicked upstairs,' so to speak, into the category of 'retired men and women' and will have to be supported by the social security system in one way or another or else be dependent on their past savings. It is almost certain that the lengthening of the working age beyond 65 will become the order of the day sooner or later, but at the same time technological progress is working to press for the shortening of the life-time working hours of each person. Here is a dilemma to be solved.

Now, the second variable – the *availability of physical resources* for Japan in the near future – has to be a matter of conjecture. The Japan Research Institute for Energy Economics has attempted to forecast two sets of supply prospects of primary energy for 2025, one 'the standard case' and another 'the energy-saving case,' as tabulated in Table 9.1. The forecast figures with the 'energy-saving' scenario, implying 27.3 per cent saving in the total compared with the 'standard' scenario, are derived from deliberately ambitious saving assumptions in the technical coefficients of the end-use energy in both industrial and household sectors. The savings are contemplated mainly in the categories of fossil fuels to the extent of reducing their

	1965	1995	2025	
			'Standard'	'Energy-saving'
Coal	457	899	907	527
	(27.0)	(16.5)	(14.4)	(11.5)
Oil	1,007	3,036	2,657	2,064
	(59.6)	(55.8)	(42.1)	(45.0)
Natural gas	20	589	1,131	499
	(1.2)	(10.8)	(17.9)	(10.9)
Hydro-power	179	189	328	328
	(10.6)	(3.5)	(5.2)	(7.2)
Nuclear	0.1	655	1,137	1,021
	(0.0)	(12.0)	(18.0)	(22.3)
New Energies	26	71	153	149
	(1.5)	(1.3)	(2.4)	(3.2)
Total	1,689	5,439	6,313	4,588
	(100)	(100)	(100)	(100)

Table 9.1 *Supply prospects of primary energy for Japan* (unit: billion kcal)

Source: The Japan Research Institute for Energy Economics

Notes: 1. Figures in brackets are percentage shares of each energy source in the year indicated.
2. 1965 and 1995 figures are 'actual' ones for fiscal years (April of the year indicated to March end of the following year). 2025 figures are forecasts for the calendar year.

share in the total from 83.1 per cent to 67.4 per cent, thus letting the nuclear category absorb the balance of electric power needed in 2025. Electric power generated by atomic plants occupied 30.5 per cent of the total in 1995 and its percentage will have to rise to 41.5 per cent by 2025 under the 'energy-saving' scenario. This is hardly practicable, as we have discussed the question earlier in the section on 'warming of the earth.' At any rate, a wishful-thinking element is manifest in the current discussion on the availability of physical resources among the official and semi-official circles in Japan, and a more realistic approach is clearly needed for all types of resources, above all in the energy field.

As for the third variable, that is *technological possibilities*, at least we can be certain that they will advance in many directions in future. And as Wassily Leontief has written:

Beginning with the second half of the nineteenth century, science began to play a very great role in technological change and now, of course, science and technology really work in tandem. Technological development now very quickly incorporates and really uses the devices, the information and the recommendations that scientists advance. . . . [In this process] labor is fast losing its position as a principal factor of production. . . . I see no limit to scientific development and I think this means that there is no limit to technological change. . . . This means that the role of labor in society will continue to diminish.[3]

Leontief goes on to make a further significant point in connection with the role of 'educated labor' as follows:

Very often we accept the idea that uneducated labor will diminish in importance but assume that educated labor will not. Obviously, automation is one of the processes that will lead to the use of less educated labor but automation and now computerization are reducing the need for educated labor too. . . . Thus the popular idea that if you have an education you will have a job has a shaky basis. Education is required to help labor adjust to changing technological requirements, but less and less educated labor is needed as processes are automated and computerized. . . . Society now responds to this problem through income transfers: free education, free health-care and income to old people, and so on, but this is just the beginning.[4]

The implication of the present-day technological development, which is pursued by Leontief in the manner as quoted above, was actually foreseen, though in a slightly different context, by Karl Marx in the middle of the nineteenth century. We have already quoted from him in the first chapter a part of the relevant passage, but here is the paragraph I have in mind:

As large-scale industry advances, the creation of real wealth depends less on the labor time and the quantity of labor expended than on the power of the instrumentalities set in motion during the labor time. These instrumentalities, and their powerful effectiveness, are in no proportion to the immediate labor time which their production requires; their effectiveness rather depends on the attained level of science and technological progress; in other words, on the application of this science to production. . . . Human labor then no longer appears as enclosed in the process of production – man relates himself to the process of production as supervisor and regulator. . . . He stands outside of the process of production instead of being the principal agent in the process of production. . . . In this transformation, the great pillar of production and wealth is no longer the immediate labor performed by man himself, nor his labor time, but the appropriation of his own universal productivity, i.e., his know-ledge and his mastery of nature through his societal existence – in one word: the development of the societal individual. . . . As soon as human labor, in its immediate form, has ceased to be the great source of wealth, labor time will cease, and must of necessity cease, to be the measure of wealth, and the exchange value must of necessity cease to be the measure of use value. The mode of production which rests on the exchange value thus collapses.[5]

Now, the conclusion appears to be inescapable that with the progress of technological possibilities the role of capital goods or instrument-alities embodying scientific know-how of all kinds will increase enormously in the process of material production in particular but also in the fields of transportation, communications and service industries, minimizing more and more the dependence on manual labour and replacing the sophisticated exercise of human intellect by automated processes. Economists tend to characterize technological change in terms of the increasing productivity of labour, but that is a somewhat ambiguous notion. If labour inputs are nearly completely eliminated, labour productivity becomes nearly infinite. To think of technical change in terms of labour productivity is a kind of hold-over from earlier times when labour was clearly the principal factor of production. But as Leontief wrote, 'labor is fast losing its position as a principal factor of production'; and this trend poses a serious problem in the field of job requirement especially in the light of a greater demand for gainful employment among the 65-or-over cohort in the coming future.

In this connection, E.F. Schumacher's discussion on the 'total social time actually engaged in real production' in Great Britain being only 3.5 per cent at present is an eye-opener. He explains his calculation as follows:

We may ask how much of 'total social time' – that is to say, the time all of us have together, twenty-four hours a day each – is actually engaged in real production. Rather less than half of the total population of this country is, as they say, gainfully occupied, and about one-third of these are actual producers in agriculture, mining, construction, and indus-try. . . . In other words, rather less than one-sixth of the total population is engaged in actual production. . . . Now, a fully employed person, allow-ing for holidays, sickness, and other absence, spends about one-fifth of his total time on his job. It follows that the proportion of 'total social time' spent on actual production – in the narrow sense in which I am using the term – is, roughly, one-fifth of one-third of one-half, i.e., 3½ per cent. The other 96½ per cent of 'total social time' is spent in other ways, including sleeping, eating, watching television, doing jobs that are not *directly* productive, or just killing time more or less humanely. Although this bit of figuring work need not be taken too literally, it quite adequately serves to show what technology has enabled us to do.[6]

Schumacher makes a further point which is reminiscent of the ethos represented by men like John Ruskin and William Morris in nineteenth century England, as when he wrote that

the type of work which modern technology is most successful in reducing or even eliminating is skilful, productive work of human hands, in touch with real materials of one kind or another. . . . We may say, therefore, that modern technology has deprived man of the kind of work that he enjoys most, creative, useful work with hands and brains, and given him plenty of work of a fragmented kind, most of which he does not enjoy at all. . . . All this confirms our suspicion that modern technology, the way it has developed, is developing, and promises further to develop, is showing an increasingly inhuman face, and that we might do well to take stock and reconsider our goals.[7]

Such characterization of modern advancing technology by the three economists with markedly divergent ideological backgrounds, whom I have quoted above, confirm the need for care in incorporating the 'science and technology' variable unqualifiedly in the equation for defining the 'needs.' No doubt, technological possibilities are an ever-present conditioning factor that cannot be ignored, but with ambivalent significance. For one thing, there has been an undeniable evolution in the nature of science itself. At least in the latter half of the nineteenth century when such scientists as G.J. Mendel, R. Koch, W.K. Röntgen and Pierre Curie were making significant contributions in unravelling the mysteries of nature, it was commonly believed quite rightly that such endeavours would redound to man's welfare as unqualified benefit. It was also believed then that it was in the nature of science that it would keep on extending its frontiers by the internal logic of its own. As we moved into the twentieth century, however, science began to lose its virginal independence, as it were, in marrying itself into what was called 'the scientific-industrial revolution' and further becoming a useful instrument in the service for war purposes. At the same time, the scope of scientific research came to be broadened not only from the elucidation of the natural world into that of human psychological, mental and life mechanisms, but also to the type of research which harbours the possibility of unbalancing of the natural order of things. It has even come to be said, à la Clemenceau, that 'science is much too serious a thing to be left to the scientists.' Thus the ambivalent significance of science and technology as a factor in the assessment of the 'needs' we are called upon to define.

As for the fourth variable in the equation for the 'needs,' that is, *the structure of demand, from the material to the spiritual*, normative considerations are bound to enter and its delineation can be quite complex. Recommendation given in *Agenda 21, the United Nations Programme of Action from Rio*, is straightforward: it is stated in the form of 'changing consumption patterns' and the basis for action in this regard is explained in the following words:

> Special attention should be paid to the demand for natural resources generated by unsustainable consumption and to the efficient use of those resources consistent with the goal of minimizing depletion and reducing pollution. Although consumption patterns are very high in certain parts of the world, the basic consumer needs of a large section of humanity are not being met. This results in excessive demands and *unsustainable life-styles among the richer segments*, which place immense stress on the environment. The poorer segments, meanwhile, are unable to meet food, health-care, shelter and educational needs. Changing consumption patterns will require a multi-pronged strategy focusing on demand, meeting the basic needs of the poor, and reducing wastage and the use of finite resources in the production process.

However, the hierarchical structure of demand relevant to the definition of 'needs' has a range as 'wide as a church door' (Shakespeare). There are apt expressions in Japanese for this range, namely, from *i-shoku-jū* to *shin-zen-bi* (from 'food, clothing and shelter' to 'truth, virtue and beauty'). This concept of *shinzenbi* was not foreign to recent generations of economists because of the famous episode of Auguste Walras edifying his son Leon (1834–1910, a most outstanding general equilibrium theorist) with a catechism that 'truth is what one cannot but believe in; virtue is what one cannot but fulfil; and beauty is what one cannot but adore. Do not let your mind go astray into things other than truth, virtue and beauty.' This broad range from the basic *ishokujū* to the value-oriented *shinzenbi* could be filled with varied types of 'needs' or the objects of consumption, such as:

- compulsive ones more or less dictated by social or institutional conditions
- discretionary ones, although often influenced by convention or current fashion
- value-oriented ones, which are independent of market valuation

The first of these types can again be classified into three sub-types, namely: (1) 'the cost of life' type, (2) 'the institutionalization of waste' type, and (3) 'the interference of income' type.

We are all aware that, within our own consumption expenditures, there are certain items which fall into the category of necessary cost, which we try to minimize as best as we can. Heating cost in a cold country would be the simplest example. High commuting cost without compensating advantages in environmental amenities, as we observe in a dense urban sprawl such as Tokyo, is another. But there are more sophisticated examples of cost-type consumption which induce citizens to part with their 'money votes' on account of certain institutional and social developments. One example of this kind relates to the widespread use nowadays of expensive burglar alarms in America to cope with the mounting incidence of burglary in homes. A news item in *The New York Times*[8] reported such development with the headline, 'Booming burglar alarm industry finds that fear of crime pays.' Whatever the explanation for the prevalence of this type of crime, citizens are more or less forced to take measures of self-protection on an individualistic basis. And the cost of burglar alarms for homes is a part of consumer expenditure, and thus constitutes a component of GNP. But it is clearly what might be called a 'cost type consumption', or a part of 'the cost of life,' and no one would dispute the statement that the smaller it is, the better.

As for the institutionalization of waste, examples are legion as popularized by Vance Packard. What is at issue here is not a moralistic assessment of extravagance or dissipation. Economists *qua* economists have nothing to say to a person who knowingly wastes something for his or her enjoyment. But when waste is institutionalized in such a way that a less wasteful alternative, which may well be preferred by consumers, is deliberately withheld from the market, we are called upon to analyse the socio-economic mechanism which makes this possible, and to draw out the necessary implications for economic welfare. It was no other than Thorstein Veblen who wrote as early as in 1904:[9]

The absorption of goods and services by extra-industrial expenditures, expenditures which, from the standpoint of industry, are pure waste, would have to go on in an increasing volume. If the wasteful expenditure slackens, the logical outcome should be a considerable perturbation of business and industry, followed by depression.

It should be possible to minimize such 'wasteful expenditures' through institutional restructuring.

'The interference of income' also often constitutes a compulsive expenditure from the standpoint of consumers. The term was used originally by the late Schumpeter who, in the light mood of cocktail conversation, jestingly disparaged the profession of American lawyers on whose services he had to depend when he went through the red tape of naturalization. Keynes, no doubt, would have sympathized with him, for he, too, apparently felt the ubiquity of lawyers in the United States as essentially redundant. The story he told in his closing speech at the Bretton Woods Conference is quite well known.[10] The 'interference of income' phenomenon can be defined as the generation of income by otherwise dispensable services, which are made indispensable through built-in institutional arrangements in the society concerned. There is usually a historical background explaining why a particular service acquires built-in indispensability in a particular society, and there is, of course, no opprobrium implied in singling out a particular profession as 'income interfering.' As a matter of fact, an 'income interfering' profession in a particular society draws often the best of brains in that society and its members distinguish themselves as outstanding citizens of the community. If lawyers serve as an example of 'interference of income' in the United States, we may say that bankers and real estate dealers do so in Japan.

Especially in the postwar period in Japan, however, a new 'income-interfering' institution has arisen prominently in the form of tutoring schools which specialize in extracurricular cramming aimed at the success in entrance examinations to élite schools and universities. The *raison d'être* of such institutions is based on the fact that a ladder from the primary school level to the few select universities via appropriately placed middle and high schools is strictly controlled by highly competitive entrance examinations at each step. Success in climbing this ladder ensures a career position in first-rate enterprises. Thus, household expenditures in sending their children to these extracurricular institutions amount to a considerable size, regarded more as an investment for the family's generational success. Probably, foreign visitors to Japan will be surprised to hear that the average salary of teachers in these tutorial schools is more than twice that of university assistant professors of comparable age. Here is a typical case of 'interference of income.'

Coming to the problem of discretionary demand, we find that the scope it covers in a modern affluent society is actually excessively wide. By definition, it is generated by individual voluntary decisions, but as Fred Hirsch has written,

> as the level of average consumption rises, an increasing portion of consumption takes on a social as well as an individual aspect. That is to say, the satisfaction that individuals derive from goods and services depends in increasing measure not only on their own consumption but on consumption by others as well.[11]

Such transformation into a social aspect is irresistibly assisted in a market-oriented economy by profit-motivated enterprises, as John Ruskin observed already in the middle of the nineteenth century.[12] The mechanism in this process is to devise countless ways in which human wants might be created and defined as *needs*. As E.J. Mishan has written: 'The fashion industry is the prime example of an activity dedicated to using up resources, not to create satisfactions, but to create dissatisfactions with what people possess – in effect to create obsolescence in otherwise perfectly satisfactory goods.[13] However, even among the most highly regarded of modern economic theorists there has been a presumption of consumer sovereignty in the market economy. Such unidirectional flow of instruction from consumer to market to producer was denoted by J.K. Galbraith as 'the accepted sequence,' against which he advanced a hypothesis of 'the revised sequence,' stating that 'instead the producing firm reaches forward to control its markets and on beyond to manage the market behavior and shape the social attitude of those, ostensibly, that it serves . . . [this] may appropriately be called The Revised Sequence.'[14] It was Gavan McCormack, who, in his critical analysis of postwar Japanese society,[15] made a special reference to

> a soft and diffuse mode in which the key roles are played by advertising agencies or by television and supermarket moguls . . . with their assigned social role . . . [to] identify and manipulate human desires, turn them into

the taste for particular commodities, and rouse those desires to the point of constituting the markets that sustain growth and profit.

Referring to Japan, he concluded: 'In no country is social life so structured around the imperatives of economic life, or are people subjected to more pressure to consume. Nowhere is the emptiness of affluence more deeply felt.'[16]

It is clear enough that discretionary demand in a materially affluent country like Japan is likely to contain a great deal of objects of consumption which may be classified as 'needs' in the context of sustainable development requirements and yet dispensable if relevant institutional restructuring is accepted. It is pertinent to recall here Arnold Toynbee's incisive remark to the effect that 'a society that is declining materially may be ascending spiritually,'[17] and to consider now the value-oriented aspect of a new life-style which developed countries in particular are called upon to formulate in the light of global concern over resource sustainability and healthy environment.

The basic point in the formulation of a new life-style, I believe, is the distinction between ends and means in the conduct of our economic life. Keynes spoke as early as in 1930 that 'the day may not be all that far off when everybody would be rich. . . . [Then] we shall once more value ends above means and prefer the good to the useful.'[18] It is significant to note that 'ends' and 'the good' are of the real physical dimension and 'means' and the 'useful' could be of the market-value dimension. In Amartya Sen's formulation:

> The market values commodities, and our success in the material world is often judged by our opulence; but despite that, commodities are no more than means to other ends. Ultimately, the focus has to be on what life we lead and what we can or cannot do, can or cannot be. I have elsewhere called the various living conditions we can or cannot achieve, our 'functionings,' and our ability to achieve them, our 'capabilities.' The main point here is that the standard of living is really a matter of functionings and capabilities, and not a matter directly of opulence, commodities or utilities.[19]

It is evidently clear that a concept like life-style has to be discussed in real physical terms or in terms of what Sen calls 'functionings' and 'capabilities' which cannot be reduced to one-dimensional value-term magnitude. By way of summary we may say that the concept of life-style can be distinguished from one-dimensional valuation of the standard of living in terms, for example, of per capita GNP in four respects, namely:

A. Positive reckoning of objects of consumption or savouring which generally defy market valuation, such as 'the scarcest of our earthly resources, natural beauty' (E.J. Mishan) or the sea-shore – 'primeval meeting place of the element of earth and water' (Rachel Carson). In other words, reversing the erstwhile policy of 'sacrificing the garden space for the sake of expanding the kitchen.'

B. Possibility of reducing existing cost through institutional restructuring, such as in the case of commuting cost that can be reduced through a more rational city planning, or many types of 'institutionalized waste,' including in the case of Japan especially, the extracurricular cramming schools.

C. Possibility of reducing consumption expenditures in the category of discretionary demand; for example, by reversing the 'Revised Sequence' back to the 'Accepted Sequence' (J.K. Galbraith), or through prevailing upon 'the brutalizing cycles of contemporary commerce' (William Morris).

D. Deliberate act of retrogression in the currently attained productivity for the purpose of giving priority to certain normative considerations.

The first three points have already been dealt with and, I surmise, could be apprehended without repetition. But the last point, D, needs some explanation. Since it was Schumacher who was most articulate in proposing this point, I take here an example from him. Earlier we cited his calculation that the 'total social time actually engaged in real production' in Great Britain was only 3.5 per cent at present. His suggestion now is to increase it sixfold to about 20 per cent with the implication that present-day productivity would be brought down to one-sixth of its present level. His argument is that 'modern technology has deprived man of the kind of work that he enjoys most, creative, useful work with hands and brains, and given him plenty of work of a fragmented kind, most of which he does not enjoy at all.' But once his proposal is accepted, 'there would be six times as much time for any piece of work we chose to undertake – enough to make a really good job of it, to enjoy oneself, to produce real quality, even to make things beautiful. Think of the therapeutic value of real work; think of its educational value.'[20] Schumacher concedes that 'it might be said that this is a romantic, a utopian, vision.' But his basic point is that 'unless we develop a new life-style which is compatible with the real needs of human nature, with the health of living nature around us, and with the resource endowment of the world,'[21] modern industrial society is likely to run into serious trouble.

Schumacher may have deliberately overstated his case for polemic effect. But we can cite no small number of examples which are illustrative of the same principle. Earlier in the first chapter I gave a pedestrian example of supplying of chicken eggs in my household some 80 years ago, which, if repeated now, would require most certainly more than six times the cost in terms of the working hours needed compared with the expense in the market purchase of the same amount of eggs. But the satisfaction obtained in conducting the entire process of chicken-egg supply as 'closed-circle' within one's household has unique welfare significance of its own. In this connection, it is of crucial importance to point out a distinction between 'work' and 'labour,' a contrasting pair of words corresponding to 'ergazesthai' and 'ponein' in ancient Greece, the former being what free citizens did in hand-crafting a jar and the latter what slaves did in polishing the master's jar. Wage or salary is a reward for 'labour' which is the antithesis of 'leisure' whereas 'work' is indistinguishable from 'leisure.' Even in the production of the basic *i-shoku-jū* (food, clothing and shelter), there could be numerous instances of our performing 'work,' spending much greater number of hours willingly in making the product with our own hands than implied in the cost for the similar marketed products.

Let me give another example from my own personal experience. Before the war, I used to cross the Pacific Ocean by steamer, taking usually two weeks from Yokohama to the west coast of the United States. Now this crossing can be done by aeroplane in something like 15 hours, that is, an improvement in transport 'productivity' of more than 20 times. But it may be agreed that the time I spent on a steamer did not mean any loss for myself since, besides enjoying direct contact with the inimitable Pacific Ocean, I could occupy myself fully with my own work while at the same time broadening my world's view through intimate association with fellow travellers. Some people even succeed in winning a life-long partner in the course of such a steamer trip. This type of transport service in a regular form is no longer available, but I would say that the reversion to the old practice will be not only a positive contribution to welfare-oriented services but also a step, though small, in the direction of reducing greenhouse gases. But alas! it was well said when F.J. Fisher wrote that 'it is history's eternal verity that as society becomes more affluent it is no longer possible to have an access to those amenities which it used to enjoy when it was poorer.'[22]

The four considerations cited above, characterizing a new life-style which is now called for in the age of global concern over resource sustainability and a healthy environment make it clear that the philosophy of growthmanship, which keeps on asking constantly what a growth rate is likely to be for the country in question, is no longer relevant in assessing the overall condition of a country's economy. We actually do go back to John Stuart Mill, whose writing I quoted at the beginning of this chapter. Mill stated quite clearly that 'a stationary condition [zero growth] of capital and population implies no stationary state of human improvement. There would be as much scope as ever for all kinds of mental culture, and moral and social progress; as much room for improving the Art of Living.' We may say that a new life-style aims at improving the Art of Living, as Mill proposed, although reorientation of one's philosophy from that of growthmanship to that of a new life-style discussed above may require a bold step like crossing the Rubicon. But as Walter Bagehot once remarked, 'one of the greatest pains to human nature is the pain of a new idea.' It seems that the time has come that now we have to expect the painful experience from the establishment circles of a country like Japan.

Notes

Chapter One   Methodological introduction

1. Adam Smith, *The Wealth of Nations*, ed. Edwin Cannan, 1904, Methuen and Co. Ltd, vol 1, p 30.
2. Paul A. Samuelson and William D. Nordhaus, *Economics*, 15th edn, McGraw-Hill, Inc., 1995, Ch. 19: Natural Resources and Environmental Economics.
3. Paul A. Samuelson and William D. Nordhaus, *Economics*, 15th edn, McGraw-Hill, Inc., 1995, pp 341–2.
4. R.F. Harrod, *The Life of John Maynard Keynes*, London, Macmillan, 1951, p 563.
5. The so-called 'Hirsch Incident' illustrates the nature of the dilemma which is characteristic of such development. Mr Donald Hirsch, a scientist engineer versed in the chloride method of producing titanium dioxide, was employed by the Du Pont Company, but apparently felt somewhat frustrated in the gigantic corporate machine of the company and responded to a help-wanted ad in a newspaper. In October 1962 he decided to move to American Potash and Chemical Company, a much smaller company in the western part of the United States. Before he joined this company, he was asked to sign an agreement, apparently a routine practice nowadays, pledging that he would 'not disclose to the company nor use, either during the interview or in the course of any possible employment with the company, any information that he knows to be the proprietary information, data, development, or trade secret of a third party.' Both Mr Hirsch and American Potash and Chemical were quite careful in this regard, but the Du Pont immediately went to court and obtained a restraining order blocking Mr Hirsch from working for American Potash on the ground that it would be 'impossible' for him to serve in his new job 'without divulging or using or being called upon to divulge or make use of his knowledge or the trade secrets and confidential information of the plaintiff.'

   This incident is eloquent enough in illustrating the essential difficulty of internalizing science or scientists within the orbit of private enterprise. But the title of the article which told this story (*Fortune*, July 1964, written by William Bowen) is actually more expressive and meaningful. It was: 'Who Owns What's in Your Head?'

6. See, for example, Kenneth E. Boulding, 'The Economics of the Coming Spaceship Earth,' *Environmental Quality in the Growing Economy*, Henry Jarrett (ed.), Johns Hopkins Press, 1966, reprinted in his *Collected Papers*, vol 2, Colorado Associated University Press, Boulder, CO, 1971, pp 383–94.
7. Kenneth E. Boulding, 'Is Scarcity Dead?' *The Public Interest*, 5 (Fall, 1966); reprinted in his *Collected Papers*, vol 3, pp 319–20.
8. Barry Commoner, *The Closing Circle*, 1971, Alfred A. Knopf, p 65.
9. Karl Marx, *Grundrisse der Kritik der Politischen Ökonomie*, Berlin, Dietz Verlag, 1953, pp 592, 593, translated into English by Herbert Marcuse in his *One Dimensional Man*, Routledge & Kegan Paul Ltd, London, 1964, pp 35–6.
10. Model, Roland & Stone, *The Scientific-Industrial Revolution*, 1957, [?], (known to have been written by Paul M. Sweezy).
11. *The New Palgrave Dictionary of Economics*, Macmillan, 1987, vol 4, p 393.
12. K. William Kapp, *The Social Costs of Private Enterprise*, Harvard University Press, 1950, p 13.
13. Adam Smith, *The Wealth of Nations*, vol II, Methuen & Co. Ltd, London, 1922, p 214.
14. K. William Kapp, *The Social Cost of Private Enterprise*, Harvard University Press, 1950, p 29.
15. S. de Sismondi, *Nouveaux Principes d'Economie Politique*, 1819, vol II, p 220.
16. Justus von Liebig, *Die Chemie in ihrer Anwendung auf Agricultur und Physiologie*, Brunswick, 1862.
17. Karl Marx, *Capital*, vol I, pp 555–6.
18. F. Engels, *The Condition of the Working Class in England in 1844*, George Allen & Unwin, 1920.
19. F. Engels, *The Condition of the Working Class in England in 1844*, George Allen & Unwin, 1920, p 64.
20. Fiona MacCarthy, *William Morris – A Life for Our Time*, Faber & Faber, 1994, p 477.
21. Fiona MacCarthy, *William Morris – A Life for Our Time*, Faber & Faber, 1994, p 348.
22. Fiona MacCarthy, *William Morris – A Life for Our Time*, Faber & Faber, 1994, p 70.
23. John Ruskin, *The Stones of Venice*, vol II, Penguin Classics p 37.
24. John Ruskin, *Unto This Last*, London: Smith, Elder & Co. 1862, Essay One, pp 3–4.
25. Quoted by James Clark Sherburne, *John Ruskin, or the Ambiguities of Abundance: A Study in Social and Economic Criticism*, Harvard University Press, 1972, p 350, footnote 31.
26. John Ruskin, *The Two Paths*, Smith, Elder and Co., London, 1859, pp 132–3.

27. Thorstein Veblen, *The Theory of Business Enterprise*, Mentor Book, 1904, pp 120–1.
28. Michael Schneider, *J.A. Hobson*, Macmillan, 1996, p 34.
29. Michael Schnieder, *J.A. Hobson*, Macmillan, 1996, p 119.
30. A.C. Pigou, *Wealth and Welfare*, Macmillan, 1912.
31. A.C. Pigou, *The Economics of Welfare*, 4th edn, Macmillan, 1950, p 134. Italics by Tsuru. It is to be noted that Pigou excluded 'psychical consequences' on the ground that his 'principal objective was the national dividend and changes in it' as he defined them.
32. A.C, Pigou, The Economics of Welfare, 4th edn, Macmillan, 1950, pp 134–5.
33. A.C. Pigou, *Socialism versus Capitalism*, Macmillan 1947, pp 43, 45.
34. Published in Tübingen in 1965.
35. K.W. Kapp, 'On the Nature and Significance of Social Costs,' 1969.
36. See R. Hueting, *New Scarcity and Economic Growth – More Welfare Through Less Production?*, translated by Trevor Preston, North-Holland Publishing Company, 1980. The page citations for quotations below are from this book.
37. Ignacy Sachs, *Transition Strategies towards the 21st Century*, Interest Publication, New Delhi, India, 1993, Foreword by M. Strong.
38. Ignacy Sachs, *Transition Strategies towards the 21st Century*, Interest Publications, New Delhi, India, 1993, second paragraph of Foreword.
39. J.M. Keynes, 'Economic Possibilities for Our Grandchildren,' *Essays in Persuasion*, Macmillan, 1931, pp 369, 372.
40. I prefer to use the word 'disruption' rather than 'deterioration' for the reason that the latter seems to have an intransitive tone, whereas the former is derived from a transitive verb. I am of the opinion that the significant aspect of the environmental problems is man-made, not natural but social in origin.
41. *Gendai Shihonshugi to Kōgai* (Present-day Capitalism and Kōgai), Iwanami, 1968, pp 14–15.
42. Barry Commoner, *The Closing Circle*, 1971, Alfred A. Knopf, p 268.

Chapter Two   Historical analysis – the prewar period

1. During the 1870s, about a decade after the Restoration year of 1868, domestically produced cotton yarns were priced at around 40 yen per *kan* (600 grams), whereas the price of imported yarns was 29.6 yen in 1874 and it declined steadily to 25.4 yen by 1879. (Cf. *Mentō Kyōshin Kai Hōkoku* [Reports of the Cotton–Sugar Promotion Concourse] No. 2, 1880, p 12)
2. J.A. Schumpeter, *Business Cycles*, 1939, p 266.
3. See Nobuko Iijima (ed), *Pollution Japan: Historical Chronology*, Asahi Evening News, 1979.
4. Article III of the 'Regulation.' Incidentally, the term *kōgai* came to be used for the first time by the Osaka Prefectural Ordinance in 1880. See

Yasunori Oda, *Kindai Nihon no Kōgai Mondai (Kōgai* Problems in Modern Japan), Sekai Shiso Sha, 1983.

5. Kujūro Fujiwara, *Osaka o Kurushimeta Baien Mondai* (The Smoke Problem – Osaka's Headache), no. 2, *Dai-Osaka*, vol 4, no. 1, November 1928.
6. Quoted from Goto's writing *Shokugyō Eisei Hō* (Public Health Legislation for Workplaces) in Namiko Kamioka (ed.), *Shiryō Kindai Nihon no Kōgai* (Documents and Data on Kōgai in Modern Japan), Shin-Jinbutsu Ohraisha, 1971, p 16.
7. See Hitoshi Koyama (ed.), *Senzen-Shōwa-ki Osaka no Kōgai Mondai Shiryō* (Documents and Data on *Kōgai*-Problems during the Prewar Showa Period), Kansai University Research Institute of Economics and Politics, *Chōsa to Shiryō*, No. 16, 1973, pp 4–5.
8. See Hitoshi Koyama, *Nishiyodogawa Kōgai – Taiki Osen no Higai to Rekishi* (Kōgai in Nishiyodogawa District – Damages and History of Air Pollution), Toho Shuppan, 1988, pp 22–5.
9. Cf. in particular Jun Ui (ed.), *Industrial Pollution in Japan*, United Nations University Press, 1992, and also Masuro Sugai, 'The Development of the Japanese Copper Industry and Environmental Destruction, 1870–', An Essay presented at the Third International Mining History Conference and Symposium on the Preservation of Historic Mining Sites, 6–10 June, 1994, at the Colorado School of Mines, Golden, CO, USA.
10. Cf. William L. Langer, *The Diplomacy of Imperialism, 1890–1902*, in two volumes, Alfred A. Knopf, 1935.
11. Reported in *Jiji Shimpō*, 29 July 1884.
12. See Ken'ichi Miyamoto and others, 'Symposium on the History of *Kōgai* in Japan,' *Sekai*, January 1971, p 76. For an episodic account with full details on the moving of the smelting plant to Shizakajima, the two-volume publication *Shizakajima* by Shoji Kimoto, Kōdansha 1971, is recommended.
13. Cf. Ken'ichi Miyamoto, 'Nihon *Kōgai* no Rekishi' (The History of *Kōgai* in Japan), *Asahi Journal*, 21 October 1970, p 5.
14. Shōji Kimoto, *Asahi Journal*, vol I, pp 88–9.
15. *Asahi Journal*, vol I, p 281.
16. By succeeding in this move, a large number of farmers were deprived of their voting rights which were based on a certain sum of land tax payment.
17. Percentage shares in the national total of copper output by each of the big four in 1910 and 1915 were as follows:

	1910	1915
Ashio	14.3	15.6
Besshi	13.3	10.5
Kosaka	12.8	12.3
Hitachi	9.8	16.0

Source: Masuro Sugai, 'The Development of the Copper Industry and Environmental Destruction, 1870s –' a paper presented for the Third International History Conference and Symposium on the Preservation of Historic Mining Sites, 6–10 June 1994, p 14.

18. Quoted in Tadanari Chiba, 'Hitachi-kōzan Engai Mondai Mukashiba-nashi ni tsuite' (Reminiscences on the Smoke Damage Problem of the Hitachi Mine), in Namiko Kamioka, *Shiryō Kindai Nihon no Kōgai*, 1971, p 214.

19. W.W. Rostow defined the concept of 'reactive nationalism' as 'reacting against intrusion from more advanced countries,' commenting further that 'in Japan, it was the demonstration effect not of high profits or manufactured consumer goods, but of the Opium War in China in the early 1840s and Commodore Perry's seven black ships in the decade later that cast the die for modernization.' (W.W. Rostow, *The Stages of Economic Growth*, Cambridge and New York, 1960, p 26.)

20. The Tripartite Intervention (16 April 1895) on the terms of peace between Japan and China had aroused a widespread sense of vendetta against Russia in any case.

21. *The Eugenics Review*, April 1937, p 16.

22. Cf. S. Kuznets and R. Goldsmith, *Income and Wealth of the United States: Trends and Structure*, 1952, p 55.

23. Lawrence Klein and Kazushi Ohkawa, *Economic Growth: The Japanese Experience Since the Meiji Era*, Richard D. Irwin, Inc., 1968, p 386.

24. Kazushi Ohkawa and Henry Rosovsky, *Japanese Economic Growth*, Stanford and Oxford, 1973, p 28.

25. Other than the three major copper mine cases dealt with in this chapter, we may single out a few important *kōgai* instances in the period between 1880s and 1920s out of a large number which are closely catalogued by Nobuko Iijima in her *Pollution Japan: Historical Chronology*, Asahi Evening News, 1979.

· (1) One of the major *kōgai* instances of the postwar period was the cadmium poisoning caused by a zinc-refining plant in the place called Kamioka. But the protest movement against the mining there started already in 1886 and became widespread especially during 1913 to 1916 over the damages caused to farm products, livestock and forest areas. The cadmium poisoning-effect began to be noticed in June 1922.

· (2) A uniquely Japanese seasoning called 'ajinomoto,' monosodium glutamate, which began to be produced by Suzuki Chemicals in the Kanagawa Prefecture in 1908, caused all kinds of pollution affecting farm and marine products through discharge of hydrochloric acid gas and starch-contaminated waste water. Protests occurred almost every year until 1927 when the company finally installed improved equipment to arrest the harmful effects of toxic gases. Meanwhile, annual indemnification was done in the form of 'sympathy payments'.

· (3) Frequent disputes which occurred over the cement dust damage caused by the Asano Cement Company from 1911 onwards are reveal-ing because the authorities sided with the Company against the claim of victim citizens citing the repercussions of WWI and then later the vital need of cement for reconstruction in the aftermath of the Great Kanto

Earthquake of 1923. In the course of these disputes also, proposals were made in vain for the transfer of location of the plant and also a temporary cessation of plant operation in the 'season of strong southerly wind.'

(4) It may be worth recording that in December 1932 Masafusa Adachi, head of the health department of the Osaka City office, advocated to make Osaka 'A Shining *Hakuto*' (smokeless city) by saying that 'it is a momentous project to place Osaka in the ranks of the cultured European metropolises as a *Hakuto*.' The term '*Hakuto*' became virtually the password of the day.

Chapter Three   Historical analysis – the postwar period I

1. For a more detailed discussion of the subject: cf. Shigeto Tsuru, *Japan's Capitalism – Creative Defeat and Beyond*, Cambridge University Press, 1993, pp 1–65.
2. Quoted in Jerome B. Cohen, *Japan's Economy in War and Reconstruction* (University of Minnesota Press, 1949, p 427) from Pauley's Report on Japanese Reparations, November 1945 to April 1946.
3. Cf. Shigeto Tsuru, *Japan's Capitalism – Creative Defeat and Beyond*, Cambridge University Press, 1993, pp 40–1. George Kennan, then the head of Planning Staff of the Secretary of State Marshall, wrote in his *Memoirs* much later that: 'The ideological concepts on which these antizaibatsu measures rested bore so close a resemblance to Soviet views about the evils of capitalist monopolies that the measures could only have been eminently agreeable to anyone interested in the future communization of Japan.' (G. Kennan, *Memoires*, Little, Brown, Boston, 1967, p 409.)
4. Reprinted in *A Key to Japan's Recovery*, edited by Japan Resources Association, 1986 p 75.
5. The memorandum was issued on 6 June 1950. Cf. F.S. Dunn, *Peace-Making and the Settlement with Japan*, Princeton: Princeton University Press, 1963, pp 99–102 for more detail.
6. Kenneth E. Boulding in his address to a Foreign Relations Dinner held at the International House of Japan on 30 January 1984, reproduced in *IHJ Bulletin*, vol 4, no. 2, Spring 1984, p 6.
7. Kakuei Tanaka, *Nihon Rettō Kaizō Ron* (Proposal for Remodelling of the Japanese Archipelago), Tokyo, Nikkan Kōgyō Shimbun-sha, 1972, p 218.
8. *Nihon Rettō Kaizō Ron*, p 124, p 115. The environmental consequences of the proposal seemed to be beyond Tanaka's imagination!
9. The population of the three largest urban areas – Tokyo, Osaka and Nagoya – increased by more than 10 million in 10 years from 1960 to 1970, from 37,380,000 to 48,260,000.
10. The number of passenger cars owned by the public per 1,000 population in Japan increased from 3.4 in 1959 to 154.0 in 1975, and already by

1969 the number of automobiles of all kinds per 1,000 hectares of flat land space was more than 1,300 in Japan, while in West Germany, the next congested country, it was 750.

11. Akitaro Kondo, *Aozora o Kaese* (Return the Blue Sky to Us), Fūbaisha, 1967, p 17.

12. Since, however, a rider to a legislation has no force of law in the legislative practice of Japan, one could not expect very much to materialize out of this clause.

13. Cf. Shigeto Tsuru (ed.), *Proceedings of International Symposium on Environmental Disruption – A Challenge to Social Scientists*, Asahi Evening News, 1970.

Chapter Four   Historical analysis – the postwar period II

1. A detailed account in English on the Yokkaichi pollution problem is given in Norie Huddle and Michael Reich with Nahum Stiskin, *Island of Dreams*: Environmental Crisis in Japan, Autumn Press, New York and Tokyo, 1975.

2. Eiji Ono, *Yokkaichi Kōgai 10–nen no Kiroku* (Yokkaichi Pollutions Recorded during the Past Ten Years), Keisō Shobō, 1971, pp 25– 8.

3. *Yokkaichi Kōgai 10–nen no Kiroku*, Keisō Shobō, 1971, pp 241–2.

4. M. Tajiri, *Rashinban no Nai Ayumi* (My Work of Life without a Compass), Tōken Shuppan, 1985, p 108.

5. See in particular M. Tajiri, *Yokkaichi, Shi no Umi to Tatakau* (Yokkaichi, Fighting in the Sea of Death), Iwanami, 1972.

6. M. Tajiri, *Rashinban no Nai Ayumi*, Tōken Shuppan, 1985, p 135.

7. *Rashinban no Nai Ayumi*, p 143. See also Hiroshi Itakura, 'Yokkaichi Ishihara Sangyō Jiken Yūzai Hanketsu o Megutte' (The Decision on the Yokkaichi Ishihara Industry Case), *Kōgai Kenkyū* Summer 1980, vol 10, no. 1, pp 49–58.

8. See, in particular, Yoshiro Sawai, *Kusai Sakana to Zensoku no Shōmon* (Testimonies on Stench Fish and Asthma), Haru Shobō, 1984, p 16.

9. For a detailed account in English on the Minamata disease case, see in particular Jun Ui (ed.), *Industrial Pollution in Japan*, United Nations University Press, 1992, pp 103–32. In Japanese, the latest, comprehensive, and most readable, account of the Minamata case is *Minamata byō Saiban* (The Minamata Disease Litigation), edited by the National Liaison Council for the Minamata Disease Victims and the Legal Defense Groups, Kamogawa Shuppan, 1997, which contains an incisive preface by Ken'ichi Miyamoto and also a detailed chronology and some 100 titles of reference publications.

10. The company changed its name a number of times since its inception. Hereafter we shall refer to it by the present name which is simply 'Chisso.'

11. Probably the best detailed discussion in Japanese of the technological advances made by Chisso can be found in Takashi Iijima, *Gijutsu no*

246 *The Political Economy of the Environment*

Mokushiroku (Revelation of Technology), Gijutsu to Ningen K.K., 1996.

12. They all had common symptoms such as severe convulsion, intermittent loss of consciousness, repeated lapses into crazed mental states, followed finally by permanent coma. Then, after the onset of a very high fever, they would die.

13. Hideyuki Kawana, *Dokument Nihon no Kōgai*, vol 1, Ryokufū-Shuppan, 1987, p 33.

14. See *Asahi Shimbun*, 26 April 1995.

15. The details given in this review on the *Asahi Shimbun* case are owed to an article by Tetsuji Shibata in *Asahi Shimbun Chōken Shitsu-hō* (Research Institute Report of the Asahi), vol 104, November 1993.

16. Article IV of the Food Sanitation Act reads in its second paragraph: 'The food, additionals, apparatus or container-package for which the standards of indication have been provided for under the provision of the preceding paragraph, shall not be sold, displayed to be offered for sale, nor be used for business, unless they bear the indication in conformity with the standards thereof.'

17. *Minamata-byō Saiban*, p 194. (See Note 9.)

18. For those readers who are able to make use of the references in Japanese, it is suggested that the following two items are particularly useful detailed accounts on the question of the responsibility of the administrative offices on the Minamata disease: Jun'ichi Fukai, 'Minamata-byō Mondai no Gyōsei Sekinin' (Administrative Responsibility in the Minamata Disease Problem), which is Ch 3 (pp 98–188) of Ken'ichi Miyamoto (ed.), *Kōgai Toshi no Saisei – Minamata* (Rebirth of Kōgai City Minamata), Chikuma Shobō, 1977, and Akio Manaki, Toshihiko Takenaka and Osamu Kato, 'Minamata-byō niokeru Kuni no Sekinin' (Responsibility of the State in the Minamata Disease) in The National Liason Council for the Kōgai Defense Groups (ed.), *Kōgai to Kuni no Sekinin* (Kōgai and the Responsibility of the State), Nihon Hyōron Sha, 1982, pp 157–84.

19. *Minamata-byō Saiban* p 82.

20. *Minamata-byō Saiban* p 20.

21. It may be recalled that we made reference to the testimony by Dr Hosokawa, head of the factory hospital of Chisso, in the bedside questioning by the court in July 1970, which provided an important clue for the court argument in favour of the disease victims. This was during the first-series law-suit.

22. Which dealt with the appealed case for the third-series law-suit and which affirmed the responsibility of the administration.

23. Earlier in 1990, both the Tokyo District Court and the Kyoto District Court had advised the 'amicable settlement' step at the time of their respective local decision on the Minamata disease case. However, the administration turned down the advice by the Cabinet decision on 29 October 1990.

24. Laying the responsibility on 'experts' is not quite fair since there are all kinds of 'experts' and those who sit on government committees are generally chosen on the basis of their known inclination to agree with the basic position of the government then in power. Still, such reference to the role of 'experts' prompted Dr Masazumi Harada, a consistent defender of the Minamata disease patients, to write a book with the title of *Who are the Ones to be Adjudged?* (*Sabakareru no wa Tare ka*), Seishoku Shobō, 1995, in which he wrote: 'The Minamata disease is a kind of mirror which brings out in reflection not only the responsibilities of the offending firm and the regulating administration but also that of experts including myself, which is serious enough.' (p 248) The book itself is one of the best objective summaries of the entire incident.

25. *The 1997 Environment White Paper*, the volume on details, edited by the Environment Agency, June 1997, p 288.

26. Manabu Kato, 'Kisha no Me' in *Mainichi Shimbun*, 2 September 1997.

27. For detailed accounts of these research visits abroad, the following publications in Japanese are suggested: Shigeto Tsuru (ed.), *Genchi ni Miru Sekai no Kōgai* (*Kōgai* in the World as Directly Observed), Chūnichi-Shimbun Tokyo Honsha, 1975, and Shigeto Tsuru (ed.), *Sekai no Kōgai Chizu* (*Kōgai* Map of the World), in two volumes, Iwanami Shoten, 1977.

28. Hideyuki Kawana, *Dokument Nihon Kōgai*, Vol 1, Ryokufū-Shuppan, 1987, p 84.

29. We say this because his final comment at the press conference was that 'Let the court judgement be as it is. But I say with Galileo that the earth still goes around the sun.' (See H. Kawana, *Dokument Nihon no Kōgai*, Vol 1, Ryokufū-Shuppan, 1987, p 314.)

30. See, for example: Tomiya Nitta's article in *Kōzan Chishitsu* (Geology of Mines), vol 22, no. 2, 1972.

31. For a technically detailed account of the post-trial steps taken in connection with the cadmium poisoning by the Kamioka Mine, see in particular: Akio Hata, *Itai Itai Byō* (the *Itai-Itai* Disease), Jikkyō Shuppan, 1994.

32. For a technically detailed discussion on this litigation, cf. Tsumoru Ushiyama, *Kōgai Saiban no Tenkai to Hōriron* (Series of *Kōgai* Litigations and the Legal Theory), Nihon Hyōron-sha, 1976, pp 169–98. This is also a useful reference for other *kōgai* trials.

33. The flight frequency of jet planes at the Osaka International Airport, as reported by the Ministry of Transportation, was as follows:

	Jet plane flights	The ratio (%) to the total flights at the airport
1964	1,540	2.1
1965	12,778	15.8
1966	26,746	30.8
1967	34,702	36.7

Cf. Hideyuki Kawana, *Document Nihon no Kōgai*, vol 8, Ryokufū Shuppan, 1993, p 25.

248   *The Political Economy of the Environment*

34. *Hanrei Roppō* (The Statute Book with Citations of Precedents), Yūhikaku, 1991, p 18.
35. In the definition given by Allen V. Kneese, 'the idea of common property resource (which should not be confused with a similar legal terminology) refers to those valuable attributes of the natural world which cannot be, or can be only imperfectly, reduced to individual ownership and therefore do not enter properly into the process of market exchange. Notable among such resources are the air mantle, our water bodies, complex ecological systems, and certain aspects of space.' Shigeto Tsuru, *A Challenge to Social Scientists, Proceedings of International Symposium: Environmental Disruption*, Asahi Evening News, 1970, p 294.

Chapter Five   From Stockholm (1972) to Rio (1992)

1. When a single exchange rate of 360 yen to $1 was unilaterally determined by the occupation authorities in April 1949, the Japanese economy was definitely in the convalescent stage, not yet able to manifest its full potential capacity. Thus it was felt that to decide on a single exchange rate for Japan in such circumstances – the rate which would *not* shut out a major part of her exports in foreign markets – was quite similar to the case of deciding on the concessional handicap for a convalescent golfer who had been absent from the course for a number of years due to sickness. If his handicap was, let us say, 18 before he fell ill, his friends might, after discussion, permit him to play with the handicap of 24 at the resumption of play. But, even with this special allowance, he may have difficulty in competing with his friends. Japan at the beginning of 1949 was in a condition similar to this convalescent golfer. But just as he might recover his pre-illness skill and thus be at an advantage as his recovery progresses, the dynamic process of recuperation enabled the Japanese economy before long to take advantage of the concessional exchange rate determined early in the process of recovery.
2. In the section on 'Earlier Lessons Forgotten.'
3. Compared with the price at the end of 1970, which was $1.8 per barrel, this meant a rise of 6.47 times.
4. We usually understand the expression 'the price revolution' to be referring to the inordinate rise of prices in European countries during the early sixteenth century and the first half of the seventeenth. It was chiefly caused by the great increase in the money supply due to the explosive rise in silver production after the conquests of Mexico and Peru.
5. *World Bank Atlas*, published by the International Bank for Reconstruction and Development, 1972, recorded the annual growth rate of population during the 1960s in most of the developing countries as ranging from 2.3 per cent for India to 2.5 per cent for Egypt and to 2.9 per cent for Brazil, and so on.

6. Cf. in particular, Wilfred Beckerman, 'Economists, Scientists, and Environmental Catastrophe,' *Oxford Economic Papers*, November 1972, pp 327–44. Also see, Gunnar Myrdal, *Against the Stream – Critical Essays in Economics*, 1975, New York: Vintage Books, pp 204–5.
7. Julian L. Simon and Herman Kahn (ed.), *The Resourceful Earth*, Basil Blackwell, 1984, p 34.
8. Cf. *The New York Times*, 18 June 1972, Weekly Review Section; p 5.
9. *New Statesman*, 16 June 1972, p 818.
10. Among the participants were Lady Jackson, who acted as chairperson, Gamani Corea, Secretary General of UNCTAD, Maurice Strong, Executive Director of UNEP, Johann Galtung and Ignacy Sachs, who cooperated in drafting the final report, and such other experts as W. Leontief, Marc Nerfin, J. Pajestka, Samir Amin, E. Iglesias, K. Kassas, Mahbub Ul-Haq, etc. For a detailed account of the discussions in the meeting, see Shigeto Tsuru, 'Kokuren Cocoyoc-Kaigi,' *Kōgai Kenkyū*, vol 4, no. 3, Winter 1975, pp 63–8.
11. Lester R. Brown, *et al.*, *State of the World 1984*, A Worldwatch Institute Report on Progress toward a Sustainable Society, W.W. Norton & Co., 1984, p xv.
12. *State of the World 1984*, p 2.
13. Julian L. Simon and Herman Kahn (ed.), *The Resourceful Earth: A Response to Global 2000*, Basil Blackwell, 1984, pp 1–2.
14. *The Resourceful Earth: A Response to Global 2000*, p 566.
15. *Environmental Policies in Japan*, Organization for Economic Co-operation and Development, Paris, 1977.
16. Quotations and pagings are from *Environmental Policies in Japan*.
17. In particular, Buichi Oishi who served from July 1971 to August 1972.
18. In the original Basic Law for Environmental Pollution Control of 1967, there was a qualifying phrase to the purpose of 'conserving of the living environment,' saying that 'harmony with sound economic development should be considered.' This phrase was deleted at the time of the 1970 'Kōgai Diet' and Ishihara commented on this as 'a kind of witch-hunting action' in his television broadcast on 21 October 1977. It was probably a novelist's way of expressing dissatisfaction with the pressure of public opinion. See H. Kawana, *Document Nihon no Kōgai*, vol 11, p 63.
19. The so-called 'Richey Report' was made public in February 1949 and served as a useful guide for the subsequent development of national parks in Japan. For details on the 'Richey Report,' see *Shizen Hogo Gyōsei no Ayumi* (The Administration of Conservation of Nature Reviewed), Environment Agency, 1981, pp 98–100.
20. Buichi Oishi, *Ozé made no Michi Ichiro to Gunshuku o Motomete* (The Road to Ozé and in Search of Arms Reduction), Sankei Shuppan, 1982.
21. Hiroshi Takasaki and Keikichi Kihara (ed.), *Irihamaken*, Japan Publishers, 1977, p 4.

22. Rachel Carson, *The Edge of the Sea*, Houghton Mifflin Company, 1955, pp vii–viii.
23. Paul Brooks, *The House of Life – Rachel Carson at Work*, Houghton Mifflin Company, 1972, pp 214–5. Quoted from Carson's letter to Rodell, dated 26 October 1957.
24. Mishan wrote: 'Privacy, quiet, and clean air, are scarce goods, far scarcer than they were before the war and sure to become scarcer in the foreseeable future. There is no warrant, therefore, for allowing them to be treated as though they were free goods.' [One could] 'imagine a country in which men were invested by law with property rights in privacy, quiet, and clean air – simple things, but for many indispensable to the enjoyment of the good life. . . . The consequence of recognizing such rights in one form or another, let us call them *amenity rights*, would be far-reaching.', (E.J. Mishan, *Growth: The Price We Pay*, Staples Press, London 1969, pp 37–8.)
25. The unstable character of Japanese rivers is best indicated by the so-called 'river contingency coefficient,' or the ratio of the maximum flux per second to the minimum at a basic point. Contrasted to the values for the Seine (34), the Thames (8) and the Donau (17), even the big Japanese rivers have values like 109 for the Shinano, 928 for the Tone and as high as 3750 for the Chikugo. (See Kazuko Tomiyama, *Mizu to Midori to Tsuchi* (Water, Greens and Ground), Chuō Kōron Sha, 1974, p 41.)
26. Notably the instance of the Isahaya Bay project in 1997 initiated by the Ministry of Agriculture, Forestry and Fisheries. A detailed account of the controversy was given in *Asahi Evening News*, 12-13 July 1997, p 5.

Chapter Six   Progress and setback in standards, compensation and assessment

1. OECD Report for Japan, p 25.
2. H. Kawana, *Dokument Nihon no Kogai*, vol. 9, 1993, Ryokufu Shuppan, p 67.
3. In fact, this was actually preceded by measures taken by a number of local governments and by a 1969 law, which was called 'Law Concerning Special Measures for the Relief of Patients with a Pollution-related Disease.'
4. For example, if the system was expected to fulfil a certain social security function, the medical aid aspect should have played a more important part.
5. As of 1986, there were 6,750 firms, paying the total charge amount of 50,423 million yen *outside* the designated areas, compared with 1,650 firms *in* such areas paying the total charge amount of 25,720 million yen.
6. Cf. in particular: Norio Suzuki, 'Kōkenhō no Kaitei o Otte' (Following Close Upon the Revision of the Pollution Compensation Law), *Kōgai Kenkyū*, vol 17, no. 1, Summer 1987, pp. 40–6.
7. *Kogai Kenkyu*, vol 17, no. 1, Summer 1987, p 45.

Chapter Seven   Pharmacological and Other Pollutions
 1. The expression used by Olle Hansson in his book: *Om SMON-skandalen*, 1977.
 2. For a detailed account of this incident in English, see Kichiro Shoji and Masuro Sugai, 'The Arsenic Milk Poisoning Incident' in Jun Ui, *Industrial Pollution in Japan*, United Nations University Press, 1992, pp 77–102.
 3. Composed of Teizo Utsumi, chief publisher of the *Jijishimpo* newspaper, Takeo Koyama, director of Tokyo Saiseikai Central Hospital, Shigeko Tanabe, lecturer of Senshu University, Ryo Masaki, lawyer, and Tasuku Yamazaki, lawyer.
 4. Reorganized in 1962 as a national organization from a regional (Okayama's) one.
 5. For a detailed discussion of this topic in English, see Norie Huddle and Michael Reich, *Island of Dreams: Environmental Crisis in Japan*, Autumn Press, 1975, pp 133–60.
 6. *Island of Dreams: Environmental Crisis in Japan*, pp 134–5.
 7. Hideyuki Kawana, *Dokument Nihon no Kōgai*, 1989, vol 3, p 296.
 8. Norie Huddle and Michael Reich, *Island of Dreams: Environmental Crisis in Japan*, Autumn Press, 1975, p 141.
 9. *Island of Dreams: Environmental Crisis in Japan*, p 138.
10. See Genshu Umeda, 'PCB Poisoning in Japan,' *Ambio*, vol 1, no. 4, pp 132–4.
11. *De samvetslosa lakemedelsbolagen Om SMON-skandalen*, 1977. The quotations here are from the Japanese translation of the book (*Sumon Sukyandaru*, 1978, Asahi Shimbun, p 172), retranslated into English by Tsuru).
12. According to the *Research Report* no. 8 of the SMON Research Council.
13. The scene in which President Hirabayashi of the Tanabé fell on his knees imploring Professor Shiraki not to make his experiment public was vividly reported in *Tokyo Shimbun*, 15 July 1975.
14. Olle Hansson, *Sumon Sukyandaru* (Japanese translation), pp 73–5.
15. *Sumon Sukyandaru*, p 120.
16. *Sumon Sukyandaru*, pp 121–8.
17. *Sumon Sukyandaru*, p 241.
18. Olle Hansson, *Sumon Sukyandaru*, p 182.
19. The sale of chinoform in Japan expanded 40 times in 14 years from 1955 to 1969.
20. Cf. Tetsuya Tanaka, *Kōdoku-Toroku Jiken* (Mine Poisoning – Toroku Incident), Sanseidō, 1981, p 128.
21. A detailed account of the incident by K. Kawahara in *Kōgai Kenkyū*, vol 7, no. 4, Spring 1978, pp 29–38 is most informative. For those who are interested in the full story, *Kiroku-Toroku* (Toroku in Records), compiled by the Society for Recording the Toroku Incident, Honda Kikaku, 1993 is highly recommended.

22. They were living quite close to one of the hearths and it had been confirmed that all seven members of the family died one after another with unmistakable symptoms of arsenic poisoning.
23. There was a second group of patients who began their suit in 1984, and among 19 persons in this group six had died by 1988.
24. Cf. Masazumi Harada, 'Minamata kara Toroku e' (*From Minamata to Toroku*), *Kōgai Kenkyu*, vol 7, no. 4, Spring 1978, pp 38–9.
25. *Kōgai Kenkyu*, vol 7, no. 4, Spring, 1978, p 39.
26. 'The Ward-Inhabitants Association' for short. 'Bokuto' means the east side of the Sumida River in Tokyo.
27. See Muneaki Tajiri 'Rokka-kuromu Jihen no Honshitsu to Kadai' (The nature of the hexavalent chromium incident and the task which confronts us), *Kōgai Kenkyū*, vol 7, no. 4, Spring 1978, pp 51–7. This article by Tajiri gives not only the details of the report mentioned here but also an excellent summary of the whole incident.

Chapter Eight   Implications of Globalized Environment Problems

1. World Commission on Environment and Development, *Our Common Future*, Oxford University Press, 1987, pp 8–9.
2. See Tanvi Nagpal and C. Foltz (eds), *Choosing Our Future: Visions of a Sustainable World*, Washington, DC, World Resources Institute, 1995. Also see, T. Nagpal, 'Voices from the Developing World: Progress Toward Sustainable Development' in *Environment*, vol 37, no. 8, October 1995.
3. T. Nagpal, *Environment*, vol 37, no. 8, October 1995, p 12.
4. *Environment*, vol 37, no. 8, October 1995, p 31.
5. *Environment*, vol 37, no. 8, October 1995, p 34.
6. Michael A. Toman, 'The difficulty in defining sustainability,' *Resources*, Resources for the Future, Winter 1992, p 3. This must be the reason that the official Japanese translation of 'sustainable development,' that is 'jizokukanōna kaihatsu,' was understood by a government official like Mr Kazuo Matsunaga, head of the Section on Environmental Policies of the Ministry of International Trade and Industry, as synonymous with 'economic growth that can be maintained.' (See *Asahi Shimbun*, 30 October 1997.) In fact, the desideratum of 'sustainable development' is cited by some business leaders (like Mr Makoto Kihara, managing director of Shin-Nippon Steel Manufacturing Company) as a kind of excuse for taking actions which might cause environmental disruption, quite similarly to the earstwhile 'harmony with sound economic development' clause which was used to qualify the Basic Law for Environmental Pollution Control of 1967. (See *Tsūsan Journal*, November 1997, pp 8–13).
7. Quoted in Steve H. Hanke (ed.), *Privatization and Development*, Institute of Contemporary Studies, San Francisco, California, 1987, pp 17–18.

8. *Privatization and Development*, 1987, p. 216.
9. See John Naisbitt and Patricia Aburdene, *Megatrends 2000 – The New Directions for the 1990s*, William Morrow and Company, Inc., New York, 1990, pp 154–77.
10. Robert Costanza, John Audley, Richard Borden, Paul Ekins, Carl Folke, Silvio O. Funtowicz and Jonathan Harris, 'Sustainable Trade: A New Paradigm for World Welfare,' *Environment*, vol 37, no. 5, June 1995, p 17.
11. *Environment*, vol 37, no. 5, June 1995, p. 43.
12. United Nations Environment Programme, *Global Environment Outlook*, 1997, p 3.
13. Andrew Jordan, 'Financing the UNCED Agenda: The Controversy over Additionality,' *Environment*, vol 36, no. 3, April 1994, p 27.
14. Heads of all the developed countries, except that of Japan, were present at the Rio Conference. And the US President Bush conveyed his message in a proud tone, speaking in part: 'I must tell you, we come to Rio proud of what we have accomplished and committed to extending the record on American leadership on the environment. In the United States, we have the world's tightest air quality standards on cars and factories, the most advanced laws for protecting lands and waters, and the most open processes for public participation. And now for a simple truth. America's record on environmental protection is second to none. So I did not come here to apologize; we came to press on with deliberate purpose and forceful action. And such action will demonstrate our continuing commitment to leadership and to international cooperation on the environment.' And yet, the US government refused to agree to the Biodiversity Convention, reportedly on account of the opposition by the biotechnology industry in their own country.
15. The official translation into English from the original Japanese. Other quotations from the text of the Law in this chapter are also from the official English version.
16. The word used in the Japanese text is 'jigyōsha' which is usually translated in English as 'enterprise agency' or 'a man of enterprise.' In view of the fact this was an official translation, I rather suspect that it was a slip which escaped the notice of the responsible official of the Environment Agency, although there is a possibility that such limitation of the coverage for application of the law was a secret wish of the Environment Agency officials.
17. Reference was given at the very beginning of Chapter One on this problem. See P.A. Samuelson and W.D. Nordhaus, *Economics*, 15th edn, McGraw-Hill, Inc., 1995, ch. 19.
18. A detailed discussion on this draft German law in Japanese can be found in Sorayasu Fujita's article in *Jichi Kenkyū*, vol 68, no. 10 and no. 11.
19. Research Group on Environment Assessment in the Environment Agency (ed.), *Nihon no Kankyō Assessment* (Environment Assessment in Japan), Gyōsei, 1997, pp 101–21.

20. Jane H. Ives (ed.), *The Export of Hazard*, Routledge & Kegan Paul, 1985.
21. Quoted from Paul Shrivastava, *Bhopal: Anatomy of a Crisis*, Ballinger Publishing Co., Cambridge, MA, A Subsidiary of Harper Row, 1987, pp 1–4.
22. See Barry I. Castleman and Prabir Purkavastha, 'The Bhopal disaster as a case study in double standards,' in Jane H. Ives (ed.), *The Export of Hazard*, Routledge & Kegan Paul, 1985, pp 215–23.
23. The summary quotation here is from *The Economist*, 15 February 1992. The quoted statement preceding this summary is from Summers' memorandum itself. His own phrasing of 'the grounds' is somewhat more technical and lengthy, as can be exemplified by his paragraph for the third ground, which is stated as follows: 'The demand for a clean environment for aesthetic and health reasons is likely to have very high income elasticity. The concern over an agent that causes a one in a million change in the odds of prostate cancer is obviously going to be much higher in a country where people survive to get prostate cancer than in a country where people under 5 mortality is 200 per thousand. . . . Clearly, trade in goods that embody aesthetic pollution concerns could be welfare enhancing. While production is mobile the consumption of pretty air is a non-tradable.' Probably referring to this paragraph, *The Economist* (15 February 1992) made a critical comment: 'Mr. Summers makes a . . . crucial assumption. He supposes that the value of a life, or years of life-expectancy, can be measured by an objective observer in terms of incomes per head – in other words, that an Englishman's life is worth more than the lives of a hundred Indians.'
24. *Bank Check*, Winter 1992, p 6.
25. Jane Ives, *The Export of Hazard*, Routledge & Kegan Paul, 1985, pp 82–5.
26. Cf. Hiroyuki Ishi, *Chikyū Kankyō Hōkoku* (Report on the Earth Environment), Iwanami Shoten, 1988.
27. *Asahi Evening News*, 23 June 1997, p 7.
28. On this question, a most incisive, critical analysis can be found in Kazuo Sumi, *ODA Enjo no Genjitsu* (Sober Reality of the ODA Assistance), Iwanami Shoten, 1989.
29. *ODA Enjo no Genjitsu*, 1989, pp 223–4.
30. *Asahi Evening News*, 9–10 October 1995.
31. J.P. Bruce, H. Lee and E.F. Haites (eds), *Climate Change 1995: Economic and Social Dimensions of Climate Change*, Contribution of Working Group III to the Second Assessment Report of the Intergovernmental Panel on Climate Change, New York: Cambridge University Press, 1996, p 22.
32. *The Economist*, 13–19 December 1997, p 14.
33. This idea, strongly championed by the US administration, makes allowances for trading pollution control credits among countries if that

would provide cheaper ways of reducing worldwide emissions. This idea is being criticized, for example by Professor Michael J. Sandel of Harvard University, as 'it creates loopholes that could enable wealthy countries to evade their obligations' and 'it may undermine the sense of shared responsibility that increased global cooperation requires.' (*Asahi Evening News*, 18 December 1997) The Kyoto protocol made it clear that there would be no trading until the next COP in late 1998.

34. 'Joint implementation' (JI) is a very limited form of tradeable permits, allowing one country to help another implement a project or change a policy so that the result is lower greenhouse gas emissions from what they otherwise would be. A typical JI scheme is presumed to entail the rich countries supplying capital to the poor. But many developing countries see JI as an effort by the rich to buy their way out of substantive commitments. Thus Japan and the United States have already set their eyes on Russia as an emissions trading partner.

35. 'Netting' is an idea to count forests as sources of absorbing CO_2. The problem is whether the forest area to be counted for this purpose should be the existing stock or the net increase after a certain base year. The Kyoto conference agreed on the latter with 1990 as the base year.

36. *The Economist*, 13–19 December, 1997, p 14.

37. The negotiators in Kyoto deferred action on several important and controversial elements, like this problem, to a subsequent meeting scheduled for Buenos Aires in the fall of 1998. For details on this matter, see Raymond J. Kopp, Richard D. Morgenstern and Michael A. Toman, 'Climate Change Policy After Kyoto,' *Resources*, Resources for the Future, Winter 1998, pp 4–6.

38. David G. Victor and Julian E. Salt, 'From Rio to Berlin: Managing Climate Change,' *Environment*, December 1994, p 30.

39. *Asahi Evening News*, 6 December 1997.

40. See *Asahi Evening News*, 6 December 1997.

Chapter Nine   A New Life-Style Sought

1. World Commission on Environment and Development, *Our Common Future*, Oxford University Press, 1987, p 9.

2. *Our Common Future*, 1987, p 8.

3. Anne P. Carter, 'Technology, Employment and the Distribution of Income: Leontief at 90,' *Economic Systems Research*, vol 8, no. 4, 1996, pp 316–17.

4. *Economic Systems Research*, vol 8, no. 4, 1996, p 317.

5. Karl Marx, *Grundrisse der Kritik der politischen Ökonomie*. (See note 9 of Chapter One.)

6. E.F. Schumacher, *Small is Beautiful*, Blond & Briggs Ltd, 1973, pp 139–40.

7. *Small is Beautiful*, pp 139–41.

8. 16 August 1970. In this connection, one cannot help recalling a discerning passage from the writings of a 'classical economist' more than a century ago, to wit: 'A philosopher produces ideas, a poet poems, a clergyman sermons, a professor compendia, and so on. A criminal produces crimes. . . . The criminal produces not only crimes, but also criminal law, and with this also the professor who gives lectures on criminal law, and in addition to this the inevitable compendium in which this same professor throws his lectures on to the general market as "commodities." This brings with it an augmentation of national wealth. . . . The criminal moreover produces the whole of the police and of criminal justice, constables, judges, hangmen, juries, etc. . . . Torture alone has given rise to the most ingenious mechanical inventions, and employed many honorable craftsmen in the production of its instruments. . . . The effects of the criminal on the development of productive power can be shown in detail. . . . Would locks ever have reached their present degree of excellence had there been no thieves? Would the making of banknotes have reached its present perfection had there been no forgers?. . . . Crime, through its constantly new methods of attack on property, constantly calls into being new methods of defense, and so is as productive as strikes for the invention of machines.' Probably few economists today can identify the author of this passage. It is from Karl Marx, *Theories of Surplus Value*, Moscow, Foreign Languages Publishing House, 1964, vol I, pp 375–6.

9. T. Veblen, *The Theory of Business Enterprise*, New York, Mentor Book, 1904, p 120. A fuller quotation was given earlier in Chapter One, pp 16–17.

10. We referred to it in Chapter One.

11. Fred Hirsch, *Social Limits to Growth*, The Twentieth Century Fund, 1976, p 2.

12. See the quotation from him in Chapter One, p 16.

13. E.J. Mishan, *The Costs of Economic Growth*, Staples Press, 1967, p 114.

14. J.K. Galbraith, *The New Industrial State*, Houghton Mifflin Company, 1967, p 212.

15. Gavan McCormack, *The Emptiness of Japanese Affluence*, M.E. Sharpe, Inc., 1996, p 288.

16. *The Emptiness of Japanese Affluence*, p 249.

17. Arnold J. Toynbee, in *London Observer*, 14 April 1974.

18. Quoted earlier in Chapter One, pp 23–4.

19. Amartya Sen, *The Standard of Living*, Cambridge University Press, 1987, p 16.

20. E.F. Schumacher, *Small is Beautiful*, Blond & Briggs Ltd, 1973, pp 140–1.

21. *Small is Beautiful*, p 142.

22. F.J. Fisher, 'The Sixteenth and Seventeenth Centuries: The Dark Ages in Economic History?' *Economica*, XXIV (1970).

Selected Bibliography (in English)

Beckerman, Wilfred, 'Economists, Scientists, and Environmental Catastrophe', *Oxford Economic Papers*, November 1972.

Biswas, Asit K. and Qu Geping (ed.), *Environmental Impact Assessment for Developing Countries*, Tycooly International, London, 1987.

Boulding, Kenneth E., 'The Economics of the Coming Spaceship Earth' in *Environmental Quality in the Growing Economy*, ed. Henry Jarett, Johns Hopkins Press, 1966.

Bowen, William, 'Who Owns What's in Your Head?', *Fortune*, July 1964.

Broadbent, J., *Environmental Politics in Japan: Networks of Power and Protest*, Cambridge University Press, 1998.

Brooks, Paul, *The House of Life – Rachel Carson at Work*, Houghton Miffin Co. 1972.

Carson, Rachel, *The Edge of the Sea*, Houghton Mifflin Co. 1955.

Carter, Anne P., 'Technology, Employment and the Distribution of Income: Leontief at 90', *Economic Systems Research*, vol 8, no. 4, 1996.

Commoner, Barry, *The Closing Circle*, Alfred A. Knopf, 1971.

Commoner, Barry, *The Poverty of Power – Energy and the Economic Crisis*, Alfred A. Knopf, 1976.

Faber, Daniel R., *Environment Under Fire – Imperialism and the Ecological Crisis in Central America*, Monthly Review Press, 1993.

Gakenheimer, Ralph (ed.), *The Automobile and the Environment*, The MIT Press, 1978.

Goldman, Marshall I., *The Spoils of Progress – Environmental Pollution in the Soviet Union*, The MIT Press, 1972.

Gresser, Julian, *Environmental Law in Japan*, The MIT Press, 1979.

Hirsch, Fred, *Social Limits to Growth*, Twentieth Century Fund, 1976.

Hitch, Charles J. *et al.*, *Resources for an Uncertain Future*, The Johns Hopkins University Press, 1978.

Hjalte, Krister, Lidgren, Karl and Stali, Ingemar, *Environmental Policy and*

Welfare Economics (transl. by Curt Wells), Cambridge University Press, 1977.

Huddle, Norie and Reich, Michael, *Island of Dreams: Environmental Crisis in Japan*, Autumn Press, New York and Tokyo, 1975.

Hueting, R., *New Scarcity and Economic Growth – More Welfare Through Less Production?* (translated by Trevor Preston), North-Holland Publishing Co., 1980.

Iijima, Nobuko (ed.), *Pollution Japan: Historical Chronology*, Asahi Evening News, 1979.

Kapp, K. William, *The Social Costs of Private Enterprise*, Harvard University Press, 1950.

Kato, Ichiro et al. (ed.), *Environmental Law and Policy in the Pacific Basin Area*, University of Tokyo Press, 1981.

Kneese, Allen V. and Bower, Blair T., *Environmental Quality and Residuals Management*, Resources for the Future, 1979.

Kopp, Raymond J. et al., 'Climate Change Policy After Kyoto', *Resources*, Resources for the Future. Winter 1998.

Krutilla, John V. and Fisher, Anthony C., *The Economics of Natural Environments*, Resources for the Future, 1975.

McCormack, Gavan, *The Emptiness of Japanese Affluence*, M.E. Sharpe, Inc., 1996.

McKean, Margaret A., *Environmental Protest and Citizen Politics in Japan*, University of California Press, 1981.

Mishan, E.J., *Growth: The Price We Pay*, Staples Press, London, 1969.

Myrdal, Gunnar, *Against the Stream – Critical Essays in Economics*, Vintage Books, New York, 1975.

Nagpal, Tanvi and Foltz, C. (ed.), *Choosing Our Future: Visions of a Sustainable World*, World Resources Institute, Washington, DC, 1995.

Naisbitt, John and Aburdene, Patricia, *Megatrends 2000 – The New Directions for the 1990s*, William Morrow and Company, Inc., New York, 1990.

OECD, *Environmental Policies in Japan*, OECD, Paris, 1977.

Olsen, Edward A. *Japan: Economic Growth, Resource Scarcity, and Environmental Constraints*, Westview Press, Boulder, CO, 1978.

Power, Thomas M., *The Economic Value of the Quality of Life*, Westview Press, Boulder, CO, 1980.

Sachs, Ignacy, *Transition Strategies towards the 21st Century*, Interest Publications, New Delhi, India, 1993.

Sax, Joseph L. and Conner, Roger L., 'Michigan's Environmental Protection Act of 1970: A Progress Report', *Michigan Law Review*, May 1972.

Schelling, Thomas C. (ed.), *Incentives for Environmental Protection*, The MIT Press, 1983.

Schumacher, E.P., *Small is Beautiful*, Blond & Briggs Ltd, 1973.

Scitovsky, Tibor, *The Joyless Economy*, Oxford University Press, 1976.

Sen, Amartya, *Collective Choice and Social Welfare*, Holden-Day, Inc., 1970.

Sen, Amartya, *The Standard of Living*, Cambridge University Press, 1987.

Shrivastava, Paul, *Bhopal: Anatomy of a Crisis*, Ballinger Publishing Co., Cambridge, MA, 1987.

Simon, Julian L. and Kahn, Herman (ed.), *The Resourceful Earth*, Basil Blackwell, 1984.

Sontheimer, Sally (ed.), *Women and the Environment – A Reader*, Monthly Review Press, 1991.

Tolba, Mostafa Kamal, *Development without Destruction – Evolving Environmental Perception*, Tycooly International Publishing, Ltd, Dublin, 1982.

Tsuru, Shigeto (ed.), *Proceedings of International Symposium on Environmental Disruption – A Challenge to Social Scientists*, Asahi Evening News, 1970.

Tsuru, Shigeto, *Japan's Capitalism – Creative Defeat and Beyond*, Cambridge University Press, 1993.

Turner, R. Kerry (ed.), *Sustainable Environmental Management – Principles and Practice*, Westview Press, Boulder, CO, 1988.

Ui, Jun (ed.), *Industrial Pollution in Japan*, United Nations University Press, 1992.

United Nations, *Agenda 21: Programme of Action for Sustainable Development – Rio Declaration on Environment and Development*, 1992.

United Nations Environment Programme, *Global Environment Outlook*, 1997.

Veblen, Thorstein, *The Theory of Business Enterprise*, Mentor Books, 1904.

Woodrow Wilson International Center for Scholars, *The Human Environment*, vol I, Bibliography, 1972; vol II, Summaries of National Reports on Environmental Problems, 1972.

World Commission on Environment and Development, *Our Common Future*, Oxford University Press, 1987.

Selected Bibliography (in Japanese)

Aragaki, Hideo, *Kuni Sakaete Sanga Horobu* (The Country Prospers While its Natural Environment is Ruined), Dobutsu-sha, 1978.

Awaji, Takehisa, *Sumon-jiken to Hō* (The SMON Incident and the Law), Yuhikaku, 1981.

Awaji, Takehisa (ed.), *Kaihatsu to Kankyō – Daiichiji-Sangyo no Kōgai o Megutte* (Development and Environment – Problems around the Primary Industries), Nihon-Hyōron-sha, 1986.

Awaji, Takehisa and Teranishi, Shun'ichi (ed.), *Kōgai Kankyō-hō Riron no Aratana Tenkai* (A New Evolution of the Theory of Kōgai Environmental Law), Nihon-Hyōron-sha, 1997.

Fujioka, Sadahiko (ed.), *[Kankyō to Kaihatsu] no Kyōikugaku* (Theory of Education on 'Environment and Development'), Dōjidai-sha, 1998.

Hanayama, Yuzuru, *Kankyō Seisaku o Kangaeru* (Reflections on Environment Policy), Iwanami Shoten, 1978.

Hansson, Olle, *Sumon Sukyandaru – Sekai o Mushibamu Seiyaku-kaisha* (The SMON Scandal – A Pharmaceutical Company which Traumatizes the World), transl. from original Swedish text by Sawada, Yumiko and Biyanale, Tamiko; Asahi Shimbun, 1978.

Harada, Masazumi, *Minamata no Shizu – Jakusha no tameno Kankyō-Shakaigaku* (A Viewpoint on Minamata – Environmental Sociology for the Weak), Rippu-Shobo, 1992.

Harada, Masazumi, *Sabakareru nowa Tare ka* (Who are the Ones to be Adjudged?), Seishoku-Shobō, 1995.

Hata, Akio, *Itai-Itai Byō – Hasseigen Taisaku 22 nen no Ayumi* (The *Itai-Itai* Disease – 22 Years in Search for the Policy towards Sources Agent), Jikkyō Shuppan, 1994.

Hoshino Yoshiro, *Shizen to Ningen – Seto-naikai ni Ikiru* (Nature and Man – Life in the Inland Sea), Iwanami Shoten, 1977.

Hyūga, Yasushi, *Tanaka Shōzō Nooto* (The Note on Tanaka Shōzō), Tabata Shoten, 1981.

Iida, Momo, *Ekorojii to Marukusu Shugi* (Ecology and Marxism), Ryokufū Shuppan, 1982.

Iijima, Takashi, *Gijutsu no Mokushiroku* (Revelation of Technology), Gijutsu to Ningen Kabushiki Kaisha, 1996.

Irokawa, Daikichi (ed.), *Minamata no Keiji – Shiranuhi-kai Sōgō Chōsa Hōkoku* (The Revelation of Minamata – Composite Research Report of the Shiranuhi Bay), in 2 vols, Chikuma Shobō, 1983.

Ishi, Hiroyuki, *Chikyū Kankyō Hōkoku* (Reporting on Global Environmental Problems), Iwanami Shoten, 1988.

Ishi, Hiroyuki, *Sansei-u* (The Acid Rain), Iwanami Shoten, 1992.

Kamata, Satoshi, *Rokkasho-mura no Kiroku* (Records of Rokkasho Village Development), in 2 vols, Iwanami Shoten, 1991.

Kamioka Namiko (ed.), *Shiryō Kindai Nihon no Kōgai* (Documents and Data on Kōgai in Modern Japan), Shinjinbutsu Ōrai-sha, 1971.

Kato, Shū, *Sugata naki Kigyō Satsujin – Jintsūgawa Kōdoku Jiken* (Amorphous Homicide by Enterprise – The Jintsūgawa Mine Pollution Incident), Tokuma Shoten, 1979.

Kawahara, Kazuyuki, 'Toroku Kōdoku-byō Higaisha no Fukken no tameni', Furon: Harada, Masazumi 'Minamata kara Toroku e – Kōgaibyō no Gainen ni tsuite', *Kōgai Kenkyū*, vol. 7, no. 4, Spring 1978 ('Mine Pollution Disease in Toroku – For the Rehabilitation of the Victims' with added comments by Harada, Masazumi on 'From Minamata to Toroku – On the Concept of the Kōgai Disease').

Kawana, Hideyuki, *Dokyumento Nihon no Kōgai* (Document: Kōgai in Japan), in 13 vols, Ryokufū Shuppan, 1987–96.

Kihara, Keikichi, *Nashonaru Torasuto* (The National Trust), Sanshōdo, 1984.

Kihara, Keikichi, *Kurashi no Kankyō o Mamoru – Amenity to Jūmin Undō* (Defence of Daily-life Environment – Amenity and the Citizens' Movement), Asahi Shimbun, 1992.

Kimoto, Shōji, *Shizaka-jima* (Shizaka Island), in 2 vols, Kōdan-sha, 1971.

Kira, Tatsuo, *Shizen-hogo no Shisō* (The Ideology of Nature Protection), Jinbun Shoin, 1976.

Kōda, Toshihiko, *Tago no Ura – Hedoro wa Kiezu* (Tagonoura – Its Accumulated Sludge does not Vanish), Asahi Shimbun, 1979.

Kondō, Akitaro, *Aozora o Kaese* (Return the Blue Sky to Us), Fubin-sha, 1967.

Koyama, Hitoshi, *Senzen Shōwa-ki Osaka no Kōgai Mondai Shiryō* (Documents and Data on Kōgai Problems in Osaka during the Prewar Shōwa Period), Kansei Daigaku – Seiji-Keizai Kenkyusho *Chōsa to Shiryō*, no. 16, 1973.

Miyamoto, Ken'ichi, *Shakai Shihon Ron*, Kaiteiban (Social Capital, revised edn), Yūhikaku, 1976.

262   *The Political Economy of the Environment*

Miyamoto, Ken'ichi (ed.), *Kōgai Toshi no Saisei – Minamata* (Rebirth of the *Kōgai* City Minamata), Chikuma Shobō, 1977.
Miyamoto Ken'ichi (ed.), *Numazu Jūmin Undō no Ayumi* (The Developing Steps of Citizens' Movement in Numazu), Nihon Hōsō Shuppan Kyōkai, 1979.
Miyamoto, Ken'ichi, *Nihon no Kankyō Seisaku* (The Environmental Policy of Japan), Ōtsuki Shoten, 1987.
Miyamoto, Ken'ichi, *Kankyō to Kaihatsu* (Environment and Dvelopment), Iwanami Shoten, 1992.
Miyamoto, Ken'ichi, *Ajia no Kankyō to Nihon no Sekinin* (Environmental Issues in Asia and the Responsibility of Japan), Kamogawa Shuppan, 1992.
Miyamoto, Ken'ichi, *Kankyō-Seisaku no Kokusaika* (Internationalization of the Environment Policies), Jikkyō Shuppan, 1995.
Miyamoto, Ken'ichi, *Kankyō to Jichi* (Environment and Autonomy), Iwanami Shoten, 1996.
Miyamoto, Tadashi (ed.), *Kōgai to Gyōsei Sekinin – Yokkaichi no Baai* (Kōgai and Administrative Responsibility – the Case of Yokkaichi), Kawade Shobō Shinsha, 1976 .
Morinaga, Eizaburo, *Ashio Kōdoku Jiken* (The Ashio Mine Pollution Incident), in two volumes, Nihon Hyōron Sha, 1982.

Nakanishi Junko, *Gesuidō – Mizu Saisei no Tetsugaku* (The Sewage Problem – Philosophy of Water Reuse), Asahi Shimbun, 1983.

Oda, Yasunori, *Kindai Nihon no Kōgai Mondai* (*Kōgai* Problems in Modern Japan), Sekai Shisō Sha, 1983.
Oishi, Buichi, *Ozé no Michi Ichiro to Gunshuku o Motomete* (The Road to Ozé and in Search of Arms Reduction), Sankei Shuppan, 1982.
Ono, Eiji, *Yokkaichi 10 nen no Kiroku* (Yokkaichi Pollutions Recorded during the Past Ten years), Keisō Shobō, 1971.

Sawa, Takamitsu, *Chikyū Ondanka o Fusegu* (Preventing the Warming of the Earth), Iwanami Shoten, 1997.
Sawai, Yoshiro, *Kusai Sakana to Zensoku no Shōmon* (Testimonies on Stench Fish and Asthma), Haru Shobō, 1984.
Shibata Kei, *Chikyū Hakai to Keizaigaku* (Destruction of the Earth and Economic Science), Minerva Shobō, 1973.
Shibata, Tetsuji, 'Minamata-byō Hōdō ni tsurte' (Concerning the Reporting on the Minamata Disease), *Asahi Shimbun Chōken Shitsuhō* (Research Institute Report of the Asahi), vol 104, November 1993.
Shōji, Hikaru and Miyamoto, Ken'ichi, *Nihon no Kōgai* (Kōgai in Japan), Iwanami Shoten, 1975.
Sumi, Kazuo, *ODA Enjo no Genjitsu* (Sober Reality of the ODA Assistance), Iwanami Shoten, 1989.

Tajiri, Muneaki, *Yokkaichi – Shi no Umi to Tatakau* (Yokkaichi – Fighting in the Sea of Death), Iwanami Shoten, 1972.

Tajiri, Muneaki, 'Rokka-kurōmu Jihen no Honshitsu to Kadai' ('The Nature of the Hexavalent Chromium Incident and the Task which Confronts Us'), *Kōgai Kenkyū*, vol 7, no. 4, Spring 1978.

Tajiri, Muneaki, *Kōgai Tekihatsu Saizensen* (Frontiers of *Kōgai* Disclosure), Iwanami Shoten, 1980.

Tajiri, Muneaki, *Yudaku no Umi* (The Oil-Contaminated Sea), Nihon Hyōron Sha, 1981.

Tajiri, Muneaki, *Rashinban no nai Ayumi* (My Work of Life without a Compass), Tōken Shuppan, 1985.

Tajiri, Muneaki, *Teigen: Tokyo-wan no Hozen to Saisei* (Conservation and Revival of the Tokyo Bay), Nihon Hyōron Sha, 1988.

Takasaki, Hiroshi and Kihara, Keikichi, *Irihamaken* (The Right to Enter the Beach), Japan Publisher, 1977.

Tanaka, Kakuei, *Nihon Rettō Kaizō Ron* (Proposal for Remodelling of the Japanese Archipelago), Nikkan Kōgyō Shimbun Sha, 1972.

Tanaka, Tetsuya, *Kōdoku Toroku Jiken* (Mine Poisoning – the Toroku Incident), Sanseido, 1981.

Teranishi Shun'ichi, *Chikū Kankyō Mondai no Seiji Keizaigaku* (Political Economy of Global Environmental Problems), Tōyō Keizai Shimpo Sha, 1992.

Tomiyama, Kazuko, *Mizu to Midori to Tsuchi* (Water, Greens and Ground), Chūō Kōron Sha, 1974.

Tsuru, Shigeto, *Gendai Shihonshugi to Kōgai* (Present-day Capitalism and *Kōgai*), Iwanami Shoten, 1968.

Tsuru, Shigeto (ed.), *Genchi ni Miru Sekai no Kōgai* (*Kōgai* in the World as Directly Observed), Chūnichi Shimbun Tokyo Honsha, 1975.

Tsuru, Shigeto (ed.), *Sekai no Kōgai Chizu* (Kōgai Map of the World), in two vols, Iwanami Shoten, 1977.

Ueda, Kazuhiro, *Haikibutsu to Risaikuru no Keizaigaku* (Economics of Waste Disposal and Recycle), Yūhikaku, 1992.

Ueda, Kazuhiro, *Kankyō Keizaigaku e no Shōtai* (Invitation to Environment Economics), Maruzen K. K., 1998.

Ui, Jun, *Jūmin o Musubu Tabi – Han-Kōgai Sekai Angya* (Tying Citizens through Travels – Worldwide Anti-*Kōgai* Pilgrimage), Chikuma Shobō, 1977.

Ui, Jun (ed.), *Gijutsu to Sangyō Kōgai* (Technology and Industrial Pollution) Kokusai Rengō Daigaku, 1985.

Ui, Jun, *Yanaka-mura kara Minamata-Sanrizuka e – Ekorojii no Genryū* (From Yanaka Village to Minanata and Sanrizuka – The Headstream of Ecology), Shakai Hyōron Sha, 1991.

Ui, Jun, *Kōgai Jishu Kōza 15 nen* (Voluntary Lectures on *Kōgai* over 15 Years), Aki Shobō, 1991.

Ushiyama, Tsumoru, *Kōgai Saiban no Tenkai to Hō Riron* (Series of *Kōgai* Litigations and the Legal Theory), Nihon Hyōron Sha, 1976.

Uzawa, Hirobumi, *Jidōsha no Shakaiteki Hiyō* (Social Cost of Automobiles), Iwanami Shoten, 1974.

Uzawa, Hirobumi, *Chikyū Ondanka no Keizaigaku* (Economics of the Warming of the Earth), Iwanami Shoten, 1995.

REFERENCE MATERIALS (IN JAPANESE) COMPILED OR EDITED BY RELEVANT ORGANIZATIONS

Shizen Hogo Gyōsei no Ayumi (Progress of the Administration of Nature protection), compiled by Kankyōchō Shizen Hogo Kyoku (The Nature Protection Bureau of the Environment Agency), 1981.

Kōgai to Kuni no Sekinin (*Kōgai* and the Responsibility of the State), ed. Zenkoku Kōgai Bengodan Renraku Kaigi (The National Liaison Conference of the Defence Council on Kōgai), Nihon Hyōron Sha, 1982.

SMON to Songai Baishō (SMON and Damage Compensation), ed. SMON Songai Baishō Kenkyukai (The Research Group on the SMON Damage Compensation), Keisō Shobō, 1986.

Kiroku-Toroku (The Toroku Incident Recorded), compiled by Toroku o Kiroku suru Kai (Society for Recording the Toroku Incident), Honda Kikaku, 1993.

Kankyō Kihon Hō o Kangaeru (Reflections on the Basic Environment Law), ed. Nihon Kankyō Kaigi (Japan Environmental Council), Jikkyō Shuppan, 1994.

Nihon no Kankyō Asesumento (The Environmental Assessment in Japan), ed. Kankyōchō Kankyō Asesumento Kenkyūkai (The Research Committee on Environmental Assessment in the Environment Agency), Gyōsei, 1997.

Minamatabyō Saiban (The Minamata Disease Lawsuit), ed. Minamatabyō Higaisha Bengodan Zenkoku Renraku Kaigi (The National Liaison Conference of the Victims and Lawyers Involved in the Mimamata Disease), Kamogawa, Shuppan, 1997.

Minamata kara Mirai o Mitsumete (Looking toward the Future from Minamata), compiled by Minamata Soshō Bengodan (The Defence Council for the Minamata Victims), published by the Bengodan itself, 1997.

Minamatabyō Saiban Zenshi (Comprehensive History of the Minamata Disease) in 4 vols, Minamatabyō Higaisha Bengodan Zenkoku Renraku Kaigi (The National Liaison Conference of the Victims and Lawyers Involved in the Minamata Disease), Nihon Hyōron Sha, 1998–9.

Index

'A Blueprint for Survival', 120
Acetaldehyde, 81, 96, 98
Ackerman, Dr Edward, 52–3, 54, 58–9
Acrylic esters, 72
Act for the Environmental Conservation of the Seto Inland Sea 1973, 57; 'Actual Conditions of Water Quality in the Watarase River', 59
Ad-hoc Group on the Berlin Mandate (AGBM), 219
Adachi, Masafusa, 244
Agano River, 96–101
Agenda 21 (Rio document), 193–201, 202, 224, 230
Agreement for the Prevention of *Kogai* in the Future 1972, 105
Agricultural Regulation Act, 215
Agriculture, 9, 27, 31–2, 32, 55–6, 215; Ashio Copper Mine, 34–5; Besshi Copper Mine, 37–40; Hitachi Mine, 41, 44; *Itai-itai* disease, 105–6; Minamata disease, 79–81, 98–9
Agriculture Experiment Station, 38
Air pollution, 3, 14, 19, 31, 128, 210–13; Copper mining, 32; Hitachi Mine, 40–4; Standards for pollution control, 140–4; Yokkaichi city, 72–7; *see also* Greenhouse effect
Air Pollution Control Act, 64, 65
Air quality, 3, 7, 141

Aircraft, 65–6, 219, 222–3
Ajinomoto, Mr (Suzuki), 97
Allied Powers, 50
Alumina, 163
Aluminium, 97
Amenity rights, 137
Amin, Samir, 249
Ammonium Sulphate, 79–80
'An Appeal to the Japanese Government', 216
'An Interim Conclusion' (Central Environment Council), 206–7
Anglo-Japanese Alliance (1902), 36
Animals, 'Dancing Cat disease', 82–5; experiments, 82–4, 102, 173; fatalities, 59, 82, 165, 211; ocean pollution, 66
Antarctic, 66
Anti-*Kogai* Movement, 79, 150–2
Aragaki, Hideo, 260
Arsenic poisoning, 147, 158–63
Arsenious acid pollution, 179–85
Asahi Evening News, 254, 255
Asahi Nenkan (*The Asahi Yearbook*), 82, 242
Asahi Shimbun, 85–6, 166–8, 172, 179–80, 246
Asano Cement Company, 243–4
ASEED, 222
Ashio Copper Mine, 33–6, 40, 41, 59
Asia Rare-Earth Company (ARE), 214–15
Assessment, Environmental Impact (EIA), 150–72, 208–10

Association for Protection ('Mamoru-kai'), 160–1
Association of Ward-Inhabitants Demanding Liquidation of Kogai in the Bokuto Area, 186
Asthmatic complaints, 72, 76–7, 147
Astrom, Ambassador (Sweden), 6, 65–7, 219
Atlantic Ocean, 136
Automobiles, exhausts, 126, 140; industry, 19, 141–2
Awaji, Takehisa, 260; Teranishi, Shun'ichi, 260

Baby teeth, 62
Baby-food poisoning, 158–63
Bacon, Francis, 2
Balloons, 41
Bank of Chosen (Korea), 80
Basar Copper Smelting Plant, 214
Basic Anti-*Kogai* Law, 151–2
Basic Environment Plan, 203–4, 206–8
Basic Environmental Law of Japan (1993), 157, 202–6
Basic Law for Environmental Pollution Control (*Kogai Taisaku Kihon Ho*), 63–9, 128, 200, 202–6, 249
Basic Policies for Environmental Conservation, 203–4
Bath-houses, 114–15
Bauxite, 163
Bay of Ise, 70, 72, 77, 78
Bay Mineral Company, 214
Beach access right (*Irihamaken*), 135–7, 206
Beckerman, Wilfred, 249, 257
Behrens III, William W., 120
Besshi Copper Mine, 36–40, 40–1, 43
Bhopal, India, 210–13
Bichromates, 188
Biochemical oxygen demand (BOD), 128
Bismuth, 32
Biswas, Asit K. and Qu Geping, 257
Black market, 49

Bones, children's, 62
Boulding, Kenneth E., 6–7, 54, 58, 240, 244, 257
Bowen, William, 257
Boxer Rebellion 1900, 45
Brain-damage, 158
Brazil, 96
Bretton Woods Conference, 232
Bribery, 34
Britain *see* Great Britain
Broadbent, J., 257
Brockhagen, Dietrich, 222
Bronchial conditions, 147
Brooks, Paul, 250, 257
Brown, Lester, 123
Brown, R. *et al.*, 249
Bruce, J.P., Lee, H. and Haites, E.F., 254
Brundtland Commission and Report, 23, 123, 195–6, 224
Bureau of Conservation of the Air, 142–3
Bureau of National Parks, USA, 129–30
Bush, George (President USA), 253
Business firms, 4, 10
Butadiene, 72
Buzen, 135

Cadmium poisoning, 101–7
Cairo Declaration (1943), 50
Calcium, 102
Calcium cyanamide, 79
Canada, 96
Cancer, 185, 187–8, 190–2
Capitalism, 4–5, 10, 27–8; social costs, 11, 19, 185
Carbide, 79
Carbon dioxide, 65–6, 219, 221–3
Carbon monoxide, 141–2
Carp streamers, 61–2
Carson, Rachel, 136–7, 250, 257
Carter, Anne P., 255, 257
Carter, James Earl (President USA), 121
Casale ammonia synthesis, 80
Castleman, Barry I. and Purkavastha, Prabir, 254

Cat Number 400 experiment, 82–4
Central Anti-*Kogai* Commission, 141–2, 148–9, 152, 202
Central Environment Commission, 209
Central Environment Council, 206–7
Central Pharmaceutical Council, 172
Chamber of Commerce, 30
'Charge method', 185–6
Chiba, Tadanari, 243
Chimneys, 42–3, 43–4, 47
China, 27, 35, 36, 120–1
Chinoform, 170–8
Chisso, 59, 79–94, 245–6
Chisui (control), 137
Chromium, 186–91
Chromium acid chloride, 185–6
Ciba-Geigy Company, 170–8
Citizens' Committee for Inquiry on the Environmental Legislation, 202
Civil Aeronautics Law, 218–19
Clean Air Act 1970 (USA), 141
Clemenceau, Georges, 230
Climate Train, 222
Clinton, William (President USA), 217, 222
Club of Rome, 119, 121
Coal, 32–3, 226
Cocoyoc Symposium, Mexico (1974), 122–3
Cohen, Bernard L., 124
Cohen, Jerome B., 244
Cold-war, 53
Commission of Living Environment, 64
Commodore Perry, 27
Commoner, Barry, 240, 241, 257
Compensation, 76, 125–7, 145–50; Hexavalent chromium *kogai*, 92; *Itai-itai* disease, 102–5; Kanemi rice-oil disease, 168–70; Minamata disease, 90–4, 99–100; Osaka airport, 107, 111; SMON schandal, 176; Toroku Mine *Kogai*, 182–5

Comprehensive Environment Law (Germany), 206
Comprehensive Research Group on EIA System, 208–9
Conference of the Parties (COP), 219
Conference of Surgical Specialists, 17th 1955, 60
'Confirmation Document' (SMON case), 176–7
Conservation, 129–39; Area categories, 130
Conservation of Nature's Environment Commission, 202
Constipation, 171
Copper, 32–47, 59
Copper Mine Poisoning Survey Commission, Third, 42–3
Copper smelting pollution, 59
Corea, Gamani (Secretary General UNCTAD), 249
Costanza, Robert *et al.*, 253
Cotton and textile industry, 27–8, 32
Council for *Kogai* Countermeasures in Yokkaichi (Yokkaichi *Kogai Taisaku Kyogikai*), 74
Covenant on Reparations for the *Itai-Itai* Disease, 104–5
Covenant on Soil Pollution Problem, 105
Creation of a Society Ensuring Sustainable Development with Reduced Environmental Load, 202–3
Crude oil, 75, 118
Curie, Pierre, 229

Damage, 25–6, 126–7
DDT, 66
De samvetslosa llakemedelsbolagen om SMON-skandalen, 251
de Sismondi, Simonde, 13, 240
de V. Graaff, J., 11
Deaths *see* Fatalities
Declaration on Environment and Development, 193–7
Declaration on the Human Environment, 122, 193–4

Deconcentration Review Board
(DRB), 52
Democratic Groups Council for
Anti-Minamata Disease
('Minsuitai'), 99
Department of State (USA), 121
'Dependence effect', 178
Dey, Suman, 210–11
Diarrhoea, 171
Dillon, George, 7
Directive 230, 51
Disease and medical complaints,
Hexavalent Chromium *Kogai*,
185–92; *Itai-itai*, 60, 101–7, 147,
152, 185; Kanemi Rice-oil,
163–70; Minamata disease, 59,
79–101, 147, 185; Yokkaichi City,
72, 76–7
Doko, Toshio, 155
Draper, William, 52
Du Pont Company, 5, 239
Ducktown, USA, 33–4
Dulles, John Foster, 53
Dumping, 186–8
Dunn, F.S., 244
Dysentery, 171

Earth Summit 1992 (Rio de
Janeiro), 23, 193–201, 215
Earth warming, 11, 219–23
Earthquakes, 98–9
East China Sea, 57
Economic activity units, 3
Economic concentrations, excessive,
51–2
Economic growth, 116–19
Economic Impact Assessment,
203–4
Economic Measures to Prevent
Interference with Environmental
Conservation, 204–5
Economic Planning Agency, 87–8
Economic and Social Council (UN),
65
Economic Stabilization Board, 59
Economic Systems Research, 255
Effluents, factory, 60, 76–8, 82–90,
102

Egashira, Yutaka (Chisso
President), 91
Ehime Prefecture, 135–6, 206
Electric Generating Company, 72
Electricity generating plants, 209
Electrochemical sector, 80
Elimination of Excessive
Concentration of Economic
Power Law (1947), 51–2
Emphysema, 147
Engels, Friedrich, 14, 185, 240
England *see* Great Britain
English Restriction Period
(1815–21), 28
Entero-vioforme, 173
Environment, 252
Environment Agency, 69, 92–4, 142,
151–7, 208–9; Establishment of,
127–9; Toroku Mine *Kogai*, 180–1
Environment Committee, Diet, 152
Environment Day, 205
Environment White Paper, 95
Environmental Disruption in the
Modern World, 67
Environmental Impact Assessment
(EIA), 150–72, 208–10
'Environmental load', 202–3
Environmental Pollution Control,
64
Environmental Right, principle of
(*kankyoken*), 205–6
Environmental Sanitation Bureau,
Ministry of Welfare, 98
Equilibrium, theory of, 13
Essay on the Principle of Polulation,
119
European Union, 220–2
Experts' Committees on Charge
System for Damage
Compensation, 146; for
Countermeasures against Soil
Contamination due to
Hexavalent Chromium, 188; on
Impact of Nitrogen Oxide on
Humans, 142–3
'External economy/diseconomy', 11

Faber, Daniel R., 257

Fabian Socialists (GB), 17
Factories, effluents, 60, 76–8, 82, 90, 102; farming, 9; sites, 55, 55–6
Factory Control Regulation (1920), 30
FAG, 67
Farben, I.G., 80–1
Farming *see* Agriculture
Fatalities, 82, 85–6, 102, 187–8, 190, 192; animals, 82, 165
Federation of Economic Organizations (*Keidanren*), 153–4
Federation of Trade Unions in the Synthetic Chemical Industries, 190
Fertilizers, 79–81, 98–9
Fifteen Year War, 45, 103
Fijioka, Sadahiko, 260
Filtering devices, 34
First World War (WW1), 30, 45, 79, 80, 103, 188
Fisher, F.J., 256
Fisheries Agency, 84, 88
Fishing, 56, 60, Bay of Ise, 72–4, 77–9; Isabela Bay, 214; Minamata Bay, 82–8, 91, 95; River Agano, 96–8
Five-Men Committee, 160
Floods, 32, 59
Fomenting Rebellion Act, 35
Food Sanitation Act (1947), 88, 246
Forest Agency, 131
Forests, 19, 32, 59, 209
Fossil fuels, 65–6, 219
Founex meeting (1971), 122
Framework Convention on Climate Change, 201, 219–21
France, 24, 36, 137
Friedman, Milton, 114
Fuchu, 101–2
Fuji Petroleum, 61
Fuji *Shimbun*, 29
Fujita, Sorayasu, 253
Fujiwara, Hisakazu, 186
Fujiwara, Kujuro, 242
Fukuda, Takeo (Prime Minister), 155, 175

Fukuoka, 85; High Court, 93, 135, 169, 176, 183
Fukuzawa, Yokichi, 36
Furukawa, Ichibei, 33–4, 36–7
Furukawa, Mr (air pollution victim), 74
Furukawa *zaibatsu*, 36–7

Gakenheimer, Ralph, 257
Galbraith, J.K., 8, 178, 256
Galvanized iron, 104
Gandhi, Mrs Indira (Prime Minister, India), 121–2
Gas, 37, 226
Gendai Shihonshugi to Kogai, 241
Germany, 2, 24, 34, 36, 53–4, 80–1, 186, 206
Global 2000 Report to the President 1980, 121–4
Global warming, 11, 219–23
Globalism, 6
Goldman, Marshall I., 257
Goto, Dr Masayasu, 167
Goto, Seichi, 145, 242
Goto, Shimpei (1857–1929), 30
Great Britain, 14–15, 17, 24, 228–9, 235; Japan's Korean expansionist ambition, 35–6; labour legislation, 185; privatization trends, 197; River Thames, 137; Roskill Committee, 114
Great Kanto Earthquake 1923, 48
Green areas, 130–1
Greenhouse effect, 65–6, 219, 222–3
Gresser, Julian, 257
Ground subsidence, 128

Hagino, Dr Noboru, 101
Hanayama, Yuzuru, 260
Hanke, Steve H., 252
Hanrei Roppo, 248
Hansson, Olle, 170, 174, 175–6, 178, 251, 260
Harada, Professor Masazumi, 89, 185, 247, 252, 260
Harbour Regulation Act (1948), 78
'Harmony Clause', 68, 151–2
Harrod, R.F., 239

Index

Hasegawa, Yasushi, 75
Hashimoto, Dr Michio, 142–4
Hata, Akio, 247, 260
HCH (agricultural chemical), 215
'High water construction work',
    137–8
Hikari Foundation, 162
Hinsu River, 101
Hirabayashi, President (Tanabe), 251
Hirose, Tadahira, 37
Hiroshima SMON Society, 176–7
Hirsch, Fred, 256, 257
Hitachi Company, 41–3, 47
Hitachi mine, 40–4
Hitch, Charles J. *et al.*, 257
Hjalte, Krister, Lidgren, Karl and
    Stale, Ingemar, 257–8
Hobson, J.A., 17–18
Hokkaido, 50, 157
Holding Company Liquidation
    Commission (HCLC), 51–2
Honshu Paper Manufacturing
    Company, 50, 60, 65
Hoshino, Yoshiro, 260
Hosokawa, Dr Hajime (Chisso),
    82–3, 246
Hosui (Conservation), 137–8
Hot-house effect, 6–7, 65–6, 219,
    222–3
Huddle, Norie and Reich, Michael,
    251, 258; with Stiskin, Nahum,
    245
Hueting, Roefie, 19–21, 23, 241, 258
Human Environment, UN
    Conference on, 21–2
Hungnum plant, 80
'Hunter-Russell' syndrome, 89
Hydro-power, 226
Hydrocarbons, 141–2
Hyuga, Hosai, 58
Hyuga, Yasushi, 260

Iba, Sadanori, 37–8
Iglesias, E., 249
Iida, Momo, 261
Iijima, Nobuko, 241, 258
Iijima, Takashi, 261
Ikeda, Bokuzen, 108, 179

'Imo Mutiny', 45
Income, family, 17
Income, Plan for doubling, 54–5
India, 120–1, 210–13
Industrial Bank of Japan, 191–2
Industrial Bank of Korea, 80
Industrial Revolution, 4, 14, 229
Industries, conglomeration of, 19
Inland lakes, 138
Inoue, Professor Yukishige, 171
Institute of Technology, Tokyo, 82
'Interference of income', 4, 232
Intergovernmental Conference
    (UNESCO), 65
Intergovernmental Panel on Climate
    Change (IPCC), 219–20
International Development
    Association (IDA), 201
International Monetary Fund
    (IMF), 216
International Social Science
    Council, 67, 151
Iodine, 96, 97
Ipoh City, 214
Irihamaken (beach access right),
    134–7, 206
Irishiken, 42
Irokawa, Daikichi, 261
Iron-works, 28
Irtami Airport, 107
Isabela Bay, 214
Ishi, Hiroyuki, 254, 261
Ishihara Sangyo Company, 78–9
Ishihara, Shintaro, 129, 142, 155
Ishokuju (food, clothing and
    shelter), 230–1
Island of Dreams, 251
'Itai-itai' disease, 60, 101–7, 147,
    152, 185
'Itami Airport', 107–8
'Itami Airport Council', 108
Ito, Mr (Mayor of Kawasaki), 143
Itochu, 214
Ittoleum, 214
Ives, Jane H., 213, 254
'Iwato Boom', 54

Jackson, Lady, 249

Japan Association of Chemical
Industries, 84
Japan Association of Conservation
of Nature, 132
Japan International Cooperation
Agency (JICA), 214
Japan Lawyers' Federation, 202
Japan Resources Association, 244
Japan Save the Ozone Network, 222
Japan Teachers Union (JTU), 180
Jiji Shimpo, 242
'Jimmu Boom', 54
Jintsu River, 60, 101, 105–6
Johnson, Stanley, 122
Joint Action Council, 100
'Joint implementation' (JI), 255
Jordan, Andrew, 253

Kabe, Tsuneo, 174–7
Kaburagi, Tokuji, 41–2, 44
Kagawa, Toyohiko, 31
Kahn, Herman, 123
Kajikawa, Kin-ichiro (Kanagawa
University), 105
Kakuei Tanaka Plan, 117
Kamata, Satoshi, 261
Kamino, Ryuzo, 167
Kamioka Mine, 101–4
Kamioka, Namiko, 261
Kamo River, 137
Kanagawa, 157, 243
Kanagawa University, 105
Kanegabuchi Chemical Industry,
164, 169, 170
'Kanekuroru' (trade name), 164,
169
Kanemi Corporation, 164–6,
169–70
Kanemi Rice-Oil Disease, 163–70
Kanemi Warehouse Company, 166,
169
Kankyo (Environment), 124–7, 134,
202
Kankyoken (Principle of
Environmental Right), 206
Kanose, 96–8
Kaplan, Mr (Canadian UN
delegate), 67

Kapp, K. William, 11–19, 22, 67,
240, 241, 258
Karafuto, 50
Kassas, K., 249
Kato, Ichiro *et al.*, 258
Kato, Manabu, 247
Kato, Mrs Shizue, 131
Kato, Sannosuke (Kanemi
Warehouse Company), 166, 169
Kato, Shu, 261
Kawahara, Kazuyuki, 180, 251,
261
Kawakami, Kenjiro, 181
'Kawamata incident', 35
Kawana, Hideyuki, 247, 250, 261
Kawasaki, 157
Kawasaki Ironworks, 214–15
Keidanren (Federation of Economic
Organizations), 153–5
Kennan, George, 244
Keynes, J.M., 4, 23–4, 46, 232, 241
'*Kichi-kogai*' (effects of military
bases), 217–19
Kihara, Keikichi, 134, 261
Kimoto, Shoji, 242, 261
Kira, Tatsuo, 261
Kiroku-Toroku, 264
Kitakyushu, 167–8
Kiyoura, Professor Raisaku (Tokyo
Institute of Technology), 84
Klein, Lawrence and Ohkawa,
Kazushi, 243
Kneese, Allen V., 67, 248; and Bower,
Blair T., 258
Kobayashi, Dr Jun, 101–2
Kobayashi, Takeharu (Welfare
Minister), 75
Kobe, 108
Kock, R. 229
Koda, Toshihiko, 261
Kogai, 23, 24–6, 31–2, 59–69;
Environment Agency, 127–8;
export and reversal, 210–16;
Kankyo, 124–7, 134, 202; major
incidents, 70–115;
pharmacopollution and other
examples, 158–92; representative
incidents, 32–47

Kogai Bureau (Tokyo Metropolitan Government), 186
Kogai Commission, 62–3
'*Kogai* Gannen', 57–8
Kogai Kenkyu, 250
'*Kogai* Session', 68–9
Kogai to Kuni no Sekinin, 264
Kombinat companies, 62, 75
Kondo, Akitaro, 245, 261
Kono, Dr Resiaku, 172
Kopp, Raymond J. *et al.*, 255, 258
Korea, 36, 45, 80, 103; Republic of, 186
Korean War, 53, 104, 107
Koyama, Hitoshi, 242, 261
Koyama, Takeo, 251
Krutilla, John V. and Fisher, Anthony C., 258
Kuhara, Mr (Hitachi), 43
Kumamoto, 98; Prefecture, 88, 90; University, 82–7, 91
Kunitake, Tadashi, 167
Kurile Islands, 50
Kurokawa Investigation Team, 74
Kurokawa Study Group, 61–2
Kuroki, Governor Hiroshi (Miyazaki), 181
Kuznets, S. and Goldsmith, R., 243
Kyoto, 137, 246
Kyoto Conference on Climate Change, 201, 219–21
Kyoto Kaigi (Joint Action Council), 99
Kyowa Sangyo Company, 163
Kyushi University Hospital, 167
Kyushu, 50, 135, 179
Kyushu Electric Power Company, 167
Kyushu University, 165

Lake Biwa, 138
Lake Nakanoumi, 139
Lake Shinji, 139
Lakes, 6, 66–7, 138–9
Land Adjustment Union, 186
Land property rights, 3
Langer, William L., 242

Law for the Compensation, etc., for Health Damages, 93–4
Law for Conservation of Nature, 128
Law for the Conservation of Nature's Environment, 131–2
Law for the Regulation of Factory Effluents, 78–9
Law for Natural Parks, 128
Law for the Partial Revision of Drugs, Cosmetics and Medical Instruments Act, 177
Law for the Prevention of Water Contamination, 128–9
Law for the Regulation of Factory Effluents (1958), 60, 88
Law to Establish a Relief Fund for Side-Effect Damage due to Pharmaceutical Products, 177
Lead, 32, 103–4
Leek, Staffordshire, 15
Leontief, Wassily, 67, 226–8, 249
Leyte Island, 214
Liantung Peninsula, 36
Liaison Association for *Kogai*-patient Families, 143
Locked particle Collectors, 34
Lung conditions, 185, 187–8, 190–2

MacCarthy, Fiona, 14, 15, 240
McCormack, Gavan, 233, 256, 258
Mackail, J.W., 15
McKean, Margaret A., 258
Maki, 221
'Mal-production/mal-consumption', 17
Malaysia, 214, 223
Malthus, Thomas, 119–20
'Mamoru-kai' (Association for Protection), 160–1
Manchuria, 45, 80
Manufactories Control Regulation 1896, 29–30
Maritime Safety Agency, 77
Market value, 1–11, 18–19
Marubeni, 214
Maruyama, Professor Hiroshi, 160–1

Marx, Karl, 13–14, 227–8, 240, 255
Masaki, Ryo, 251
'Matsue Resolution 1985', 138–9
Matsukata Deflation 1881–5, 28
Matsumura, Dr., 61–2
Matsumura Research Corps, 62
Matsuoka, Yuji, 186
Matsuyama District Court, 135–6, 206
Mead, Margaret, 121–2
Meadows, Dennis L., 120
Meadows, Donnella, 120
Media coverage, 85, 87
Medical Care, 147, 168–9, 178
Medical Instruments Act, 177
Mei County, 101
Meiji Japan, 28, 33–4, 45–6, 103, 137, 237
Mendel, G.J., 229
Mental retardation, 158
Mercury, 87–9, 91, 96, 96–7, 99
Metals, 32
Meteorological conditions, 41
Methyl-mercury, 82, 87, 91, 98–101
Michalski, W., 19
Miki, Takeo (minister), 133, 142, 152
Military bases, 216–19
Milk, powdered, 159
Mill, J.S., 15–16, 224, 237
Minamata disease, 59, 79–101, 147, 185
Minamata kara Mirai o Mitsumete, 264
'Minamata Three-Day Talk', 93
Minamatabyo Saiban, 246, 264
Minamatabyo Saiban Zenshi, 264
Mine Poisonings Survey Committee, Second, 35
Mining, 32–44, 59, 97, 179–85
Mining Act, 182, 184
Minister of Agriculture, 55
Minister of Agriculture and Commerce, 39
Minister of Welfare, 64
Ministry of Agriculture and Forestry, 87, 165, 168, 169–70
Ministry of Construction, 128, 131

Ministry of International Trade and Industry (MITI), 78, 84, 87, 153–4
Ministry of Transportation, 113
Ministry of Welfare, 86–8, 91, 98, 103–5, 129, 159–60, 169–75; Environment Agency establishment, 127–8; 'Minsuitai' (Democratic Groups Council for Anti-Minamata Disease), 99
Mishan, E.J., 137, 235, 250, 256, 258
Mishima, 61–2
MIT group, 120
Mitsubishi Kasei Corporation, 214
Mitsubishi Monsanto Company, 164
Mitsubishi-Shell, 70
Mitsui Metal-Mining Company, 102–4
Miyakubo village, 38
Miyamoto, Ken'ichi, 242, 261, 262
Miyamoto, Tadashi, 262
Miyazaki, 182; Prefectural Office, 180–1; Summary Court, 184; University, Agriculture Department, 179
Miye Prefecture, 171
Miye Thermal Plant, 72, 74
Mizushima kombinat, 134–5
Model, Roland and Stone, 240
Monazite, 214
Monitoring procedures, 209
Monobe, Governor (Tokyo), 143
'Mori *Konzern*' (financial and industrial combine), 96
Mori, Nobuteru, 96–7
Morinaga Company, 158–9, 161–2
Morinaga, Elizaburo, 262
Morris, William, 14–15, 17, 229
Municipal Health Centre, Yokkaichi, 72
Municipal Research Institute on Public Health, 31
'Muskie Law', 141–2
Mutual Help Association of the Minamata Disease Families, 90
Myrdal, Gunnar, 258

Nagahama, 135–6
Nagano Prefecture, 172
Nagasu, Governor (Kanagawa), 143
Nagoya, 75, 85; High Court, 104
Nagoya Industrial Laboratory, 163
Nagpal, Tanvi and Foltz, C., 196, 252, 258
Naisbitt, John and Aburdene, Patricia, 198, 253, 258
Nakajima Mining, 179
Nakanishi Junko, 262
Naphtha, 72
National Association of the Minamata Disease Patients, 94
National Environment Policy Act (NEPA), 204
National Federation of Kanemi Rice Oil Victims Associations, 167
National Heredity Research Institute, 61
National Liaison Council for SMON Associations (Suzenkuyo), 174
National Park Agency, US, 129
National Parks Law (1957), 130
National Public Health Agency, 142
National SMON Society, 174
Nature, conservation of, 129–39
Nature Conservation Act, 131
Nature Conservation Charter, 132, 132–3
Navigation, 78
'Needs', 224–5
Negative externalities, 3
Nerfin, Marc, 249
Nervous disorders, 170–8
'Netting', 255
Neutralization plant, 40
New Statesman, 249
Nickel, 97
Nigata, 96–101; Prefecture, 91, 96, 221; Public Health Section, 96; University Medical Faculty, 96
Nigata Organic-Mercury Victims Association, 99–100

Nihon Light Metal Company, 162–3
Nihon no Kankyo Asesumento, 264
Niigata Prefecture, 97, 101, 172
Niihanma smelting plant, 38
Nippon Chemical Industrial Company (NCI), 186–92
Nippon Chisso Company *see* Chisso Company
Nippon Kogyo-sho, 40–1
Nishida, Elichi (Minamata factory chief), 84–5
Nitrogen oxides, 140–4, 148–9
Nitta, Tomiya, 247
Noguchi, Shitagau, 79–81
Noise Abatement Act, 65
Noise pollution, 19, 66, 107–15, 206, 217
North/South, 23, 210, 215; concept of, 21
Nuclear power, 226
Nuclear testing, 7, 11
Numazu, 61–2
Nylon, 5

Occupational disease, 185–92
Oceans, 65
Octonal, 81
ODA Enjo no Genjitsu, 254
ODA (official development assistance), 215–16
Oda, Yasunori, 241–2, 262
Odour, offensive, 128
OECD (Organisation for Economic Cooperation and Development), 10, 258; Environment Committee, 125; Report for Japan, 140, 250; Review, 124–7, 140, 145
OECF (Overseas Economic Cooperation Fund, 214
Official development assistance (ODA), 215–16
Ohkawa, Kazushi and Rosovsky, Henry, 243
Oil, 120–1, 134
Oishi, Buichi (Environment Agency), 131, 134, 152, 249, 262
Okamoto, President, 104

Okayama, Prefecture, 159, 160, 171; Public Health Department, 159; University, 101–2, 159; University Hospital, 160
Okinawa, 49, 216, 218
Okubo, Toshitaka (Osaka Prefecture Governor), 30
Olsen, Edward A., 258
Omoto, Mr Shimpei, 104
Ono, Eiji, 75, 245, 262
OPEC (Organisation of Petroleum Exporting Countries), 120
Opium War (China), 27
Organisation for Economic Cooperation and Development *see* OECD
Organization of Petroleum Exporting Countries (OPEC), 120
Osaka, 29, 64, 85, 108, 244; Chamber of Commerce, 29–30; Court of Appeals, 44; District Court, 107, 161; High Court, 113, 114, 206; Prefecture, 28–31
Osaka Alkali Company, 44
Osaka Association of Manufacturing Industries, 30
Osaka Coal-gas Company, 31
Osaka International Airport, 107–15, 150, 206, 247–8
Osaka *Jiji Shimpo*, 29
'Oshidashi' (push out), 35
Ota, Kaoru, 190
Our Common Future, 123, 255
Overall Medical Countermeasure Service, 94
Overseas Economic Cooperation Fund (OECF), 214
Oxygen, 66
Oxyquinoline, 171
Oze National Park, 133

Pacific Ocean, 57
Pacific War (1941), 81, 107, 129
Packard, Vance, 16, 231
Pajestka, J., 249
Paralysis, 158
Park administration, 130

Patents, 5
Pauley, Mr (The Pauly Reparation Mission), 50
PCBs (polychlorinated biphenyl compounds), 134, 163–9
Pearl Harbor, 50
Perforated nasal septa, 187–8
Perry, Commodore, 27
Pesticides, 215
Petrochemical industry, 60, 70–1, 89
Petroleum, 118
Pfeil, Dr (medical specialist), 185–6
Pharmaceutical companies, role of, 178
Pharmacological pollution, 158–92
Philippines, 214, 223
Philippines Sintering Corporation (PSC), 214
Phosphorus, 102
Photochemical smog, 141
Physical handicap, 147
Pigou, A.C., 6, 17–19, 210, 241
Planning, 19
Poaching, 77
Poisoning, 98–101, 101–7, 158–63, 163–70
Polluters Pay Principle (PPP), 10, 146, 148
Pollution *see* Air pollution; Radioactive pollution; Soil pollution; Water pollution
Pollution abate battles, 127, 150
Pollution Compensation Law, 150
Pollution-Related Health Damage Compensation Association (PRHDCA), 148
Pollution-Related Health Damage Compensation Law, 127, 146, 146–50, 156, 183–4
Polycholorinated byphenyls (PCBs), 134, 163–9
Polyvinyl chloride, 81
Popham, Captain Walter, 129
Population, world, 7, 119–20, 225
Port Arthur, 36
Potassium iodide, 188
Power, Thomas M., 258
Prefectural Parks, 130

Prefectural Research Convention, Japan Teachers Union, 180
President's Council on Sustainable Development (PCSD), 200
Private compensation, 126
Private enterprise, 5, 10, 60–1
Privatization and Development, 253
Profit-and-loss systems, 5
Property rights in land, 3
Protest movements, 31–2, 60, 72–4, 93, 218; Ashio, 34–6; Asia Rare-Earth Company, 214
Prud'homme, Professor Remy, 125
Pulp, chemical, 60
Puri, Swaraj, 210–11

Quasi-National Parks, 130
Qureshi, Shakil, 210–11

Radioactive pollution, 7, 62
Railway engines, 19
Randers, Jorgan, 120
Reclamation plan 1969, 56–7
Refuse, 186
Relief Measure Fund, 162
Remodeling of the Japanese Archipelago, Plan for, 54–5
Research Group on Environment Assessment in the Environment Agency, 253
Research Group on the Peculiar Minamata Disease, 84
Research Institute of Labor Sciences, 191
Residents' control, 125
Resources, 2–3, 7, 11, 225–6
Resources Committee (*Shigen Iinkai*), 59
Resources Research Council (*Shigen Chosa Kai*), 59
Restoration of Human Rights, 55
Retired Employees' Association, 190
Review of Environmental Policies in Japan, 125
Rice, 32, 33, 49
Rice-oil disease, Kanemi, 163–70
Rich, Bruce, 213
Richey, Charles A., 129–30, 249

Rio de Janeiro Earth Summit (1992), 23, 193–201, 215
Riots, 72–4, 86
Risui (utilization), 137
Rivers, 60, 66–7, 137, 138; see also under name
Road surfaces, 19
Rodell, Marie, 137
Rogai Research Committee, 74
Rontgen, W.K., 229
Rostow, 27
Rostow W.W., 243
Rotary kilns, 186
Royalties, 5
Ruskin, John, 9–10, 15–16, 229, 240
Russia, 35, 36, 45, 50
Russian Revolution (1917), 45

Sachs, Ignacy, 67, 241, 258
Saionji, Kinmonochi, 37
Saito, Masatake, 180
Saito, Professor Bunji, 179
Sakhalien, 50
Salt, 79
Samuelson, Paul A. and Nordhaus, William D., 239, 253
Sandel, Professor Michael J., 255
Sano, Dr Tasuo, 191
Sapporo, 176
Sato, Eisaku, 103
Sawa, Takamitsu, 262
Sawai, Yoshiro, 245, 262
Sax, Joseph L. and Conner, Roger L., 67, 259
Schelling, Thomas C., 259
Schneider, Michael, 17, 241
Schumacher, E.P., 228–9, 235–6, 255, 256, 259
Schumpeter, Joseph, 4, 48, 241
Scitovsky, Tibor, 259
Scoping, 209
Screening, 209
Seashore, 6, 135–6
Second World War, 81
Seki, Tenshu, 41–2, 44
Sen, Amartya, 234, 256, 259
Seto Inland Sea, 38, 57
Sewage, 128

Sewage Control Act, 128
Sexual assaults, 217
Shaw, G.B., 17
Sherburne, James Clark, 240
Shibata Kei, 262
Shibata, Tetsuji, 262
Shigen Chosa Kai (Resources Research Council), 59
Shigen Iinkai (Resources Committee), 59
Shikaaki, Takasaki, 29
Shikoku, 50
Shimizu, 61–2, 162–3
Shimoda, 27
Shin-Daikyowa Petrochemical Naphtha centre, 75
Shin-Nihon Metal Company, 163
Shinsui (savouring), 138
Shinsuiken (Water-savouring right), 137–8, 206
Shinzenbi (truth, virtue and beauty), 230–1
Shiohama, 71, 72
Shiono, Monnosuke, 38
Shiraki, Professor Hirotsugu, 172–3, 251
Shizakajima, 38, 39
Shizen Hogo Gyosei no Ayumi, 264
Shizuoka Prefecture, 61
Shoji, Hikaru and Miyamoto, Ken'ichi, 262
Shoji, Kichiro and Sugai, Masuro, 251
Showa Denko Corporation, 96–101
Showa Hiryo (Fertilizer) Corporation, 97
Showa Kogyo, 97
Showa Yokkaichi Petroleum, 75
Shrivastava, Paul, 254, 259
Shultz, George P. (US Secretary of State), 197–8
Siam (Thailand), 45
Silk, 5, 32–3
Silver, 103
Simon, Julian L. and Kahn, Herman, 123–4, 249, 259
Singh, Moti (Bhopal district collector), 210–11

Sino-Japanese War (1894–5), 28, 34
Sintering process, 214
Siting development projects, 125; factories, 55, 55–6
Smith, Adam, 1–3, 8, 12–13, 15, 239, 240
Smog, 141
Smoke, 37–8, 41–2
Smoke Prevention Ordinance 1913, 29
Smoke Regulation Act 1962, 40
Smoke and Soot Control Act 1962, 65, 74
SMON Research Council, 173, 251
SMON scandal, 170–85
SMON to Songai Baisho, 264
'Social costs', 11–24
Socialist League, England, 14–15
Soil, pollution, 128, 218; restoration, 105–6
Soke dispersion system, 42
Solatium, 34
Sonoda, Sunao (Minister of Welfare), 103
Sontheimer, Sally, 259
South *see* North/South
Soviet Union, 50
Special Action Committee on Facilities and Areas in Okinawa (SACO), 218
'Special Research Group on the Niigata Mercury Poisoning Incident', 97
Standards, 125, 140–57
Standing Committee on Environmental Disruption, 67
Staphylococcus poisoning, 159
'Status Judgement Council', 94
Steam, 2
Steel manufacturing industry, 142
Stench fish incident, 72–4
Stockholm Conference on Human Environment 1972, 20–1, 65, 92, 116, 119–24, 131, 151–2, 193
Strong, Maurice (Secretary General, 23, 122
Strontium-90, 62

Subacute myelo-opticoneuropathy, 170
Subsidence, ground, 128
Sulphur, 37, 72
Sulphur Dioxide, 72, 148, 149, 150
Sulphurous acid, 40, 42–4, 79
Sumi, Kazuo, 262
Sumitomo, 37–40
Sumitomo Chemical, 61
Sumitomo Metal Mining Company, 179, 181, 184
Sumitomo Metal Processing Corporation, 58
Sumitomo Shoji, 214
Sumon Sukyandaru, 251
Supreme Court, 113–15, 170, 183–4
Sup'ungho dam, 80
Sustainable development, 202–3
Suzenkyo, 176, 177
Suzuka River, 72
Suzuki Committee, 191
Suzuki Company, 97, 243
Suzuki, Dr A. Takeo, 142–4, 188–9
Suzuki, Governor Shun'ichi (Tokyo), 156
Suzuki, Norio, 250
Sweden, 125, 219
Switzerland, 171
'Sympathy' money, 90–1

Taisaku Kaigi, 191
Taisho era, 47
Tajiri, Muneaki, 77–9, 187–91, 245, 252, 263
Takamatsu High Court, 161
Takasago, 134
Takasaki, Hiroshi and Kihara, Keikichi, 249, 263
'Take Over Korea Policy' 1873, 45
Takeda, 171, 175
Takemura, Masayoshi (Shiga Prefecture), 138
Tamura, Dr Zengo, 172
Tanabe Company, 171, 174–5
Tanabe, Shigeko, 251
Tanahashi, Kan'ichi (President NCI), 188, 192

Tanaka, Kakuei (Prime Minister), 54–5, 117–18, 244, 263
Tanaka, Shozo (Diet member), 34, 40, 46
Tanaka, Tetsuya, 251, 263
Tapajos river, 96
Target practice, 218
Tayama Prefecture, 105–6
Tea, 32–3
Technology, 5, 9–10, 13, 65, 80, 225–30
Tennessee Valley Authority (USA), 33
Teranishi Shun'ichi, 263
Thailand (Siam), 45, 223
Thalidomide, 170
Thames, River (GB), 137
Thatcher, Mrs Margaret (Prime Minister GB), 197
'The Agreement for the Prevention of *Kogai* in the Future' 1972, 106
The Asahi Yearbook (*Asahi Nenkan*), 82, 85
The Association of the Members of the City of Takasato, 134
The Compensation for *Kogai* Health Impairment Act 1974, 105
The Ecologist, 120
The Economist, 254, 255
'The Eleven-City Majors Council', 113
The Emptiness of Japanese Affluence, 256
The Limits to Growth, 119–21
The Mutual Help Association, 90–1
The National Environment Policy Act, US (NEPA), 151
The New York Times, 231, 249
The Pauley Reparation Mission 1945, 50
The Resourceful Earth, 121, 123, 249
'The Revised Sequence', 233
The Tripartite Intervention, 243
The Ward-Inhabitants Association, 187, 252
Thorium, 214

Tide land, 138
Tohoku Electric Power Company, 221
Tokugawa shogunate, 27, 29
Tokushima, 159; District Court, 162, 165
Tokyo, 35, 64, 85–6, 93, 157, 188; District Court, 174, 175, 192, 246; Edogawa ward, 186; High Court, 144, 144–5; Institute of Technology, 82, 84, 85; Metropolitan Government, 186, 187, 188, 191; Universities, 36, 81, 172–3, 186–7; University Hospital, 190; water front and bay side areas, 138, 141
Tokyo Electric Generation, 61
Tokyo Resolution, 67–8
Tolba, Mostafa Kamal, 215, 259
Toman, Michael A., 197, 252
Tomkiyama, Kazuko, 250, 263
Tomugawa, 33
Tone River, 35
Toroku Mine, Kogai, 179–85
Toskill Committee, 109–20
Toyama, District Court, 103; Prefecture, 101–2, 105
Toyanaka, 108
Toynbee, Arnold, 234
Toyokura, Dr Yasuo, 172
Training flights, 219
Treaty of Peace (1951), 50–1
Trials, 77, 78, 90
Tripartite Intervention, 35, 245
Truman Doctrine (1947), 53
Tso-Lin, Chang, 45
Tsubaki, Professor Tadao, 96, 172
Tsuchida, Judge Isamu, 192
Tsuru, Shigeto, 244, 245, 249, 259, 263
Turner, R. Kerry, 259
2050 Project, 196

Ueda, Kazuihiro, 263
Ugalo, General Kazushige, 80
Ui, Jun, 242, 259, 263
Ul-Haq, Mahbub, 249
Umaokoshi, 71

Umeda, Genshu, 251
UNESCO, 65, 67
Union Carbide, 211, 212
United Kingdom *see* Great Britain
United Nations Army, 53
United Nations Conference on Environment and Development (UNCED), 219
United Nations Conference on Trade and Development (UNCTAD), 122
United Nations Environment Programme (UNEP), 122, 200–1, 253
United Nations (UN), 21–2, 65, 93, 259; Conference on the Human Environment 1972, 6; General Assembly, 6, 200, 219
United States Agency for International Development (USAID), 197
United States of America *see* USA
Urban pollution, 32
US-Japan Security Treaty, 216, 219
USA, 33, 45, 50, 53–4, 73, 143, 151–4, 200; Audit Board, 215; Council on Environmental Quality, 121; Dallas-Fort Worth International Airport, 109; global warming, 220–2; interference of income', 232; Japan's National Parks, 129–30; Long Beach, California, 71; military bases, 216–19; New England coast, 136–7; NIH research grant, 102; St Louis research project, 62; Security Pact, 107–8; Stockholm Conference, 120–1, 123; witnesses from, 183
Ushiyama, Tsumoru, 247, 264
Utsumi, Teizo, 251
Uzawa, Hirobumi, 264

Veblen, T., 256
Veblen, Thorstein, 16–17, 231–2, 241, 259
Vegetation, mogi-resistant, 41

Vibration, 128
Victor, David G. and Salt, Julian E.,
    255
von Liebig, Justus, 13, 240

Wakayama Prefecture, 171
Walras, Auguste, 230
Ward, Barbara, 6
Waste Disposal, 6
Waste-water drains, 129
Watanabe, Professer Keigai
    (formerly Kumamootot
    University), 85
Watarase River, 33–5, 59
Water Contamination Prevention
    Act, 187
Water pollution, 19, 60, 65, 128, 147,
    218; Copper mining, 32
Water Quality Conservation Act
    1958, 60, 77–8, 88
Water vapour, 66
Water-savouring right, 137
Water-savouring right (*Shinsuiken*),
    137, 206
Weapons, 193–4
Welfare Ministry, 97
Welfare state, 10
West Germany, 53–4
West Virginia Institute, 212
Western Federation of Economic
    Organizations, 58
Wind survey, 62

Woodrow Wilson International
    Centre for Scholars, 259
World Bank, 216
World Bank Atlas, 248
World Commission on Environment
    and Development, 252, 255, 259
World Environmental Conference
    on Lakes and Marshes, 138
World Health Organisation (WHO),
    67
'World Population Year' 1974, 120

Yalta Agreement (1945), 50
Yalu River, 80
Yamakawa, Kenjiro, 36
Yamamoto, Mr Yoshimasa, 143–4
Yamazaki, Tasuku, 251
Yanaka, 35
Yawata, 28
Yokkaichi, 60–1, 70–9, 145, 187;
    Master Plan, 70–1
Yokkaichi *Kogai Taisaku Kyogikai*
    (Council for Kogai
    Countermeasures in Yokkaichi),
    74
Yonezawa, 173–4
Yukijurushi Company, 159
Yusho, Kanemi, 166

'*Zaibatsu*', 37, 51, 53, 80, 81, 103
Zenkyo, 160
Zinc, 32, 102, 103, 103–4